The Superstar Roadmap

How Ordinary People Build Extraordinary Careers

Dr. Myra S. White, J.D.

D1527536

Work Intelligence, Inc.

The author is grateful for permission to
include the following copyrighted material.

Excerpts from interviews published on the Academy of
Achievement's Achiever Gallery on their website:
www.achievement.org

———

The Superstar Roadmap
How Ordinary People Build Extraordinary Careers
Copyright © 2012 by Work Intelligence, Inc.
ISBN 978-0-9849449-0-3
All rights reserved.

Published by Work Intelligence, Inc.
223 Dolphin Cove Court
Bonita Springs, FL 34134-7456
978-405-3136
www.workintelligence.com

———

To Kyle who started me on my journey to success.

To Elizabeth who has sustained and supported me on my journey.

To Tieh-Su Wu who has kept me moving forward.

To my Mother who taught me the magic of stories and how to have fun.

To Karina Furman who worked tirelessly to make this book possible.

To my former students who inspired me to write this book.

To Shahbaz Khan, my marketing guru.

May the eyes of your heart be enlightened.
From Paul in Ephesians, 1:18

Coming Alive

"We are all born Superstars." —*Lady Gaga*

Each of us has a superstar hidden in us waiting to come alive. *The Superstar Roadmap* shows you how to bring that superstar to life. It teaches you what they forget to teach you in school and at work—namely the steps that you need to take to be successful at what you love to do.

People often fail to fully express their inner superstar, not because they lack talent and ability, but because they get lost along the way. Even Lady Gaga struggled. When she began her career playing small clubs in New York, she received standing ovations in some but in others she was booed off the stage.

This is because success is a process which involves a series of steps. It doesn't happen overnight but you can avoid a lot of wrong turns and make more progress if you know how to do it.

The Superstar Roadmap lays out the steps that have worked for others. It is based on a study of how 60 ordinary people became superstars. It differs from other books because it goes beyond just telling you the steps that superstars take. It also shows you how to take those steps using examples and stories from the lives of people who have become superstars.

This "how to" component is critical to your success. Think of it in terms of taking a tennis lesson. You arrive at the court in your new tennis outfit eager to become a good tennis player. The coach hands you a racquet and ball and says, "All you need to do is hit the ball across the net so it lands within the lines in the opposite court." You try this. Sometimes the ball falls in the court but a lot of times it doesn't go where you want and it certainly wouldn't win you any points. You turn to the coach and say, "OK, but how do I hit winners?"

He replies, "Well to do that, you need to learn what the pros do. You hold the racquet this way, bring it back at this angle, step into the ball, swing though with a circular arc and aim the ball at a place where your opponent can't return it." Suddenly you realize that there are approaches and techniques that you can use whether you are a beginner or seasoned player that will make hitting winners much easier than just whacking at the ball.

Becoming a superstar is similar. Like hitting a tennis ball, there are actions and techniques that will ensure that you hit winners at each step along the way. Understanding these techniques and knowing how to use them can make the difference between the ball going in the net versus zooming past your opponent's out-stretched racquet. Just like in sports or any other endeavour one of the best ways to become good at it is to learn the techniques and strategies that the pros use. This is what *The Superstar Roadmap* teaches you.

Jack Welch not only knew that he needed to build power and influence to become CEO of GE but he also knew the concrete actions that he needed to take to do this.

The superstars in this book come from a wide range of fields of endeavor ranging from business to medicine to sports. They were chosen because they achieved something of value for others. They produced products or services that improved the quality of people's lives, created jobs for others or lifted people's spirits through their art or athletic feats.

Included with these superstars are the characters from *The Wizard of Oz*. As you may recall, *The Wizard of Oz* is the story of how Dorothy, a naïve girl from Kansas, teams up with the Scarecrow, who is always falling apart, the Tin Man, who keeps getting stuck in one place and the Lion, who is afraid of everything. Together they journey across Oz and achieve their dreams. They slay the

Virginia Rometty, the new CEO of IBM, relates how early in her career she almost turned down a big job at IBM because she was afraid that she wasn't ready to take on such a high level job.
New York Times,
Nov. 11, 2011, p. B2.

Wicked Witch of the West, which frees the inhabitants from the Witch's reign of terror and makes them into superstars in the land of Oz. These characters with all their flaws serve to remind us that no matter how inadequate we may appear or feel, we all have the potential to make valuable contributions to the world around us.

Even more importantly, as Dorothy and her companions dance and sing down the yellow brick road, they show us that the journey can be fun. Superstars know this. One of the distinguishing features of the superstars in this book is that they all love what they do and find it fun. This is because tapping into what is best in us fills us with the same sense of joy and exhilaration that athletes experience when they are in the zone.

Tip for the Road

Becoming a Superstar is not about changing who you are. It is about changing what you do.

—M. Myra S. White

Featuring the Following Superstars

Andre Agassi Winner of eight Grand Slam tennis singles titles; the only tennis player to win each of the four Grand Slam singles titles, the Masters, the Davis Cup, and an Olympic gold medal.

Madeleine Albright First female Secretary of State of the United States.

Alan Alda Actor who also writes and directs feature films; played Hawkeye on the popular television series *M*A*S*H*.

Woody Allen Academy Award winning film director, writer, actor, and comedian.

Lance Armstrong Seven-time winner of the Tour de France and well-known cancer survivor.

Fantasia Barrino Popular singer; 2004 winner of the *American Idol* talent competition.

Jeffrey Bezos Founder and CEO of the Internet company Amazon.com.

Richard Branson British entrepreneur who founded the Virgin Group, which now includes more than 400 companies. They include Virgin Atlantic Airways; Virgin Mobile; Virgin Trains; and Virgin Fuel, which provides cheap green fuel.

Sergey Brin Co-founder of the Internet company Google, Inc.

Zbigniew Brzezinski National security advisor to President Jimmy Carter.

Warren Buffett Berkshire Hathaway chairman and CEO whose ability to spot undervalued companies and purchase them cheaply has made him and the people whose money he invests extremely wealthy; in five decades he has amassed a fortune of over $44 billion, most of which he is currently donating to the Bill and Melinda Gates Foundation.

Susan Butcher Four-time winner of the Iditarod, the 1,150 mile dog sled race across Alaska.

Dr. Ben Carson Celebrated pediatric neurosurgeon who is Director of Pediatric Neurosurgery at Johns Hopkins; in 1987 made medical history by being the first surgeon to successfully separate conjoined twins joined at the head.

Johnny Cash Grammy winning country singer and songwriter who sold over 50 million albums and received multiple country music awards.

Bill Clinton Former President of the United States.

Hillary Clinton Secretary of State; former senator from New York and former First Lady.

Sasha Cohen United States Figure Skating Ladies Champion in 2005 and silver medalist at the 2006 Winter Olympics.

Deborah Copaken Kogan Photojournalist whose work has appeared in *Time, Newsweek,* and *The New York Times.*

Donny Deutsch Chairman and former CEO of Deutsch Inc, one of America's top ad agencies; former host of the talk show, *The Big Idea.*

Corey Dillon Former premier running back for the New England Patriots who gained over 1000 yards in 2004; helped the Patriots win Super Bowls XXXVIII and XXXIX.

Michael Eisner Former chairman and CEO of The Walt Disney Company.

Larry Ellison Founder, chairman, and CEO of Oracle, one the world's largest developers of computer-based management information systems.

Roger Federer Winner of 16 Grand Slam tennis singles titles.

Richard Feynman A Nobel Prize winning physicist who during WWII worked on the Manhattan Project to build the atomic bomb.

Carly Fiorina Former CEO of Hewlett-Packard.

Lady Gaga American singer and song writer known for her flamboyant costumes and performances.

Bill Gallagher Co-founder of A D S Financial Services Solutions, a major provider of technological and consulting services to financial institutions.

Bill Gates Co-founder and chairman of the computer software giant, Microsoft.

J. Paul Getty Founder of Getty Oil Company and one of the world's first billionaires.

Katharine Graham Former CEO, chairman, and publisher of *The Washington Post;* one of the most powerful women in America during the period she headed the *Post*.

John Grisham Only American writer to author a number-one bestselling novel of the year for seven years in a row (1994–2000); has sold more than 250 million copies of his books worldwide.

Justine Henin-Hardenne Winner of seven Grand Slam tennis singles titles.

Billie Holiday American singer who is considered one of the greatest female jazz voices of all time.

Bill Hewlett Co-founder of the Hewlett-Packard Company, a leading producer of computers and peripherals.

Lee Iacocca Former president of Ford Motor Company and former CEO of Chrysler; saved Chrysler from certain bankruptcy and rebuilt it into a viable company.

Phil Jackson A National Basketball Association (NBA) coach who has won 11 NBA championships.

Steve Jobs Founder and former CEO of Apple who was responsible for the design and development of the Macintosh computer and the iPod, iPhone, and iPad.

Michael Jordan Former professional basketball player who led the Chicago Bulls to six NBA championships.

Wynonna Judd A Grammy award winning country music singer who has had over 20 number one singles.

Jeong H. Kim Founder of the telecommunications company Yurie Systems, which he sold in 1998 to Lucent Technologies for over $1 billion.

Larry King Former host of the nightly interview program, *Larry King Live,* which was one of television's longest running shows.

George Lucas One of America's most successful independent directors and film makers who is best known for his movies *American Graffiti, Star Wars,* and the *Indiana Jones* series.

Peter Meyers Mediator and labor lawyer; inducted into the prestigious College of Labor and Employment Lawyers in 2005.

Andrea Mitchell NBC News chief foreign affairs correspondent and anchor of MSNBC's *Andrea Mitchell Reports.*

Charles Ogletree Harvard Law School Jesse Climenko Professor of Law and founding and executive director of the Charles Hamilton Houston Institute for Race and Justice; in 2006 named by *Ebony* magazine as one of the 100+ Most Influential Black Americans.

Dave Packard Co-founder of Hewlett-Packard Company, a leading producer of computers and peripherals.

Larry Page Co-founder and CEO of Google, Inc.

Ben Richardson Former vice chairman and chief of operations at Gant Electronics.

Anita Roddick Founder of the international retail chain The Body Shop.

Virginia M. Rometty CEO of IBM.

Bob Schieffer Chief Washington correspondent for CBS who also serves as anchor and moderator of *Face The Nation,* the Sunday public affairs broadcast.

Stan Shih Co-founder and former chairman and CEO of the Acer Group, the Taiwanese computer maker.

Donna Shirley Leader of the team that built the *Sojourner,* the first solar-powered rover to explore the surface of Mars.

Fred Smith Founder, chairman, and CEO of FedEx.

George Soros Founder and chairman of Soros Fund Management, one of the most profitable hedge funds in the industry; founder of The Soros Foundations, which works to promote democracy, human rights, and economic and social reform around the world.

Michael Steinhardt One of the most successful money managers in the history of Wall Street.

Martha Stewart Business mogul and media personality who has transformed American homes and gardens.

Margaret Thatcher The United Kingdom's first female prime minister.

Roy Vagelos Former chairman and CEO of Merck known for attracting top research scientists and developing new, groundbreaking drugs.

Sam Walton Founder and former chairman and CEO of Wal-Mart.

Jack Welch Former CEO of General Electric.

Oprah Winfrey Former host of *The Oprah Winfrey Show,* one of the highest-rated programs of its type in television history; founder of Harpo Productions, Inc., the Oprah Winfrey Network, and *O,* the Oprah magazine; considered by many to be the world's most influential woman and the only African-American billionaire.

John Wooden One of college basketball's greatest coaches, he won 10 NCAA national championships at UCLA; first person admitted to the Basketball Hall of Fame both as a coach and player.

Tiger Woods Winner of 14 major golf championships; considered one of the most successful golfers of all time.

Bob Woodward The *Washington Post* reporter who helped uncover the Watergate scandal that led to Richard Nixon's resignation; author of twelve best-selling nonfiction books.

Follow Dr. White

Twitter: @DrMyraWhite

Facebook.com/SuperstarRoadmap

Go to www.SuperstarRoadmap.com for

The *Ask Dr. White* Blog, Motivational Exercises,

and Much More

Contents

Forgotten the story of *The Wizard of Oz*?
See the Appendix for a summary of the story.

The Power of Oz

The Wizard of Oz with its colorful sets and memorable songs is more than just an entertaining story. With its highly flawed characters it helps dispel the myth that we need some sort of "right stuff" to become superstars. Instead it shows us that with courage and persistence we all have the power to succeed despite our imperfections. In the story the scarecrow never lets the fact that he is continually falling down and losing pieces of his insides deter him from achieving his goal of getting a brain. He just gets back up and stuffs the straw back into his body. The tin man doesn't let getting stuck in one position stop him from acquiring the heart that he desperately desires. He just finds someone to oil him and goes on his way. The lion similarly doesn't let his overwhelming fear of almost everything keep him from obtaining the badge of courage that he needs to overcome his fears. Instead he continues forging ahead on his trembling legs.

Superstars Are Ordinary People

Like the characters in *The Wizard of Oz*, real-life superstars start out just like the rest of us. They rarely look like the "beautiful people" who grace our television screens. Moreover, they have both strengths and weaknesses as well as fears that they may fail. All have had to overcome difficult challenges.

Richard Branson, the founder of the Virgin empire of businesses, has dyslexia. Jack Welch, formerly CEO of General Electric, stutters. Oprah Winfrey has had to come to terms with the psychological scars left by a childhood of sexual abuse. Lance Armstrong, a seven-time winner of the prestigious Tour de France, had to put his blossoming career on hold while he battled cancer. After a year of grueling treatments he then had to overcome serious self-doubts about his ability to again compete at the highest level.

Most superstars also lack the glamour that we associate with being a superstar. Bill Gates has been described as a "nerd." A 1994 *Playboy* interview with him began, "His glasses are smudged, his clothes are wrinkled, his hair is tousled like a boy's."[1] Sam Walton, who founded Wal-Mart, had a quiet unassuming presence. Even after he made his first million he would introduce himself as a little guy in retail from Bentonville, Arkansas. When the president of the National Mass Marketing Retail Institute first met Sam Walton, he recalls thinking, "Who is this guy? He looks like an undertaker."[2]

What makes people such as these become superstars is not their external appearance or special talents. Like the characters in The Wizard of Oz, they become superstars because they understand the steps that they need to take and the techniques and strategies they need to use to achieve their dreams.

Becoming a Superstar
Takes More than a Diploma

When Dorothy, the Scarecrow, the Tin Man, the Lion and Toto triumphantly return to the Emerald City after defeating the Wicked Witch of the West, the Wizard of Oz awards the Scarecrow a brain by presenting him with a doctoral diploma in "thinkology." The Wizard explains that the diploma will let the Scarecrow think the same deep thoughts as people at universities. Delighted, the Scarecrow begins reciting the Pythagorean Theorem.

To be a superstar in the workplace, we need more than a diploma. Like the Scarecrow, many of us have a diploma or even a series of diplomas. These diplomas provide us with credentials and open doors to opportunities. They are like the thrusters that launch rockets into space. They get us off the launching pad, but they don't determine the success of our mission. As the Wizard points out, having a diploma means that we can think the type of deep thoughts that are rewarded in school. Once we leave school, however, we are on a different playing field. To become a superstar on this field, we need a new set of strategies and techniques.

Only a few of the superstars whom you will read about in this book excelled in school. Most did not graduate at the top of their high school or college classes and some never even graduated from college. Richard Branson, founder of the Virgin empire, struggled in secondary school because he had dyslexia. As a result, he was hopeless at any type of test, including IQ tests, and never attended college. Because dyslexia was not yet a recognized learning disability, his teachers thought that he was stupid and lazy and would often thrash him for his poor performance.[3]

Donna Shirley, leader of the Mars Exploration Program that landed the first rover on Mars, did so poorly in the aeronautical engineering program at the University of Oklahoma that in her senior year she changed her major to journalism in order to graduate. After working for a few years in the aeronautical industry, she realized that she needed an engineering degree to be taken seriously. She returned to the University of Oklahoma where with some difficulty she finally completed the engineering degree that she had earlier abandoned. She relates, "I eked out a D in Advanced Electrical Engineering by promising the professor that I'd never touch anything electrical as long as I lived if he'd just let me pass."[4]

Other superstars have become passionately involved in their future careers before they finished college and lost interest in academics. Bob Schieffer, chief CBS Washington correspondent and anchor of *Face the Nation*, started working as a journalist at a local radio station when he was still in college. He loved his job so much that going to school became secondary for him. He completed his degree but did the bare minimum to graduate.[5] Bill Gates was so fascinated by computers and starting his own company that he never finished his undergraduate degree at Harvard. Google's founders, Larry Page and Sergey Brin, started building their search engine while doctoral students at Stanford. They became so absorbed in developing it that they abandoned their doctoral studies.[6]

Why School Smarts Don't Guarantee Success

The reason that being "school smart" doesn't ensure that we will become a workplace superstar is because the techniques and strategies that lead to high grades in school are different from those that make people top achievers in the workplace. We need a different type of brain to excel in the workplace than in school. To be "school smart" we must be good at memorization, rote learning, taking tests, and following instructions. Doing well requires conforming to a highly structured environment where our behavior is closely controlled and little opportunity exists to set our own individual goals or to experiment with different ways of doing things. In addition, we must pay close attention to what teachers want because they choose our goals, set the timelines, decide what we should study and, most importantly, determine the standards for success.

Students who are superstars in a school environment are the ones who know and use the techniques and strategies that lead to top grades in school. In 1981 researchers Karen Arnold and Terry Denny began following the careers of 81 students in Illinois who graduated first in their high-school class.[7] In interviews these valedictorians repeatedly told Arnold and Denny that they did well in school because they worked hard and knew how to play the game, not because they were the brightest students. One student astutely commented, "I'm not the smartest person in the school. I just know how to get good grades."[8] Jack Welch, former CEO of General Electric, has similarly commented in his autobiography that he wasn't the "resident genius" in his Ph.D. program in Chemical Engineering at the University of Illinois. He received a Ph.D. because he worked hard and attracted powerful mentors at the university who supported and encouraged him.[9]

In contrast to the highly structured environments that exist in schools, the world of work is strikingly different. It is a chaotic and unpredictable environment where we must continually deal with the unexpected, take risks, and set our own goals. Moreover, there is typically no one to encourage us or tell us whether we are on the right road. We must instead build our own road in an environment where there are no agreed-upon right answers or feedback on how we are doing. To be a superstar in this world, we need a different set of techniques and strategies than those that worked in school.

Unfortunately, schools don't teach us how to make the transition from school to work. Being smart is not enough after we leave school. None of the valedictorians that Arnold and Denny followed have to date become superstars in the workplace. Even having a high IQ doesn't help us make this transition from school to work or guarantee that we will become a superstar. In 1921 Dr. Lewis Terman, a Stanford psychologist, began following 1,521 children with genius level IQs to determine how they fared in life. In a follow-up study thirty-nine years later, it was found that only four percent of the men in the group had achieved exceptional financial success. A further analysis compared the 100 top achieving men in the group with the 100 poorest achieving men. A key difference was that the top achieving men had parents of superior socioeconomic status who could teach them the techniques and strategies that they needed to use to become superstars. The low achievers lacked this advantage.[10]

While some of us are lucky enough to have parents or mentors who teach us the techniques and strategies needed to become a superstar, for others of us the world of work can be a frustrating and at times an overwhelming experience. To become superstars in this world and ultimately achieve our dreams, we need to learn what others have done to become the best at what they do. This book will show you the road map that they have followed and the techniques and strategies that they have used to get where they wanted to go.

The Superstar Road Map

When Dorothy asks Glinda, the good witch of the North, how to start for the Emerald City, Glinda tells her that it is always best to start at the beginning.

Below is a description of the steps in the superstar roadmap that you will learn in the chapters that follow.

Step 1: Know Yourself

The key to becoming a superstar lies in understanding our mini-strengths and identifying what we passionately care about in this world.

Step 2: Know Where You Are Going

Superstars know what they want to achieve. To become superstars we must commit ourselves to a mission and then pursue it relentlessly.

Step 3: Know How to Get There

Our ability to become a superstar depends on more than doing a good job. We must also understand how to build power and influence.

Step 4: Know How to Create Your Personal Success Syndrome

To become a superstar we must strategically use the personal powers that we have to acquire more powers.

INTRODUCTION: THE POWER OF OZ

Step 5: Know How to Give and Get Help

No man or woman is an island. Superstars don't do it alone. They have lots of help from others and they remember in turn to help others.

Step 6: Know How to Manage Your Emotions

Our emotions can be one of our biggest stumbling blocks to becoming a superstar. Understanding how to control our fears and anxieties is essential to becoming a superstar.

Step 7: Know How to Manage Your Performance

There are key times when we must deliver our best performances. To do this we must learn techniques that let us perform at our peak when it counts most.

Step 8: Know How to Deal with Risk and Adversity

The journey to becoming a superstar is never easy. There are always unanticipated roadblocks and periods of deep despair when it seems that we will never succeed. To survive we must learn how to overcome failure and believe in ourselves.

Step 9: Know How to Have Fun

Superstars love what they do. We must choose a path that we find fun and that expresses the joy of who we are and what makes us special.

To effectively use the techniques and strategies in this book we must have the heart that the Tin Man wanted, the courage that the Lion sought, and, most importantly, persistence. We must also realize that no one becomes an instant superstar. Like Dorothy, we must proceed down the Yellow Brick Road one step at a time. Oprah Winfrey, one of America's best-known superstars, has wisely commented that no one skyrockets to the top.[12] Her journey to becoming a superstar began as a child when she gave her first Easter speech in church at the age of three.[13] It was only many years later that she became an American household name.

We must also remember the advice that Glinda gives to Dorothy at the end of *The Wizard of Oz*: The power to become a superstar lies within. Sasha Cohen, who won the 2006 United States national ladies figure skating championship, had to learn this before she could win. Sasha is a beautiful skater who combines strength with elegance, but in the past the mental side of her performance had defeated her. At world and national competitions she was a chronic runner-up who left the podium with only a second place medal. She tried new coaches in hopes of finding one who would show her how to conquer her competition anxiety, but she still didn't win. Finally, she realized that the key to becoming a superstar lay within herself. Returning to her old childhood coach, she began to focus on her training and performance rather than winning medals. In the 2006 American championships she turned in an almost flawless performance and finally achieved her dream of winning the national championship.[14] In the chapters that follow you too can become a superstar by learning how to use the power to win that lies within you.

Visit www.achievement.org to find superstars whom you admire. Read their posted interviews to learn how they built their careers.

Take a Moment to Reflect

A person doesn't have to be famous or rich to be a superstar. Think of someone you know who is a superstar at what they do.

On the page below, describe the things that this person did to become successful.

Know Yourself

At the end of *The Wizard of Oz*, Dorothy learns that the power to return to Kansas lies within her. Like Dorothy, we all have special powers within us, but to use them we first must honestly appraise who we are. We must understand both our strengths and weaknesses and know what we passionately like to do.

Superstars are acutely aware of their strengths and also their weaknesses. This allows them to capitalize on what they do well and use others to do things that they don't do well. Richard Branson, founder of the Virgin Group, soon realized after he started his first business that he was good at sales but not good at managing the money. To manage the money he recruited his best friend.

The second important key to becoming a superstar is knowing what speaks to our heart. Superstars listen to their hearts because what is in their hearts gives them the desire and drive that they need to achieve great things. Oprah has built her empire by pursuing her passion for connecting with people and helping them improve their lives. For Oprah, making a lot of money has just been a byproduct of doing what she likes to do.[1] When we know our strengths and what speaks to our hearts, we too can become unstoppable like Oprah.

Identify Your Special Mini-Strengths

Soon after Dorothy leaves Munchkinland she finds the Scarecrow hanging from a nail on a pole in a field. She tries to get him down but she can't figure out how to do it. The Scarecrow says, "Of course I'm not bright about doing things but if you'll just bend the nail down in the back, maybe I'll slip off. . . ." [2]

Despite the Scarecrow's self-deprecating manner, he knows that he is good at solving three-dimensional mechanical problems. It is one of his mini-strengths. As a result, he doesn't hesitate to tell Dorothy how to bend the nail so he will slip off the pole. Carefully following his instructions, Dorothy uses her manual dexterity to bend the nail in the right direction and the Scarecrow is immediately released. Like Dorothy and the Scarecrow, we all have small mental and physical behaviors that we do exceptionally well. These are our mini-strengths. They make what we are doing so easy that it never occurs to us that others struggle with such tasks. As a result, we often fail to see our mini-strengths. To become a superstar we need to identify our mini-strengths and learn how to capitalize on the advantage they give us in the workplace.

People have a wide range of mini-strengths. If we look at our family and friends, we will find a rich panorama of mini-strengths. In my family, my sister is like the Scarecrow. She can solve three-dimensional mechanical problems. When anything mechanical broke in our house, we always took it to my sister to repair. By just looking at it, she could see what was wrong. My mother is extremely good at focusing on small details. This makes her an excellent proofreader. Before I submitted my dissertation for my Ph.D. at Harvard, my mother carefully read every word and corrected my grammar and spelling. My stepfather had a great eye for landscape design. He knew how to trim the bushes and shrubbery in the state park that he managed to create visually beautiful backgrounds. My best friend in college could make his voice resonate and echo across any room. Capitalizing on this, he became a powerful and compelling public speaker.

In identifying our mini-strengths, we must be careful not to mix them up with our accomplishments. Our degrees, expertise and job experience are accomplishments. Similarly being a doctor, mechanic, manager, or graduate of a particular school is an accomplishment. In contrast, our mini-strengths are the behaviors that we use to produce these accomplishments. They are the building blocks out of which we create our greatest achievements.

By knowing our mini-strengths and effectively using them, we increase our ability to become a superstar. When researchers watch people's brains in action using modern scanning technologies, they find that if people have to pay attention to too many things at once, their brains become overloaded and their performance drops.[3]

This drop in performance is what happens when we ignore our mini-strengths and try to excel at a task that we find difficult to do. We have to pay so much attention to every detail of what we are doing that we use up valuable brainpower. The result is that we have none left over to devote to the parts of the task that are critical to doing it well and producing an exceptional outcome.

Superstars know how to conserve brain power. They avoid tasks they do badly that overload their brains; instead they focus their energies on doing tasks that maximize their use of their mini-strengths.

Another advantage to knowing our mini-strengths is that this knowledge gives us enormous freedom to pursue a wide range of jobs and careers. Mini-strengths are portable. They aren't linked to particular types of jobs or careers. We can use them to shine in many different types of pursuits. For example, being extremely good at solving problems in three dimensions can help us become a superstar dentist, carpenter, architect, scientist, or even a patent attorney. Being good at

13

analyzing processes and being able to break them down into a series of small tasks can help us become a superstar software developer or a great dinner host because this mini-strength is key to excelling at both jobs. To write software we must break the task that we want to computerize into smaller ones that can be performed by the computer. To successfully host a large dinner party, we also must break the task down into a series of smaller tasks that either we or someone else can perform. We need to create a guest list, keep track of which guests have accepted and declined, decide on a menu, and buy food, to name just a few of the many little tasks that we must identify and execute to make a dinner party successful.

Enormous variety exists in the types of mini-strengths that people have used to become superstars. There is no fixed set of mini-strengths that are essential. What superstars have in common is that they know what their mini-strengths are and they use them to excel. Below are descriptions of the mini-strengths that Jack Welch (former CEO of General Electric), Oprah (host of the highly popular Oprah Winfrey Show), Lawrence Ellison (founder of Oracle), Dr. Ben Carson (world renowned pediatric neurosurgeon), Lee Iacocca (former president of Ford and CEO of Chrysler), and Anita Roddick (founder of The Body Shop) used to become superstars. As these examples illustrate, each relied on very different sets of mini-strengths.

Jack Welch

In 1980 Jack Welch was selected to be CEO and Chairman of General Electric. During the next 20 years, he transformed General Electric into an innovative and lean organization that delivered growth year after year. To become a superstar he relied heavily on his mini-strengths as a relationship builder, information collector and analytical thinker.

Relationship Builder Jack Welch's ability to build strong relationships with powerful people above him who served as mentors helped him at every point in his climb to becoming a superstar. While completing his university degrees and moving up the corporate ladder at General Electric, he found mentors who supported and promoted him. Even when he made dramatic mistakes, such as blowing up a pilot plastics plant early in his career at General Electric, his mentors stepped in and protected him.[4]

Information Collector and Analytical Thinker Jack's ability to profitably manage General Electric's various businesses lay in his skill at finding out what was really going on in the plants that he managed. On plant visits he would question managers for hours on every facet of plant operations, analyze their responses, and then ask more questions. His ability to drill down to the details and collect extensive information from managers helped him to anticipate problems and make good business decisions.[5]

Oprah Winfrey

Oprah Winfrey's talk show has won more than 25 daytime Emmy awards. It has been syndicated in 122 countries and for 19 consecutive seasons has been the most popular talk show on American television. In 1988 Oprah founded her production company, Harpo. Its success has made her one of the wealthiest women in the world.[6] Two key mini-strengths that Oprah used to become a superstar are her abilities to emotionally connect with others and to identify and use the mini-strengths of others.

Emotionally Connects with Others Oprah's ability to forge emotional connections with her audience and guests is what makes "The Oprah Winfrey Show" unique and has been central to her acquiring worldwide popularity. Audiences feel that Oprah is tuned-in to them and what they want to know. Oprah's producer, Debbie DiMaio, describes the connection viewers feel with Oprah:

One of Oprah's greatest gifts is her ability to ask the question that is on the tip of the tongue of everyone watching at home. . . . Audiences come to me and say, "You know, I feel like I know Oprah Winfrey. I feel like she's a friend of mine. And she always asks what I want to know."[7]

Oprah also connects with her guests. By listening to guests without judging them and sharing her own problems with them, she puts them at ease. Guests feel comfortable talking to her about personal problems and dark periods of their lives. Dick Maurice, entertainment editor of *The Las Vegas Sun's* showbiz section and a guest on Oprah's show, describes how Oprah draws you out and makes you feel important.

She had a special quality about her that made her unique. There was this way she had of looking at you, and you felt that, when you were talking to her, the only person she was thinking about was you.[8]

Identifies and Uses the Mini-strengths of Others Oprah's ability to identify mini-strengths in others and find ways to use them at Harpo is one reason for Harpo's success. This strength helped Oprah discover Dr. Phil. In 1996 Oprah was sued by a group of Texas beef ranchers for commenting on the air that she was reluctant to ever eat another hamburger after learning about mad cow disease. Her lawyer hired Dr. Phil to coach her for the grueling process of testifying and being cross-examined by plaintiff lawyers. In working with Dr. Phil, Oprah observed that he had a special talent for identifying people's psychological blocks and telling them how to overcome them. After the trial Oprah recruited Dr. Phil to appear on her show. She believed that the type of practical straightforward advice he provided was what her viewers needed to hear. In 2002 Harpo partnered with Paramount Domestic Television to create the "Dr. Phil Show." It was an instant success.[9]

Lawrence Ellison

In 1977 Lawrence Ellison founded Oracle, currently the world's leading developer of computer-based information management systems. His major mini-strengths are thinking logically and challenging the status quo. These have been ideal for becoming a superstar in the evolving computer software arena.

Logical Thinker and Challenger of the Status Quo Larry's ability to see logical flaws in the reasoning of experts and authority figures and his courage to challenge them has served him well as an entrepreneur in the rapidly changing high tech business. In this business you must continually question traditional approaches and ideas about what is possible because new technology is always making old ways of doing things inefficient. Survival requires constant innovation.

Larry Ellison began questioning experts and authority figures when he was still a child. Even at a young age he saw that many of the things that adults told him didn't add up or make sense.

> I don't think that my personality has changed much since I was five years old. The most important aspect of my personality, as far as determining my success goes, has been my questioning conventional wisdom, doubting the experts, and questioning authority. While that can be very painful in relationships with your parents and teachers, it can be enormously useful in life.
>
> I had some teachers when I was very young whom I thought were telling me things that weren't true. When I tried to ask questions, they basically wanted me to parrot back what they said. They really weren't interested in discourse with a child, or debate with a child. They said this was true, and "You are smart if you can repeat back to me exactly what I said to you." I had a real problem with that as well. I had very strong authoritarian figures, both in school and at home, which served as wonderful examples of how not to be.[10]

Dr. Ben Carson

Dr. Ben Carson is a pioneer in the field of pediatric neurosurgery. Raised in a poor African-American neighborhood in Detroit by a single mother, Dr. Carson became Director of Pediatric Neurosurgery at Johns Hopkins Hospital at the age of 33. As a surgeon he has developed techniques that make it possible for children with previously hopeless brain injuries and pathologies to now lead normal lives. Using these techniques he made medical history in 1987 by separating conjoined twins who were joined at the head.[11] Two mini-strengths, his superb eye-hand coordination and ability to see in three dimensions, have played a key role in his achieving superstar status as a surgeon.

Eye-hand Coordination Operating on the brains of children requires enormous eye-hand coordination. One slip of the hand can cause extensive neurological damage or even death. A key factor in Dr. Carson's success is his superb eye-hand coordination, or what he calls his "gifted hands." Dr. Carson initially didn't realize how exceptional his eye-hand coordination was. While a student at Yale he often played table soccer with classmates. He had picked up the game quickly and easily but did not give it much thought. It was only when a classmate told him years later that they had named certain plays, "Carson shots" that he realized how exceptional his eye-hand coordination was and that it played a major role in his success as a surgeon.[12]

Ability to See in Three Dimensions Dr. Carson's ability to see in three dimensions makes it possible for him to perform delicate brain surgeries on children without complications. When surgeons operate on the body, they often can see only one side of the structure on which they are working. This is particularly true in brain surgery where a surgeon enters the brain from one side of the head. The ability that Dr. Carson has to see in three dimensions and visualize what is on the other side of a structure increases his success rates. In reflecting on his high success rate, Dr. Carson notes that surgeons who lack this mini-strength "just don't develop into outstanding surgeons, frequently encountering problems, constantly fighting complications."[13]

Lee Iacocca

At Ford Motor Company Lee Iacocca developed the Ford Mustang and eventually rose to be president. In 1978 after being fired by Henry Ford II, he became president of Chrysler. When he took the job, he knew that Chrysler was on the verge of bankruptcy, but he soon discovered that it was in even worse shape than he had thought. He later related, "[I] felt like [I] had just signed on to captain the Titanic."[14] His rescue of Chrysler from certain bankruptcy has made him a legend in the halls of American industry. A key strength that made Lee Iacocca a superstar in the automobile industry was his ability to influence others.

Influences Others Lee Iacocca's ability to influence others helped him throughout his career at Ford and Chrysler. His success in sales at the dealership level resulted in him being noticed early in his career by Ford executives and promoted to an upper level management position at Ford headquarters. This same strength helped him to motivate and energize his team while developing the Ford Mustang. Later in his career after leaving Ford, he used his ability to influence others to save Chrysler from bankruptcy. At the time, Chrysler's financial situation was so dismal that even banks refused to lend it money. With nowhere to go Iacocca approached the U. S. Congress. He testified before the Senate and House and met with members of Congress and the president. Using his ability to influence others, he convinced Congress to take the unprecedented action of providing Chrysler with a loan.[15]

Anita Roddick

In 1976 Anita Roddick opened her first Body Shop in Brighton, England in which she sold natural beauty products in hand-filled bottles. Six months later she opened a second store, eventually building The Body Shop into an international presence with stores throughout the world. She accomplished this by relying heavily on three of her core mini-strengths: her creative energy, attention to detail, and ability to relate to customers.

Creative Energy Anita Roddick has always been filled with creative energy. After she graduated from college, she taught school. Her classroom was in constant flux. She was always changing the chairs and desks around and putting up new pictures on the walls. She spent hours preparing innovative lessons that used drama and music to bring subjects to life.[16] It was this same creative energy that helped her make The Body Shop so unique and innovative. As a consumer of beauty products, Anita had always been dissatisfied with having to spend money for large bottles of cosmetics wrapped in fancy packaging when she didn't know if she would even like the product. When she started her store, she decided that it would be much more practical to let customers buy cosmetics in small sizes without the expensive and fancy packaging. So in her first shop she sold cosmetics in five sizes. The cheapest containers that she could find were bottles used by local hospitals to collect urine samples. Because she couldn't afford to buy very many bottles, she came up with the idea of making the bottles reusable. Customers could refill the bottles or even bring in their own bottles.[17]

Attention to Detail When Anita opened her first Body Shop, she attended to every detail that might sell her products. She prepared hand-written labels for each product that described what was in it, where the ingredients came from, and what the benefits were. To attract customers into her store, she created an elaborate set of lures, which included putting sandwich boards on the street, spraying exotic perfumes near the doorway, and hanging dried flowers from the ceiling.[18]

Customer Relations Anita first realized that she was good at customer relations when she and her husband, Gordon, opened a restaurant. Initially she cooked and Gordon dealt with customers. This was a disaster. Gordon's brusque manner and impatience with customers drove them away, whereas the kitchen under Anita's reign looked like a bomb had exploded. Realizing that this arrangement didn't use their mini-strengths, they switched roles. Gordon stayed in the kitchen and Anita dealt with customers. Soon their business was thriving.[19]

This ability of Anita's to relate to customers proved key to The Body Shop's instant success. Anita enjoyed explaining products to customers. Soon people of all ages and backgrounds began stopping by the shop to talk to her. Even men felt comfortable just coming in to browse. Anita also created a "perfume bar" and showed people how to mix their own perfumes which people found to be great fun.[20]

All of the people described above have become superstars, but each has used different mini-strengths. As their stories illustrate, there are many paths to the top. We don't need one particular set of mini-strengths. Rather what is important is that we identify our mini-strengths and then use them to skip down the Yellow Brick Road to our Emerald City.

Know Your Weaknesses

In *The Wizard of Oz,* the Tin Man tries to avoid crying because he knows that his tears make him rust. The Scarecrow avoids fire because he knows that it will consume him.

To become a superstar we also need to be aware of our weaknesses and avoid putting ourselves in situations where they can hurt us. Despite the pressures that we feel to be superstars in all areas of our life, none of us does everything well. We all have weaknesses. By seeing our weaknesses clearly and by honestly acknowledging them, we can minimize their potentially damaging effects on our ability to become a superstar. If we ignore them, we are likely to trip over them and create major disasters for ourselves. Moreover, when we take jobs or pursue careers requiring mini-strengths that we don't have, the struggle of trying to succeed can undermine our confidence

21

and cause other people to classify us as losers rather than winners. Oprah has commented:

> I think that the ability to be as good as you can comes from understanding who you are, and what you can and cannot do. What you can't do is far more important than what you can do, if what you can't do is going to keep you from flying as high as you can.[21]

Superstars tune-in to their weaknesses and find ways to avoid them. In some cases they change their career path. Jeffrey Bezos, founder of the Internet company, Amazon, originally wanted to be a physicist.

> I went to Princeton to study physics. . . . Things went fairly well until I got to quantum mechanics. There were about 30 people in the class by that point and it was so hard for me. I just remember there was a point where I realized I'm never going to be a great physicist. There were three or four people in the class whose brains were so clearly wired differently to process these highly abstract concepts. I was doing well in terms of the grades that I was getting, but for me it was laborious hard work. For some of these truly gifted folks-it was awe inspiring for me to watch them because in a very easy, almost casual way, they could absorb concepts and solve problems that I would work 12 hours on, and it was a wonderful thing to behold. At the same time, I had been studying computer science and was really finding that it was something I was drawn toward. I was drawn to that more and more, and it turned out to be a great thing. So I found—one of the greatest things Princeton taught me is that I'm not smart enough to be a physicist.[22]

Lance Armstrong, the elite world-class bicycle racer, similarly realized as a child that he wasn't good at sports like football that used balls and required eye-hand coordination.

> In Plano, Texas, if you weren't a football player you didn't exist. . . . I tried to play football. But I had no coordination. When it came to anything that involved moving from side to side, or hand-eye coordination—when it came to anything involving a ball, in fact—I was no good.[23]

Once Lance acknowledged this weakness, he went out and tried different sports until he found bike racing which didn't require eye-hand coordination. Using his amazing core physical mini-strengths, he soon made a name for himself as a top racer.

Roy Vagelos, former CEO of the pharmaceutical giant, Merck & Co., Inc., also took his weaknesses into consideration when he selected his career path. In high school he discovered that he was hopeless at rote memorization. He was so bad that the principal of his high school suggested that he read his valedictorian address. Taking his weakness into consideration, Roy chose a career in biochemistry and medicine that didn't depend heavily on rote memorization and instead, used his excellent problem solving skills.[24]

Once we acknowledge and accept our weaknesses, we can further reduce their impact by finding other people to do the things that we don't do well. Sam Walton, founder of Wal-Mart, has commented, "I think my style as an executive has been pretty much dictated by my talents. I've played to my strengths and relied on others to make up for my weaknesses."[25]

In the mid-1960s Sam Walton became overwhelmed by the problems involved in effectively managing the merchandizing and replenishment systems for Wal-Mart's ever-increasing numbers of stores. He decided that computers, which were just beginning to play a role in businesses, would solve these problems. So he enrolled in an IBM computer school for retailers. He knew that he wouldn't be any good at computers, but he figured that it would be a great place to look for a smart computer person.[26]

Richard Branson also has always been quick to find others to compensate for his weaknesses. In the early 1970s he was struggling to get his first major business, Virgin Mail Order Records, off the ground. He soon realized that he was not good at the financial side of the business and immediately recruited his childhood friend, Nik, to manage the money. As a result, Virgin Mail Order Records thrived. Nik kept track of every penny and even got the group to turn off the lights when they left rooms and make quick phone calls to save money.[27]

It is also important to be aware that our mini-strengths can turn into weaknesses if we use them in the wrong place. Oprah became a talk-show host because she was on the verge of being fired from her job as a television news reporter. Her ability to emotionally connect with people and experience their pain was a handicap in the news business.

> My openness was the reason why I did not do well as a news reporter. Because I used to go on assignment and be so open that I would say to people at fires—who've lost their children—"That's okay. You don't have to talk to me." Well then you go back to the newsroom and the news director says, "What do you mean they didn't have to talk to you?" I'd say, "But she just lost her child, and you know I just felt so bad."
>
> So, I didn't do very well. I'd go to funerals of people and not go in. I wouldn't want to talk to them, disturb them, have them cry on the air.[28]

Larry Ellison, founder of Oracle, wisely never attempted to be part of the traditional corporate world. In such an environment where rules and procedures are important, Larry's mini-strengths of challenging experts and questioning conventional ways of doing things would have been a liability. By choosing to be an entrepreneur, he selected an arena in which his mini-strengths were truly an asset and didn't become a weakness.

Accepting our weaknesses is essential to becoming a superstar. Only by finding a path that doesn't depend on them can we express our true potential. Once we are aware of our weaknesses, we can have others handle what we don't do well and we can then capitalize on what we do best.

Listen to Your Heart

When the Wizard of Oz presents the Tin Man with a heart shaped watch, the Tin Man immediately knows what to do. He holds the watch up to his ear and says, "Listen! Look it ticks!" [29]

To be a superstar we need to follow the Tin Man's lead and put our heart to our ear and listen to what it tells us. Knowing our mini-strengths and weaknesses is just one part of becoming a superstar. It is equally important to know what speaks to our heart. Becoming a superstar requires long hours of work. It doesn't happen instantaneously. We can only sustain such effort and commitment when we act from our hearts and do something that we love to do. To be a superstar, we must—like the Tin Man—listen to our heart.

Superstars pursue activities that speak to their heart. Michael Steinhardt, a Wall Street superstar, became fascinated with investing while still in high school. He started buying stocks with whatever money he had. He would take the train from his home in Brooklyn to downtown Manhattan where he would spend the day at brokerage houses reading annual reports and watching the ticker tape.

> I liked watching my stocks go by on the ticker tape. I learned their symbols and I charted the progress of companies I was interested in. The noise of the ticker only exacerbated the delirium of the environment. Not only did you see the ticker, you heard it too. The greater the activity in the market, the more rapid the sound of the ticker. There was, then, a certain music to the market, and when its tempo increased, it became that much more exciting.
>
> My interest in the market was so intense that it dwarfed any other pursuits. I knew I wanted to work on Wall Street and, once I had made up my mind, I never thought about any other career. It was not work, it was joy. I had come to love the risk taking associated with trading, and the rush when the risk pays off.[30]

Deborah Copaken Kogan, the brilliant photojournalist, was interested in photography as a child but she really fell in love with it in college. She didn't just love taking pictures. She loved the entire process, including developing pictures in the chemical baths that photographers use.

When I got to college and started shooting pictures myself, my appetite for the medium was insatiable. I shot at least eight and sometimes fifteen rolls of film a day.[31]

I loved to press the shutter, to freeze time, to turn little slices of life into rectangles rife with metaphor. I loved to collect the rectangles, like so many souvenir trinkets, to gaze at them, study them, find the one that best summarized a particular lived moment. I loved the smell of the black-and-white chemicals. Loved to dip a naked piece of white photographic paper into a bath of developer and watch the image miraculously materialize, watch life, a moment, reborn. Loved rescuing the ever-darkening image, saving it from blackness with my tongs, immersing it into the stop bath, then into the fixer, imagining all those silver crystals stopping, fixing, imagining my little rectangle living on forever.[32]

Sam Walton was equally enthralled with the process of finding goods to sell and then figuring out how to get people to buy them.

It's almost embarrassing to admit this, but it's true: there isn't a day in my adult life when I haven't spent some time thinking about merchandising. . . . It has been an absolute passion of mine. It is what I enjoy doing as much as anything in the business. I really love to pick an item—maybe the most basic merchandise—and then call attention to it.[33]

Following his passion for merchandising, Sam constantly searched for better and cheaper ways to sell and display products. He regularly visited other retail stores looking for ideas. During his first retail job at J. C. Penney's in Des Moines, Iowa, he spent his lunch hours checking out stores on the block where he worked.[34] In Newport, Arkansas where he started his first store, he regularly strolled across the street to visit the store of his major competitor, John Dunham, to look for ideas on how he might do things better.[35] Even on family vacations Sam would stop and visit stores along the way.[36]

Sam also read everything that he could about merchandising. If he found a new idea that he thought was promising, he would find out more about it. On one occasion, he was so intrigued by an article about two stores in Minnesota that had started using self-service that he hopped on a bus and went to visit them to see how it worked. He liked the idea and implemented it in his store in Bentonville, Arkansas, making it the third self-service store to open in the country.[37]

The other process that Sam loved was finding bargains. After he opened his first Ben Franklin store in Newport Arkansas, he realized that he could make more money if he purchased his products directly from manufacturers and wholesalers rather than buying them through the Ben Franklin franchise. As soon as he closed his store for the day, he would hook up a trailer to his car and drive to Tennessee and Missouri looking for deals on merchandise to sell in his store.[38]

When, like Sam Walton, we listen to our hearts, we find that we have enormous energy for our work. We become fully engaged in what we are trying to achieve and are always willing to go the extra mile. It is this energy that propels us forward and helps us become superstars.

Hear the Special Beat
of Your Own Heart

When Dorothy and the Scarecrow find the Tin Man frozen in place, they carefully oil him. After finishing, Dorothy tells him that he is now perfect. The Tin Man replies, "Bang on my chest if you think I'm perfect." Dorothy lifts her hand and does as he asks. The Tin Man's chest emits a hollow echo. As it fades, the Tin Man explains that the tinsmith forgot to give him a heart. Lamenting about his lack of a heart, he imagines what it would be like to have a heart. He sings, "I hear a beat. How sweet! Just to register emotion. . . . "[39]

The Tin Man considers himself defective because he doesn't have his own heart. He wants to hear his heart beat, not someone else's heart. He knows that we can't become superstars unless we are in tune with the special beat of our own hearts.

Sometimes it is difficult to hear our own heart. Society's external drums promising riches and glamour beat so loudly that they drown out the sound of our own heart. We become caught up in what Jeffrey Bezos, founder of Amazon, calls the "hot passion of the day."[40] As Bezos points out, there is always a "hot passion of the day" that is hard to resist. When everyone else seems to be following it, we feel left out or not "cool" if we don't march to its beat. Applications to graduate schools show how we become captivated by the "hot passion of the day." Making lots of money has been "hot" in recent years. As a result, business school applications have spiked. Applications to law schools, which were previously "hot," have now fallen off. Before this, everyone wanted to attend medical school because being a doctor was considered prestigious and glamorous.

The Internet revolution in the mid 1990s is another example of how we become swept up in the "hot passion of the day." When the Internet became "hot," people abandoned college and stable careers to start Internet businesses. Others worked at start-ups for low salaries or no salary at all in exchange for stock options that they hoped would one day make them rich. In 2000 when the bottom fell out of Internet stocks and easy money disappeared, most of these dreams turned to dust.

Jeffrey Bezos stresses how important it is to not get caught up in these "hot passions of the day" and instead hear the beat of your own heart.

Do something you're very passionate about and don't try to chase the hot passion of the day. I think that we actually saw this. I think that you see it all over the place in different contexts, but I think that we saw it in the Internet world quite a bit, where, at sort of the peak of the Internet mania in—say 1999—you found people who were very passionate about something [else but] they left that job and decided, I'm going to do something on the Internet because it's almost like the 1849 Gold Rush in a way. [During the Gold Rush] everybody who was in shouting distance of California [went]. . . . They might have been a doctor but they quit being a doctor and started panning for gold. It almost never works. Even if it does work according to some metric, financial success, or whatever it might be, I suspect it leaves you ultimately unsatisfied.[41]

We also don't always hear the special beats of our own hearts because we listen to parents, teachers and friends instead of our own hearts. They can push us to do what is practical or "best for us" rather than what our own heart tells us. Even years after we have moved beyond their influence, their words can continue to ring in our ears and keep us from doing what speaks to our hearts. While their advice is based on a desire for our success, only we know what is in our heart. When we listen to others, we can end up spending our days doing work that we don't like. A woman included in Arnold and Denny's study of valedictorians has lamented that she became a doctor because she listened to others instead of what she wanted. Another valedictorian focused on grades in school because he was trying to be the "good son" rather than following his passion for art.[42]

Superstars listen to the beat of their own hearts even when others think that they are on the wrong track. Susan Butcher, the famous dog musher who won the Iditarod four times, went to Alaska after high school, despite her parents' protests. They felt that she should go to college, but Susan didn't listen. She loved animals and wanted to be in a place where she would be directly connected to nature. She never regretted this decision.

> If you have a passion, no matter how many people criticize that passion . . . you have to go with your dream, which is certainly what I have done. Which has brought my life great fulfillment.[43]

George Lucas, director of *Star Wars* and *American Graffiti*, recalls how people around him thought that he was crazy to go to film school. From their perspective he would never be able to earn a living. Despite their warnings, he listened to the beat of his own heart because he loved the process of making movies.

> I decided to go to film school because I loved the idea of making films. I loved photography and everybody said it was a crazy thing to do because in those days nobody made it into the film business. I mean, unless you were related to somebody, there was no way in. So everybody was thinking I was silly. "You're never going to get a job." But I wasn't moved by that. I set the goal of getting through film school, and just focused on getting to that level. . . .[44]

Even if we don't hear the special beat of our own heart at first, we should keep trying. Superstars continue to listen for the beat of their own heart even when they start out on the wrong track. Anita Roddick had a number of false starts before she decided to start The Body Shop. After she left college she taught school. Next, she and her husband started a bed and breakfast. When their customers disappeared at the end of the summer, they transformed it into a residential hotel. They then opened a restaurant. These ventures were moderately profitable but none was a grand success. After three years they were physically and emotionally exhausted. One evening they sat down and both agreed that they couldn't continue.[45] It was at this point that Anita started to hear the special beat of her own heart. She had always been intrigued by the beauty of women in under-developed areas and the ways in which they used natural products from their environment on their bodies and hair. In her early twenties during her travels through developing countries, she often stopped and observed how women cared for their bodies.

> I loved to watch native women's beauty and bathing rituals; I was fascinated by their ingenuity, and made it my business to talk to women wherever I went to find out what they used on their bodies. I saw women using as a shampoo, a kind of green mud that worked wonderfully. I saw women eating pineapple, then rubbing the inside of the skin onto their faces.[46]

Following her passion for natural body products, Anita decided to open The Body Shop, a store that would provide women with these products at reasonable prices.

Lee Iacocca didn't initially hear the beat of his own heart. In college he studied engineering and then entered Ford's prestigious engineering internship program. One day after spending an entire day designing a clutch spring and making a detailed mechanical drawing of it, he heard the beat of his own heart loud and clear. He thought, "What on earth am I doing? Is this how I want to be spending the rest of my life?"[47] He realized that he wanted to work with people rather than machines. He was passionate about influencing and motivating others, not designing automobile parts. After much negotiation he convinced Ford to let him try sales. It was his ability to be honest with himself and hear the beat of his own heart that started him on his journey to becoming a superstar in the automobile industry.

No matter where we are in our career, it is never too late to listen to the special beat of our own heart. Some of us don't hear this beat until we have worked for a number of years. While in the past people were expected to pick a career and stick with it for the rest of their lives even if they intensely disliked it, today we have more choices. It is acceptable to change careers no matter how old we are. When we consider that during our lives we can spend more than 80,000 hours at work, this is a long time to be toiling away at something that doesn't fulfill us or provide us with the joy of accomplishment that comes from following our hearts. Moreover, by not following our hearts, we may physically kill our hearts. The stress and unhappiness of doing something we dislike contributes to heart disease, a leading cause of death. Like the Tin Man we must insist on listening to our own heart and follow what it tells us. Not only will this make us a superstar but it will also bring us more happiness and a longer life.

Find Your Winning Combination

After Dorothy's house lands with a crash in Oz, she opens the door and looks around in delighted amazement. When Glinda, the good witch, arrives, Dorothy eagerly peppers her with questions about Oz. As she travels down the Yellow Brick Road to the Emerald City, Dorothy is intrigued by the Scarecrow and the Tin Man's predicaments and invites them to come with her to Oz. She even gets the Lion to join them. By the time Dorothy and the group reach the Emerald City, the Scarecrow, the Tin Man and the Lion are committed to helping Dorothy return to Kansas.

Dorothy could have remained barricaded in her house after she lands in the strange land of Oz. Instead her love of adventure and exploring new things soon lures her out of the house. By combining her passion for new things with her mini-strengths, which include curiosity, charisma, and the ability to influence others, she is soon on her way to becoming a superstar. On her way to the Emerald City her curiosity helps her discover the Scarecrow and the Tin Man. Attracted by Dorothy's charisma, they decide to become part of her team. Dorothy also convinces the Lion to join them by using her ability to influence others. The help of the Scarecrow, the Tin Man and the Lion becomes instrumental to her success. Without them, she would never have reached the Emerald City or defeated the Wicked Witch. Moreover, through all the ups and downs on her journey, Dorothy still has great fun because she is doing something she likes.

Once we have identified our mini-strengths and what speaks to our heart, we must, like Dorothy, combine them in ways that give us an edge. This is not always a simple task because we are multi-dimensional. We have many mini-strengths and most of us like to do more than one thing. The filmmaker and executive producer George Lucas believes that the best way to find our winning combination is to watch ourselves in action.

> You keep going through the things that you like to do, until you find something that you actually seem to be extremely good at. It can be anything. There are lots of different things out there. It's a matter of moving around until you find the one for you, the niche that you fit into.[48]

Lucas used this approach to discover that making films was a perfect way for him to combine his mini-strengths with something that he loved to do. He recalls:

> Suddenly everything came together in one place. All my likes, everything I actually seemed to have a talent for was right there. I said, "Hey, this is it. I can do this really well. I really love to do it."[49]

Like all superstars, he found a winning combination where his mini-strengths and what spoke to his heart merged.

When we find this winning combination it strikes a deep chord in us. It feels right for us. Oprah discovered her winning combination when she did her first talk show. As a talk show host, she combined her ability to emotionally connect with others with her love of learning about other people's lives. She relates, "From the very first day I did my first talk show, I knew it was the right thing to do."[50] I said, "I'm home. I'm home. I know this is what I am supposed to be doing."[51] Tiger Woods found the perfect winning combination for himself in golf where he combines his eye-hand coordination and physical prowess as a golfer with his passion for competing. In a *60 Minutes* interview he commented, "I love to compete. That's the essence of who I am."[52]

This search for our winning combination can be an ongoing process. Many superstars take initial wrong-turns. Oprah first worked as a television news reporter before she discovered that being a talk show host was the winning combination for her. Lee Iacocca started at Ford as an engineer. After 9 months, he realized that marketing and sales were a better fit for him. Before Anita Roddick opened her first Body Shop, she had a number of different careers.

In looking for our winning combination, we also need to be aware that the world is continually changing. As a result, new ways of combining our mini-strengths and what speaks to our hearts are always emerging. When Jeffrey Bezos decided that he wanted to start a computer company, Internet businesses didn't exist. Once the Internet became a viable business option, he decided that an Internet computer company would be a perfect way to combine his mini-strengths and love of computers. Like Jeffrey Bezos, we must remain attuned to the opportunities in the world around us and the ways in which they can become vehicles for combining our mini-strengths with what we like to do.

In searching for our winning combination, we also need to pay attention to the subtle clues that others provide. People often intuitively sense when we haven't found our winning combination and start trying to change little things about us so that we will fit better with what we are doing at the moment. Their suggestions can be valuable signals that we may not be in the right place for us. When Oprah became a co-anchor of the evening news in Baltimore, the assistant news director had a feeling that something wasn't working well. He thought it was her appearance. He told her, "Your hair is too long. It is too thick. Your eyes are too far apart. Your nose is too broad. Your chin is too wide. And you need to do something about it." Oprah relates, "They sent me to this chichi, pooh-pooh salon. And in a week I was bald. Just devastated. I had a French perm and it all fell out."[53] This push to cosmetically change Oprah ended when she began to do talk shows. Once she combined her mini-strengths with what she liked to do, she exuded a genuineness that transcended her appearance. As a result, producers and directors forgot about how she looked.

The other key to finding our winning combination is to remain focused on who we are and what is special about us. It is easy to become enthralled with imitating someone whom we idolize rather than just being ourselves. When Oprah started as a newscaster, she wanted to be another Barbara Walters.

> When I first started out . . . I was pretending to be somebody I was not. I was pretending to be Barbara Walters. So I'd go to a news conference, and I was more interested in how I phrased a question, how eloquent the question sounded, as opposed to listening to the answer.[54]

Oprah never became good at being Barbara Walters because she has different mini-strengths. One of Barbara Walter's mini-strengths is her ability to probe guests for important details and ask them tough questions that they don't want to answer, whereas Oprah excels at emotionally connecting with her guests. Once Oprah abandoned the idea of being Barbara Walters, she was able to forge her own path and find the route that led her to becoming a superstar.

Being committed to who we are also means doing it our way. Johnny Cash relates how he learned this lesson from his voice teacher when he was twelve.

> I was singing some popular country song of the day. . . . I didn't sing it like the artist had sung it on the radio. [My teacher] said, "You're a song stylist."
>
> She said, "Always do it your way."
>
> And from the age of 12, I didn't forget that. But that was the way I had to do it, because it was the way it was with me. I had to do it my way. I couldn't read those notes, singing those great songs, like a lot of those singers could, but I could do it my way—the way it felt good to me.[55]

Johnny Cash's teacher gave him good advice because it was the unique quality of Johnny Cash's voice that helped him become a superstar.

Jack Welch learned a similar lesson about the importance of being himself when he became vice-chairman of General Electric. As a young manager climbing through the management ranks, he often worried that he didn't fit the mold of the typical General Electric manager. He states, "I remember the tremendous pressure to be someone I wasn't."[56] When he became vice-chairman, he decided to cultivate the mature and polished image that he believed a vice-chairman should project.

> At one of my earliest board meetings in San Francisco shortly after being named vice-chairman, I showed up in a perfectly pressed blue suit, with a starched white shirt and crisp red tie. I chose my words

carefully. I wanted to show the board members that I was older and more mature than either my 43 years or my reputation. I guess I wanted to look and act like a typical GE vice-chairman.[57]

After the meeting one of the directors came up to him and touched his suit. He said, "Jack, . . . this isn't you. You looked a lot better when you were just being yourself."[58]

Once we know our mini-strengths and what speaks to our heart, we can become a superstar in any arena. Whether we are enthralled with music, law, computers or business we can find a way to use our mini-strengths in that arena. When Dr. Ben Carson entered medicine, he didn't know what area of medicine he would practice. With his gifted hands and ability to see in three dimensions, he could have gone into any area of surgery, but he discovered that he was fascinated by the brain. Michael Eisner, former CEO of Disney, became interested in literature and theatre while in college. After college he tried writing plays and novels but soon realized that he didn't have the mental stamina to finish them and writing wasn't one of his mini-strengths. Instead, he realized that he enjoyed managing creative people and he did it well. This led to his becoming an executive superstar in the television and movie industries.[59]

When we find our winning combination and "do it our way" we increase our ability to become a superstar because we don't waste energy trying to be someone we aren't. We instead can skip down the Yellow Brick Road with confidence and use the best in us to meet any challenge.

TAKE A MOMENT TO REFLECT

What are your mini-strengths? Are you using them to build your success?

On the page below, make a table with a column listing your mini-strengths and one next to it that describes how you are using each mini-strength to build your career.

STEP TWO

Know Where
You Are Going

Dorothy knows where she is going. She is determined to return home to Kansas. Despite many ups and downs, she never wavers from her mission. To become a superstar, we too must have a mission that is vitally important to us. Without such a mission, it is easy to wander through careers, and often life itself, and never accomplish anything of value. When I was in college, I hitch-hiked through Europe one summer. I had no specific agenda. Each morning I stuck out my thumb with only a vague destination in mind. Often I changed where I was going depending on who offered me a ride. I traveled across the Swiss Alps to Austria instead of south to Italy because a student on his way to Salzburg, Austria picked me up. I had a fabulous time that summer but this approach is not a recipe for becoming a superstar.

Superstars have missions. They know what they want to accomplish. Moreover, they choose missions in which they intensely believe. To maintain their momentum, they create short-term challenges and goals that energize and empower them. They also retain the flexibility needed to capitalize on new opportunities and find different routes when they encounter roadblocks. Finally, superstars never lose sight of where they are going.

Choose a Mission

Soon after Dorothy's house lands in Munchkinland, Glinda arrives in a magical bubble of light. As soon as the opportunity arises, Dorothy asks Glinda, "Which is the way back to Kansas?" [1]

Dorothy has a definite mission which guides her on her way through Oz. Choosing a mission is an important first step on our journey to becoming a superstar. Without one, it is difficult to know whether we are going in the right direction or even if we are making progress. Superstars start their journeys with a vision of where they want to go. Jack Welch decided early in his career at General Electric that he wanted to be CEO.[2] From the time George Lucas entered film school, he was determined to make movies.[3] Donna Shirley dreamed of traveling to distant planets from the time that she was a small child.[4]

Missions don't have to be detailed plans. Most superstars initially start with just a direction. They expand and elaborate on their mission as they move forward. When Richard Branson left secondary school, he was clear about the fact that he wanted to start businesses but he didn't know exactly what type. Sam Walton made retail his mission after discovering as a management trainee at J. C. Penney how much he loved selling people merchandise. At that point, he didn't know what he wanted to do in retail. It was only three years later after completing his military service that he decided to open his own variety store. The idea of starting Wal-Mart didn't occur to him until many years later.[5]

The value of having a mission is that it gives us a direction and increases our chances of success by delineating the steps that we need to take to get to our destination. If we lack a mission, we can waste time aimlessly moving between different jobs and even careers. When Donny Deutsch, the advertising mogul, graduated from college, he wasn't sure what he wanted to do. He was attracted to advertising so he accepted a job at Ogilvy & Mather, a large prestigious New York advertising firm steeped in years of tradition. Donny soon found the firm's culture so oppressive that he left and went to California where he did nothing for six months.[6] When he returned to New York, he went to work at his father's small advertising agency as an account executive, but his heart was not in it. His father finally said to him, "You're not taking this seriously. Take a walk. Find work you love."[7] So Donny sold Gitano jeans at a flea market. It was six months later when his father considered selling his agency that Donny found his mission. Feeling that his father wasn't really ready to sell, Donny decided to build his father's agency into a major player in the advertising world. Once Donny embraced this mission, the actions that he needed to take to get there became obvious. He started searching for bigger and better accounts, using every strategy he could devise. In less than a year he acquired the Pontiac Dealers Association account, which was four times the agency's usual account size. This account set him on the path to building the agency into a billion dollar media business.[8]

A mission also serves to attune us to opportunities that we would have missed if we didn't know where we were going. When opportunities arise that further our mission, we are more likely to seize them and spring into action. Even as a child, Richard Branson was always clearly focused on where he was going and quick to grab opportunities to get there. When Richard was five, his Auntie Joyce promised him 10 shillings if he learned how to swim while they were on summer holiday. This became Richard's holiday mission. Each day he spent hours in the cold sea trying to swim but had no success. At the end of holiday Aunt Joyce told him not to worry, "There's always next year." Richard, however, didn't want to wait until next year. On the drive home he spotted a river through the car window. Seeing it as his last chance to learn how to swim before the holiday ended, he pleaded with his father to stop. After the car came to a stop, Richard tore off his clothes, raced down to the river, and leapt in, wearing only his underpants. A powerful current dragged him downstream while he desperately tried to keep his head above water. Pulled under by the water, he felt his foot hit on a stone on the bottom. He pushed off and suddenly he was swimming.[9] If Richard had not been on a mission to learn how to swim, he wouldn't have noticed that they were driving by a river. It was his awareness of what he wanted to achieve that attuned him to the opportunity and moved him to action.

George Lucas was similarly quick early in his career to seize opportunities. When he entered film school, he knew that he wanted to make movies. As a result, he didn't wait until he left film school to make a movie. While his fellow students lamented that they wished that they could make a movie, Lucas leapt right in and made a movie in his first class.

> The first class I had was an animation class. It wasn't a production class. And in the animation class they gave us one minute of film to put onto the animation camera to operate it, to see how you could move left, move right, make it go up and down. They had certain requirements that you had to do. You had to make it go up and you had to make it go down, and then the teacher would look at it and say, "Oh yes, you maneuvered this machine to do these things." It was a test.

> I took that one minute of film and made it into a movie, and it was a movie that won about 25 awards in every film festival in the world, and kind of changed the whole animation department. Meanwhile all the other guys were going around saying, "Oh, I wish I could make a movie. I wish I was in a production class."[10]

Jeffrey Bezos's mission when he graduated from Princeton was to start a computer business but he decided that first he should acquire some business experience. Ten years later when the Internet developed, he saw his opportunity. He didn't hesitate. He leapt into the water and started building Amazon into a viable business. He relates:

> I knew that when I was 80, I was not going to regret having tried this. I was not going to regret trying to participate in this thing called the Internet that I thought was going to be a big deal. I knew that if I failed I wouldn't regret that, but I knew the one thing that I might

regret is not ever having tried. I knew that would haunt me every day, and so when I thought about it that way, it was an incredibly easy decision.[11]

When we have a mission, we don't get lost. We aren't afraid to take action. Like Richard Branson, George Lucas, and Jeffrey Bezos, we leap into the river without worrying whether we will drown. Our attention is directed outside of ourselves on our environment searching for opportunities that will help us pursue our mission.

Focus on What You Want to Achieve

After Dorothy's house lands on the Wicked Witch of the East, she is declared a national heroine in Munchkinland. The Munchkins have a celebration in her honor and give her the keys to the city. Dorothy dutifully accepts their accolades, but she doesn't linger to bask in their adoration. She is soon on her way to the Emerald City to ask the Wizard for help.

Dorothy is not interested in the fame and glory that the Munchkins bestow on her. She is focused on returning to Kansas. Superstars, first and foremost, are intent on achieving things that they feel are important. They see money and fame as simply one of the rewards that they may receive for their achievements. Oprah's first priority is to help people improve the quality of their personal lives. She has commented, "My focus has never, ever for one minute been money—I would do this job, and take on a second job to make ends meet if nobody paid me."[12]

Sam Walton's mission similarly was never money. In the 1950s people in rural areas were served by small stores that couldn't afford to carry large inventories and charged high prices for the products that they sold. Sam Walton's mission was to change this. In his stores he wanted to provide rural people with the same wide array of products that people in cities could buy and at the same low prices.[13]

> Money never has meant that much to me, not even in the sense of keeping score. If we had enough groceries, and a nice place to live, plenty of room to keep and feed my bird dogs, a place to hunt, a place to play tennis and the means to get the kids good educations—that's rich.[14]

Fame also held little interest for Sam Walton. He just wanted to live modestly outside of the limelight. He rarely called attention to himself. He was appalled when the media descended on his home in Bentonville, Arkansas after Forbes magazine in 1985 named him the "richest man in America." When he received an invitation to one of Elizabeth Taylor's many weddings, he commented, "Why in the world . . . would I get an invitation to Elizabeth Taylor's wedding out in Hollywood?"[15]

Richard Branson, the "rebel billionaire," also has never been driven by money and fame. He starts businesses because he wants to provide better service and products to people at cheaper prices. Even after Virgin Music made 660,000 pounds in 1973 from the release of Michael Oldfield's first album, *Tubular Bells*, Richard continued to live frugally and put the money that he earned into expanding his business. He relates:

> We still paid ourselves tiny wages, we still all lived in each other's pockets, and we reinvested all the money we earned from *Tubular Bells* into new artists and building up the company.[16]

Warren Buffett's mission has always been to figure out ways to invest money that will bring steady long-term returns. Money just indicates how good a job he is doing. His disregard for material wealth is seen in his simple life-style. He still lives in the same house in Omaha that he bought in 1958 for $31,500. When in 1999 he auctioned off his twenty-year old wallet at a charity function, he commented:

> There's nothing special about the wallet. It goes back a long time. My suits are old, my wallet's old, my car's old. I've lived in the same house since 1958, so I hang on to things.[17]

Despite the fact that making money and becoming famous has never been their primary mission, Oprah, Sam Walton, Richard Branson and Warren Buffett have acquired lots of it. This is because they provide people with goods and services that they need and want. When we do something that people value and appreciate, they will open their wallets and rain admiration on us. Oprah is rich and famous because people are eager to improve their personal lives. Warren Buffett is rich and famous because his investment strategies have made many other people millionaires. Wal-Mart became a billion dollar company because Sam Walton focused on finding ways to please customers.[18]

Richard Branson's financial empire similarly rests on the fact that he understands what people want and need. One of the first questions that he asks himself when deciding whether to enter a particular type of business is whether he, his family or his friends would want to buy its products or services. He started his mail order record business because he saw that his impoverished friends still spent money on records. He realized that he could save them and others money by selling records through the mail. He bought a computer game company after he saw how much his children loved to play video games.[19] His focus has always been on providing products and services that people value and want to buy.

By concentrating first on providing goods and services that other people value and need, we are more likely to ensure our long-term success. While we may acquire short-term success by ignoring the interests of others, it is unlikely to last. The leading characters in the Enron scandal were superstars for a few years but ultimately their ruthless pursuit of money and fame resulted in their downfall. In contrast, people like Oprah, Richard Branson, Sam Walton and Warren Buffett have achieved long-term success because they have concentrated on producing products and services that benefit others.

Believe in Your Mission

When the Tin Man stands before the Wizard of Oz to receive his heart, the Wizard booms, "You don't know how lucky you are to not have one." The Tin Man says, "But I, . . . I still want one." [20]

The Tin Man intensely believes that he needs a heart to make him human. He doesn't care if the Wizard thinks it is a good idea. He is deeply committed to having a heart so he can be compassionate and caring. To become a superstar, we must choose a mission that is intensely important to us. It may not make sense to others but we need to believe in its value and be totally committed to it.

Superstars strongly believe in the value of their missions and fiercely embrace them. It is the strength of their belief that generates the unshakable commitment that they have to achieving these missions. Anita Roddick started The Body Shop because she deeply believed in the power of natural beauty products from around the world to nourish and improve women's skin. This belief in the value of her products was a key factor in making her first Body Shop in Brighton, England successful. She recalls:

> Talking about products was never a chore. Passion persuades, and by God I was passionate about what I was selling. I loved to tell people where the ingredients had come from, how they were used in their original state and what they could do. [21]

Fred Smith started Federal Express because he intensely believed that as reliance on technology increased, there would be a critical need for an integrated air and ground system that quickly and reliably delivered packages to the right place at the right time.

> I was very convinced that the idea was the central feature of the new economy. That without a system like this, it simply wasn't going to be able to work. So I was in every sense of the word, a zealot. . . . I felt very strongly that this needed to be done, that it was something that would be extremely useful to people and that it would make the

economy and society and the system work much better than it would work absent that.[22]

When we have such a powerful belief in our mission, other people's opinions don't matter to us. We are undeterred by criticism. Warren Buffett doesn't worry about what other people think about his investment decisions. He conceives of his work as analogous to painting the Sistine Chapel and is unconcerned about the comments of critics.

> If I want to paint blue or red on the canvas, I can do it. No one criticizes. Someone else may not like the painting, but I like it.[23]

Billie Holiday, the famous African-American jazz singer, similarly ignored public opinion when she included "Strange Fruit" in her repertoire. This powerful song portrays brutally lynched African-American men hanging from Southern trees like strange fruit. Billie Holiday first sang the song in 1939 in a Greenwich Village café. As the notes of the song faded away, there was silence. She recalled later, "There wasn't even a patter of applause when I finished. Then a lone person began to clap nervously. Then suddenly everyone was clapping."[24] Billie Holiday sang "Strange Fruit" because she believed that lynching should stop and people needed to feel the horror of it. While some people praised her for singing the song, others vilified her. Irate whites would at times verbally abuse her, and some clubs refused to let her sing. Her record company, Columbia Records, wouldn't record "Strange Fruit" because they were afraid it would offend their Southern buyers. Despite the outpouring of criticism, Billie Holiday continued to sing "Strange Fruit" because she believed in its message.[25] Ultimately, it increased her fame.

Even repeated rejection doesn't stop superstars when they believe in what they are doing. John Grisham, the popular contemporary novelist, spent years writing his first novel, *A Time to Kill*. He would arrive at his office at five in the morning and write before he started work. When he finally completed the manuscript, 28 publishers rejected it. He eventually found an unknown publisher who was willing to print a short run and Grisham, through Herculean efforts on his part, was able to sell 5,000 copies. The lack of popularity of his first book didn't stop Grisham because he believed in his mission. He wrote a second novel, *The Firm*. This time he was more successful. The book became a bestseller and was made into a movie.[26]

To become a superstar we must choose a mission in which we intensely believe. When we pick this type of mission, we will be willing to pursue it to the ends of the earth. The opinions and criticism of others won't stop us. We will, like the Tin Man, be driven to persist, no matter what setbacks occur along the way.

Create Short-Term Challenges

Just as Dorothy and the Scarecrow finish oiling the Tin Man, the Wicked Witch appears. Cackling, she tells the Scarecrow that she'll stuff a mattress with him. Turning to the Tin Man, she proclaims that she will make a beehive out of him. She then throws a ball of fire at the Scarecrow.

After they put out the fire, the Scarecrow turns to Dorothy and declares, "I'm not afraid of her. I'll see that you get safely to the Wizard now, whether I get a brain or not! Stuff a mattress with me! Hah!"

The Tin Man echoes the Scarecrow's comments. He tells Dorothy, "I'll see you reach the Wizard, whether I get a heart or not. Beehive—bah! Let her try and make a beehive out of me!"[27]

Rather than being intimidated by the Wicked Witch, the Scarecrow and the Tin Man are challenged. Their outrage at the Wicked Witch's threats energizes them and makes them determined to protect Dorothy. They vow to raise their performance to higher levels to help her reach the Emerald City.

Superstars welcome challenges. They know that there is a powerful link between being challenged and performing at our highest levels because we try harder when we are challenged. Roy Vagelos believes that the competitive challenges he faced as CEO of Merck were an important source of his success.

I loved the competition and still do. It brought out the best in me and, I've observed, in most of us. Competition is what keeps my juices running. . . .[28]

The key to capitalizing on the power of challenges is to break our mission into short-term challenges that are at the right level of difficulty for us at our present skill level. Elite athletes don't start by focusing on winning a Gold Medal at the Olympics. They create short-term challenges that are tailored to their abilities and what they can do at the moment. Once they meet a challenge, they raise the bar by creating a harder one for themselves.

Sam Walton loved to challenge himself but he always chose short-term challenges that he had some hope of reaching based on where he was in his career. When he opened his first Ben Franklin store in Newport Arkansas, he decided that he would make it the most profitable one within Arkansas in five years.[29] In addition, he decided that he would outdo his biggest competitor, John Dunham's Sterling Store, which was directly across the street. Sam met his challenge of surpassing John Dunham within three years.[30]

Two years later in his fifth year of operation, Sam met his other challenge, which was to be the number one Ben Franklin store in Arkansas. As sometimes happens when we set the right short-term challenges for ourselves, Sam exceeded his goal. His Ben Franklin not only became the number one Ben Franklin within Arkansas but also within the six-state region.[31]

In choosing short-term challenges we must also guard against picking ones that are too easy and thus, not really challenges at all. When we choose non-challenges, it is hard to muster the energy that we need to perform at our highest levels. We become apathetic and never get around to actively pursuing our mission. At General Electric Jack Welch was keenly attuned to the close link between success and choosing short-term challenges that were sufficiently challenging. After he became CEO, he saw that many of GE's businesses were no longer actively pursuing business and that the company was about to be left behind due to increasing foreign competition. To create a short-term challenge that would energize these businesses, he announced that any GE business that was not No. 1 or No. 2 in its market must find a way to become No. 1 or No. 2 or it would be fixed, sold, or closed. This short-term challenge helped him transform GE from an aging giant into an agile competitor that has entered the twenty-first century as a contender.[32]

Knowing how important short-term challenges are, superstars don't wait for them to arrive at their doorstep. They actively seek them. Once they meet one challenge, they find another. Richard Branson didn't instantaneously build his Virgin empire. He built it by creating a series of short-term challenges for himself. After he made one business successful, he would start a new one and see if he could make it equally successful. He particularly liked being the underdog. In 1998 he launched Virgin Cola to see if he could seize some of Coke's massive market share.

> The Virgin Cola launch in New York in May of 1998 exemplifies the type of business challenge that I love. . . . I like to think that Virgin will be able to use the experience that we've built up during the first half of my life to give Coke its first proper competition. Coke's size doesn't intimidate me-the dinosaurs didn't last forever either. If any brand can give Coke a serious run, it's Virgin.[33]

The series of short-term challenges that Roy Vagelos continuously created for himself ultimately led him to his becoming CEO of Merck. Each time Roy met one challenge, he went out and found a new one. After finishing his medical residency, he took a position as a researcher in biochemistry at the National Institutes of Health (NIH). This was a significant challenge for him because he lacked a Ph.D. in biochemistry. Ten years later after he had established himself as a respected researcher in the field, he decided that he needed a new challenge. He took a job heading Washington University Medical School's ailing biochemistry department, which had lost its former status as one of the top biochemistry departments in the country. He notes, "Being part of Washington University's first-rate medical school was important, but the hook was really the challenge of rebuilding the school's biochemistry department."[34] Once he had successfully returned the department to prominence, he accepted the challenge of putting Merck's research labs on the cutting edge of biochemical research.[35] After he accomplished this, he decided to learn the business side of the pharmaceutical industry with the goal of becoming CEO of a company. Reviewing his career moves and his wife's partnership in his career, he has reflected:

> We changed our lives decisively about every ten years. Each time the move came when we began to feel we'd accomplished most of what we'd set out to do. When that happened, a new challenge became appealing.[36]

Creating short-term challenges for ourselves adds zest to our journey to becoming a superstar. It keeps us fully engaged in what we are doing. Moreover, each time we reach a short-term challenge, it empowers us. The excitement that we experience energizes us and fuels our drive forward to our ultimate destination.

Be Flexible

When Dorothy and the group finally reach the Emerald City and stand before the Wizard of Oz, he mocks them in a loud voice that echoes across the hall. Trembling in fear they huddle together thinking that their cause is hopeless. Finally the Wizard proclaims, "The beneficent Oz has every intention of granting your request! . . . but first you must prove yourselves worthy by performing a very small task. Bring me the broomstick of the Wicked Witch of the West!"[37]

As Dorothy travels through Oz, her mission expands in ways that she could not have anticipated. On her way to the Emerald City, she rescues the Scarecrow and the Tin Man and then becomes involved in helping them fulfill their dreams. Once

51

she gains entrance to the Wizard, he declares that he will only help them if they take a side-trip to the Wicked Witch's castle and bring him back her broomstick.

Most journeys to success are similar to Dorothy's trip. They unfold in ways which we hadn't planned. Opportunities arise that we didn't foresee. We must take detours and side-trips, which weren't on our original route. To succeed in the face of this uncertainty, we must remain committed to our mission but still be flexible enough to negotiate and, where possible, capitalize on these unexpected twists and turns in the road.

Superstars remain flexible. As they proceed, they are open to enlarging their ideas of what they can do. Jeffrey Bezos founded Amazon to sell books online but he soon discovered that there were many other items that people would buy online. Amazon now sells a wide array of products from music CDs to kitchen appliances. Bill Gates started out writing the behind-the-scene operating systems that make our computers run smoothly. He then realized that people needed good application software to take full advantage of their computers and developed his Microsoft Office packages. J. Paul Getty, who amassed a huge fortune in oil, started out as a producer of crude oil. During the Depression when the shares of refineries and pipeline companies plummeted in value, he purchased shares in these companies and expanded his company into an integrated oil "well to consumer" company.[38] Oprah never planned to be a talk show host but when the television station where she worked bumped her out of news and made her a talk show host, she was open to the change.[39] As it turned out, her flexibility launched her career.

Dr. Ben Carson was equally flexible while building his career. His initial route to becoming a top neurosurgeon didn't include a stop in Western Australia. When a colleague from Australia proposed that he work in Australia for a year after he completed his residency, he immediately discounted the suggestion. Johns Hopkins Hospital had already offered him a position. Despite this, he and his wife explored the idea.

They discovered that he would have more opportunities to acquire valuable surgical experience in Australia than at Johns Hopkins. With some trepidation, they decided to take this unprecedented step and spend a year in Western Australia. As it turned out, during the year in Australia he acquired more surgical experience than most doctors obtain in a lifetime.[40]

Superstars also reshape their missions to fit the ever-changing world around them. When Larry King was a child, radio was the primary medium of home entertainment. Television did not exist. When television began to supplant radio, Larry didn't hesitate to move from radio to television.[41] Margaret Thatcher's initial mission when she graduated from Oxford was to become a Member of Parliament.[42] After she became a Member of Parliament and was invited to join the Cabinet, she set out to be Chancellor of the Exchequer, the most powerful Cabinet position below the Prime Minister.[43] Margaret didn't consider becoming Prime Minister because she believed that the party was not yet ready to be led by a woman.[44] When later in her career Prime Minister Edward Heath's government fell apart and there were no strong candidates to replace him as head of the party, Margaret adjusted her mission and put her name forward. She was elected head of her party and when the Conservative Party subsequently returned to power, she became Britain's first female Prime Minister.[45]

Fred Smith has maintained Federal Express's dominance in the overnight delivery field by keeping pace with changes in technology. He has made sure that Federal Express always provides customers with the latest electronic services.

> As time changed and markets changed and peoples' expectations changed, we changed with them. For example, when it became obvious that people wanted to interface with FedEx electronically, many years before people were doing this, we built an electronic interface system that allowed them to do business with us. When the Internet came on the horizon, we built versions of that that allowed people to interface with FedEx over the Internet.[46]

The flexibility that we need to become superstars also requires that we be ready to take alternate routes when our way is blocked. No matter how carefully we plan our route, it is hard to know if the road that we have chosen will be passable when we get there. Superstars find other routes when they run into roadblocks. When Jeong H. Kim, founder of Yurie Systems, started his telecommunications company in the early 1990s, he planned to raise venture capital to finance the development of his products, but no one would fund him. His efforts were blocked at every turn. To acquire the money that he needed, he turned to consulting and put all the money that he earned into his company. In 1998 Jeong Kim sold his telecommunications company to Lucent Technologies for over a billion dollars.[47]

Bob Woodward, the reporter who was instrumental in unearthing the Nixon Watergate scandal, had to change his route when he first started his career. After leaving the Navy, he had his heart set on working at the *Washington Post*. He convinced Harry Rosenfeld, the metropolitan editor, to let him work at the *Post* for two weeks for no pay in hopes that they would recognize his talent as a reporter. None of the 17 articles that Woodward wrote during those two weeks were published by the *Post*. At the end of the two weeks, the deputy editor at the *Post* decided that Woodward lacked the skills needed to be a reporter and it would take too long to train him. In short, he was "hopeless." Woodward's short stint at the *Post* made him even more committed to being a reporter. So he took a detour. He went to the *Montgomery County Sentinel* in Maryland and soon was scooping the *Post*'s reporters. His successful detour to the *Sentinel* ultimately convinced the *Post* to hire him.[48]

This type of flexibility is essential to becoming superstar. A powerful commitment to our mission doesn't mean that we can't make changes and adjustments based on what we encounter along the way. If we don't do this, we can miss out on important opportunities or run into serious trouble. Fred Smith has commented, "Very rarely have I ever seen any busi-

STEP TWO: KNOW WHERE YOU ARE GOING

ness or major undertaking that goes in a straight line."[49] Thus, we must balance our commitment to our mission with an openness to zigzagging and improvising based on the terrain.

Keep Your Eyes on the Horizon

When Dorothy meets the Scarecrow, she stops and helps him off the pole but she doesn't linger long. As soon as the Scarecrow has recovered his balance and can walk, Dorothy is back on the Yellow Brick Road on her way to the Emerald City with the Scarecrow at her side.

Even though Dorothy must at times interrupt and change her route, she remains focused on what she ultimately wants to achieve. Superstars never lose track of their long-term mission. Once they decide on a mission, they hold onto it tightly. Like the early pioneers who traveled across the vast American continent by using distant landmarks to guide them, superstars keep their eyes on the horizon.

Once Larry King decided as a child that he wanted to be on the radio, he began practicing for his debut.

> When I was five years old, I would lie in bed and look at the radio. I wanted to be on the radio. I don't know why. I was magically attuned to it. I would listen to these voices, and then as I got a little older—and just a little older, 7 or 8—I would imagine myself doing what they were doing. I would actually stand up, sit down, I'd go to the mirror, and I would say, "The Romance of Helen Trent," as if I were the announcer.[50]

After finishing high school, Larry's grades weren't good enough for him to attend college. Instead, he worked at odd jobs but he didn't abandon his dream. He continued to hold onto it and, despite the skepticism of those around him, tell people that one day he was going to be on the radio. His best friend's father would put his arm around Larry and say, "What are you, nuts? What are you, a pipe dreamer?"[51] Larry didn't blink. He remained focused. It was this ability to keep his eyes fixed

55

on the horizon that ultimately led him to fulfill his mission to be on the radio.

Fred Smith formulated his idea for Federal Express while he was still in college. Even though he entered the military immediately after graduating from college, the seed was planted and growing within him. His vision of the need for a company that provided prompt accurate overnight package delivery was only reinforced by his observations of how ineffective the military was at getting supplies to the right place at the right time. Once he left the military, he started raising money to found Federal Express.[52]

Bill Clinton also always kept his eyes on the horizon. Early in his life he decided that his mission was to become a politician. After graduating from law school, he returned to Arkansas to teach and began his political career almost immediately by running for a seat in the United States House of Representatives. He failed to win but was undeterred. He next ran for Attorney General and was elected. Soon after the election, he was back on the road traveling around the state giving speeches and meeting with people in order to build an even stronger political support network for his next run for office.[53]

When we keep our eyes on the horizon, it is easier to resist the temptation of pursuing attractive opportunities that aren't part of our mission. If George Lucas hadn't kept his eyes fixed on the horizon and resisted such temptations, *American Graffiti*, the film that launched his career, would never have been made. After Lucas developed the idea for *American Graffiti*, it took him two years to raise the money that he needed to hire a screenwriter. The screenwriter whom he hired then failed to follow his story layout and instead turned the movie into a "hotrods to hell" story rather than the coming-of-age story that Lucas envisioned. With no money left to hire a new screenwriter, Lucas had to write the screenplay himself. While writing it, he kept receiving calls from producers offering him lots of money to do flashy movies with no story lines. Even though he desperately needed the money, he turned them down because he knew that these projects didn't fit with his mission of making movies that told stories and explored deeper life issues. He recalls his personal struggle to keep his eyes on the horizon.

> I had to constantly turn down vast sums of money while I was starving, writing a screenplay for free that I didn't like to write, because I hated writing. But I did finish it. I did write the screenplay, and eventually I got a deal to make the movie.[54]

Bill Clinton was similarly tempted early in his career. The chief counsel for the House Judiciary's Committee invited Bill to work with him on the inquiry into whether President Nixon should be impeached because men under his command burglarized the Democratic Party's Watergate offices. The chance to work on an inquiry into one of the major political scandals of the twentieth century was a great opportunity for a young lawyer. Bill Clinton didn't accept the invitation because his goal was to be a politician, not a lawyer. In recalling his decision he has noted, "A lot of your life is shaped by the opportunities that you turn down as much as those you take up."[55]

At times it is easy to lose sight of the horizon. We all experience cloudy days where it is hard to remain focused. Even superstars lose their way at times. What distinguishes superstars from others is that they look up when skies clear to make sure that they are still heading in the right direction and make changes if they have veered off course. In 1977 Donna Shirley gave birth to her daughter. When she returned to her job at the Jet Propulsion Laboratories, she received uninteresting assignments that were not advancing her career. She started asking questions and discovered that the managers who made assignments thought that now she was a mother, she wouldn't want a "real job." She also realized that during the 1970s she had taken her eyes off the horizon. She had become involved in alternative energy projects rather than space projects which were her real passion. Shirley immediately set out to get her career back on track. She met with key managers and soon was assigned to lead a project studying the feasibility of sending a spacecraft to orbit Saturn and drop probes into its atmosphere.[56]

To succeed we must be clear about where we want to go and what we want to accomplish. Once we choose a mission, we must make sure that we keep our eyes on the horizon and steadily and surely move toward it.

TAKE A MOMENT TO REFLECT

What is your mission? What do you want to accomplish in this world?

On the page below, describe your mission and what you want to accomplish.

Know How To Get There

Once Dorothy decided to go to the Emerald City to see the Wizard of Oz, she had to figure out how to get there. Glinda, the good witch, told her, "All you do is follow the Yellow Brick Road." Even though this sounded simple, Dorothy's journey to see the Wizard proved to be much more complicated than just following the Yellow Brick Road. Before she had traveled very far, she came to a fork. Dorothy said to Toto, "Now which way do we go?" The Scarecrow who was hanging on a pole in the adjacent cornfield pointed to the right and replied, "That is a very nice way." Then he pointed to the left and said, "It's pleasant down that way too." Dorothy commented to Toto, "That's funny. Wasn't he pointing the other way?" In response the Scarecrow crossed his arms and pointed in both directions and said, "Of course, people do go both ways!"[1] The road to becoming a superstar can be similarly confusing. It is often unclear which is the best way to go. Sometimes we need to go in several directions at once. To get where we are going, we need to think strategically, build a strong power base, and learn to motivate others.

Think Strategically

After Dorothy is captured and taken to the Wicked Witch's castle, the Scarecrow, the Tin Man, the Lion, and Toto rush to the castle to rescue her. When they arrive at the castle gates and see the Witch's Wonkie guards, they realize that they will never get into the castle by using brute force. Instead, they capture three Wonkie guards, take their uniforms, and disguise themselves as guards. They then march into the castle at the end of a line of guards.

The Scarecrow, the Tin Man and the Lion find a way into the castle by using strategy. To become a superstar, we must think strategically. Driving a tank through the obstacles that we face rarely gets us where we want to go. Instead, we must carefully plan our moves. After each move, we need to stop and evaluate how effective it was and then make adjustments so that our next move will be even more effective. We must also prepare for what Stan Shih, founder of Acer, calls "bottlenecks" which can sabotage our plans. To deal with these bottlenecks we must have a "Plan B" or even a "Plan C." As Stan Shih points out, we don't have to choose the right plan the first time to become a superstar. Rather, it is our ability to formulate and roll out alternate plans in the face of bottlenecks that ensures our rise to superstar status.[2]

Once we start thinking strategically we become proactive. Instead of just reacting to events, we control what happens. Dr. Ben Carson discovered the power of thinking strategically at a young age. When he was eight, his father left. His mother toiled valiantly to support him and his brother, but it was not easy growing up poor and African-American in Detroit, Michigan. Dr. Carson learned that by carefully planning his moves he could become an actor on his world rather than a victim of it.

> Once I recognized that I had the ability to pretty much map out my own future based on the choices that I made, and the degree of energy that I put into it, life was wonderful. . . . I saw my situation as temporary, meaning that I had full power to change it and that completely changed my outlook.[3]

Richard Branson built his Virgin Empire using strategic thinking. His first business was a magazine called *Student* which he started with some friends before he left secondary school. Unlike his partners, Richard soon saw that *Student*'s days were numbered and decided to start a new business selling discount records by mail. Rather than immediately disbanding *Student*, he realized that it was a great medium to use for launching his new business because it targeted the same market as his discount record business.[4]

Richard has continued throughout the years to strategically modify and change his businesses based on the bottlenecks that he has encountered. When he ran into trouble selling records by mail due to a two-month postal strike, he opened a discount record store in London. He next started an all-night recording studio because he learned that bands couldn't find places to record that had flexible hours.[5] By carefully calculating his moves, Richard steadily expanded into other parts of the music business, eventually making Virgin into a major record label. From there, he branched out even further creating the large complex of Virgin businesses that today provide everything from cola to train service.

Superstars like Richard also apply strategic thinking to the smallest details of what they do. Before choosing where to open his first discount record store in London, he and his best friend, Nik, spent hours measuring pedestrian traffic patterns to identify the best place to locate the store.

> Nik and I spent a morning counting people walking up and down Oxford Street compared with people walking along Kensington High Street. Eventually we decided that the cheaper end of Oxford Street would be the best site. We knew that we couldn't rely upon people knowing about the Virgin record shop and making a special trip to buy a record, so we had to be able to attract passersby into the shop on impulse. At the exact point where we counted the most people walking along the street, we started looking for an empty property.[6]

When in 1976 Stan Shih of Taiwan founded Acer with his wife and three friends with only $25,000 in capital, he used strategy to overcome their lack of funding. By forming partnerships with dealers and distributors in the neighboring countries of Indonesia, Malaysia, Singapore and Thailand, he was able to make Acer into a multi-national company without a major infusion of cash. In explaining his strategy he compared it to the Japanese game, Go.

> It is like the strategy in the Japanese game Go—one plays from the corner, because you need fewer resources to occupy the corner. Without the kind of resources that Japanese and American companies had, we started in smaller markets. That gives us the advantage because these smaller markets are becoming bigger and bigger and the combination of many small markets is not small.[7]

Margaret Thatcher also used strategy to become a superstar. When she entered Oxford, she joined the Oxford University Conservative Association. Most of her fellow students belonged to the Labour Club which contained livelier and more interesting people than the Conservative Association. Nina Bawden, a fellow student, asked her why she hadn't joined the Labour Club. Nina relates

> [Margaret] admitted, the Labour Club was just at the moment more fashionable . . . but that in a way unintentionally suited her purposes. Unlike me she was not 'playing' at politics. She meant to get into Parliament and there was more chance of being 'noticed' in the Conservative Club just because some of the members were a bit stodgy.[8]

Michael Eisner, Disney's former CEO, took a similar strategic approach during the early years of his career at ABC. He sought places to work within the company where there was less competition and it was easier to shine. He relates, "I always went into an area that was in last place, with a philosophy that you can't fall off the floor."[9] His success in these areas was instrumental in making him a superstar.

Superstars also use strategic thinking to make decisions. Dr. Carson often must decide whether to operate on difficult surgical cases where the chances of success are low and the risks of death are high. He describes his approach as follows.

It simply has to do with me asking the questions: What's the best thing and what's the worst thing that happens if I do something? What's the best thing and what's the worst thing that happens if I do nothing? On the basis of those four questions, I can determine whether I should do something or not. If the best thing that's going to happen if I do nothing is that they're going to die, then I certainly don't have anything to lose by doing something.[10]

We can apply this same type of strategic thinking to making decisions. We can identify the best and worst possible outcomes of each course of action including what will happen if we do nothing. We can then weigh the results in terms of which action will take us where we want to go.

Get on the Playing Field

After Dorothy and the Scarecrow start down the Yellow Brick Road, Dorothy sees an apple tree. She reaches to pick an apple. The tree slaps her hand and accusingly says, "How would you like someone to come along and pick something off you." The Scarecrow turns to Dorothy and says, "Come along, you don't want any of those apples. The tree asks, "Are you hinting my apples aren't what they ought to be?" The Scarecrow replies, "Oh, no! It's just that she doesn't like little green worms!" Angrily the tree pelts them with apples.

Busily collecting the apples, Dorothy discovers the Tin Man standing frozen in place. In a barely audible voice, he begs Dorothy to oil him. The Scarecrow immediately grasps the situation and rushes to help. Together he and Dorothy rescue the Tin Man.[11]

When Dorothy first finds the Scarecrow, he is helplessly hanging from a pole in a field. Even after she takes him down, he can barely stand and he literally keeps losing pieces of his straw insides. He hardly seems like the type of person Dorothy would like on her team. Despite the Scarecrow's initial rocky start, he soon proves invaluable. By suggesting that the apple tree has worms, he gets the apple tree to throw more apples at Dorothy than she can possibly eat. When Dorothy finds the Tin Man, the Scarecrow instantly pitches in to help oil him and interpret the Tin Man's garbled speech. Dorothy begins to regularly turn to the Scarecrow for assistance. The Scarecrow has made himself an important player on Dorothy's team through his efforts to help her and his attractive manner.

Like the Scarecrow, getting on the playing field is one of the first major hurdles that we face in becoming a superstar. Until people have confidence in our abilities and trust us, they are reluctant to give us responsibilities and important assignments. To overcome people's reservations and get onto the playing field, superstars rely heavily on three personal powers. These are effort, expertise, and attractiveness. The beauty of these powers is that we all have them or can easily acquire them. They are at our disposal whether we are just graduating from school with a diploma in-hand or are many years into our career.[12]

Effort solely depends on how hard we are willing to work. When we expend effort, we show commitment and an eagerness to do a good job. Bill Clinton launched his political career in Arkansas by the enormous effort that he put into his first run for office. Despite little hope of success, he worked tirelessly from dawn to the late hours of the night meeting people, giving speeches and shaking every hand he could find. Even though he didn't win, the effort that he put into the campaign convinced people that he was a serious political contender and it later helped him be elected attorney general of Arkansas.[13]

Expertise is another power that we can use to get on the playing field. We can acquire it through education, training and on-the-job experience. With expertise, we become valuable to others because of the special skills and knowledge that we have to offer. Madeleine Albright paved her way to becoming Secretary of State by obtaining a doctorate in foreign policy.[14] Alan Alda, who played Hawkeye in the famous television show *M*A*S*H*, couldn't afford acting lessons when he first started his career. Instead, he developed his acting skills by obtaining lots of on-the-job experience. He said "yes" to every job he was offered, not just to earn money, but to acquire expertise. He writes:

To be young, and out of work and an actor is to say yes to everything. Can you ride a horse? *Certainly.* Can you play the trumpet? *Oh yes.* How tall are you? *How tall do you need?*

You take any acting job you can get—not just to be able to live, but to also learn how to act.[15]

Ultimately, Alan Alda's increasing expertise got him on the playing field and enough jobs to earn a living as an actor.

Attractiveness is also an important power that we can use to get on the playing field. It entails making ourselves likeable and projecting a positive image and appearance. The media lead us to believe that our physical beauty is all that counts but it is actually only a small part of being attractive. Researchers have found that people judge physical attractiveness based on a person's clothes and how well they care for themselves and not just their physical beauty.[16] These are characteristics under our control and easily attainable. We can wear clothes that flatter us and we can also keep fit.

Even more important than our external appearance is being likeable and having good social skills. In *The Wizard of Oz*, the Tin Man, the Scarecrow, and the Lion all lack physical beauty but their amusing ways make them highly likeable. Woody Allen, the actor and film director, is another example of a person who is not physically attractive but has effectively used humor to endear himself to millions.

Good social skills and manners also make us more attractive. Everyone likes to be around people who are kind, caring, compassionate and considerate. Charles Ogletree, a Harvard law professor and top criminal defense and civil rights lawyer, always greets people with a warm accepting manner even if he disagrees with them. Moreover, he never has anything bad to say about other people even if they are on the opposite side of an issue about which he deeply cares. He accepts them for who they are and respects their right to hold a different view of the world than himself.[17]

Being a good listener similarly contributes to our social attractiveness. In our contemporary culture, the art of listening is becoming lost. People primarily want to listen to themselves. As a consequence, listening to others is a powerful tool because so few people use it. When we listen to people, they feel important and valued and they then associate these positive feelings with us. During one of my most successful job interviews, I barely talked. Instead, I listened while the interviewer enthusiastically talked about the work that the job entailed. By the end of the interview, his enthusiasm had become associated with me and I was offered the job.

The powers of effort, expertise, and attractiveness are not just important when we first start our journey to becoming a superstar. They continue to be highly valuable wherever we are in our career. By using them effectively, we can gain access to bigger and better playing fields. The table below summarizes these powers and shows how superstars have used them throughout their careers to build success.

POWERS THAT GET US ON THE PLAYING FIELD

EFFORT Being willing to go the extra mile to make sure a job is done well and finished on time.

EXAMPLE Sam Walton expended enormous effort in building Wal-Mart. He was not content to receive reports on how his stores were doing. He bought a plane, obtained a pilot's license, and personally visited Wal-Mart stores to make sure that they were being run properly. Before his Saturday morning meetings with his executive team, he went to the office at two in the morning to review the weekly numbers.[18]

EXPERTISE Specialized knowledge and skills that others around us don't have.

EXAMPLE During her travels to remote areas of the world, Anita Roddick became an expert on the natural organic potions that women in developing countries use to beautify their bodies. She used this expertise to create the unique beauty products that The Body Shop sells.[20]

ATTRACTIVENESS The degree to which people like us, feel that we are similar to them, and want to work with us. Physical attractiveness is only a small part.

EXAMPLE: Richard Branson has always been extremely likeable. People want to work for him. As a result, he has easily attracted top people to help develop his businesses. Patrick Zelnick left Polygram, a French record distributor, to set up Virgin's highly successful Megastore in Paris after meeting Richard at a dinner with his boss. His boss later commented to Richard, "When you're invited to dinner, you are not supposed to walk off with the cutlery. . . ."[19]

Get Noticed

After Dorothy kills the Wicked Witch, the group returns to the Emerald City to give the Wizard the Witch's broomstick. Astounded to see them, the Wizard says, "Can I believe my eyes? Why have you come back?" Dorothy then puts the broomstick at the foot of his throne and announces that they melted the Wicked Witch. Impressed, the Wizard responds, "Oh you liquidated her. Very resourceful."[21]

By killing the Wicked Witch of the West, Dorothy and the group gain the attention of the "Great and Powerful Oz." He recognizes them as a group that can effectively deal with troublesome witches. We need this same type of recognition and attention to become a superstar. Just getting on the playing field is not enough. We must make sure that powerful people, who control access to important positions and valuable resources, notice our accomplishments.

Superstars get noticed by strategically using the powers of visibility, relevance, and a positive track record.[22] Visibility involves doing things that attract the attention of influential people and decision makers who control the resources that we need to succeed. Within an organization there are senior people above us in the hierarchy who have the power to promote us, supply us with funds for our projects, give us good assignments, or provide us with access to other influential people. If we are not part of an organization, then we must identify the people on whom our success depends and get their attention. For entrepreneurs this is often people with money to invest in their business. For professionals and small business people, it is potential clients and customers. When we are looking for a job, it is the people who have the power to hire us.

Madeleine Albright used visibility to get her first job in the government. After her children entered school, she decided to return to the workplace. She wanted a job that combined her interest in foreign policy and politics. She realized that to obtain such a job she had to get someone important in government to notice her.

> To get started I needed proper credentials and the backing of someone with enough faith to help me, not out of charity but because he (that's how it was) would recognize my value, either to him or to some project.[23]

Madeleine chose Beauvoir, a private girl's school, as an arena where she would have an opportunity to be seen by influential people and gain visibility. Many of the children at the school had parents who held high-level political and governmental positions in Washington. At Beauvoir, Madeleine first volunteered to run a campaign to recruit African-American students and increase scholarship funds available to them. She did such a good job that she was invited to join the Beauvoir board of trustees and run their annual fund drive. This was a great opportunity to be seen by powerful alumni who were a key source of fund drive contributions. Her success running annual fund drives generated even more visibility for her. People began to ask her to raise funds for political campaigns and sit on the boards of nonprofit organizations. Ultimately, the visibility that she acquired through these activities led to a paid job as Maine Senator Edmund Muskie's chief legislative assistant.[24] Moreover, this visibility stayed with her throughout her career in Washington. In reflecting on her career in her book, *Madam Secretary*, Madeleine Albright states that it all began when she first sat on Beauvoir's board of trustees.

> It may sound crazy, but no one would be reading this book had I not been asked to be on the Beauvoir board of trustees and run the annual fund drive beginning in the fall of 1969.[25]

We too can acquire visibility by getting to know influential people and making them aware of our accomplishments and talents. Such people often like to advise more junior people and help them shape their careers. They find it flattering and energizing. Within organizations, savvy successful senior people are also open to relationships with junior people because they realize that they are a valuable source of information about what is happening at the lower levels of the organization.

Cultivating relationships with more senior people in an organization also protects us from being exploited. My students often complain that their managers take advantage of them by claiming credit for their work. We can protect ourselves from this by forming relationships with senior people and keeping them informed about our accomplishments and ideas. This way when our manager tries to claim credit for our work, the senior person will quickly realize that it is our work.

Another way to acquire visibility is to take the lead in presentations and speak up at meetings. Researchers have found that the person who makes a project presentation to upper management becomes identified with the success of the project.[26] To make sure that we are recognized for our contributions, we must step forward to do such presentations. This also holds true for meetings. Speaking up provides us with visibility even if we don't say anything particularly insightful. People are more likely to remember us than what we actually said. Moreover, our participation shows others that we are committed to the task at hand and an important contributor. A female friend of mine at Harvard Law School once commented on the large amount of airtime that men in our classes consumed.

They would speak at great length during classroom discussions, whereas women either rarely talked or made their comments so brief and succinct that they barely created a ripple in the classroom. The men, however, clearly knew something that the women didn't. They understood how important visibility is to becoming a superstar. When women subsequently asked professors for recommendations, professors often didn't know who they were.

The second power that superstars use to get noticed is relevance. It involves accomplishing things that are closely aligned with an organization's main objectives. By killing the Wicked Witch of the West, Dorothy, the Scarecrow, the Tin Man and the Lion gained relevance because they rescued the inhabitants of Oz from a dangerous and feared tyrant. Madeleine Albright acquired relevance in her work as a fundraiser because money is the lifeblood of political campaigns and nonprofit organizations. By raising money for these groups, she performed a critical function that was directly linked to their organizational survival and success.

Like Madeleine Albright, we can make ourselves relevant by seeking assignments and positions that are closely aligned with key priorities and goals of an organization. Within corporations, people from finance often rise to the top because money is extremely important and closely watched by those in power. Other highly relevant activities within businesses are related to the production and sale of profitable products and services. At General Electric, Jack Welch initially worked on the development of new plastics. As an emerging market in the 1960s and '70s, this area was highly relevant to General Electric's future. Michael Eisner moved up the corporate ladder at ABC because he produced successful television shows that were key to ABC's survival.

A third power that we can use to get noticed is a positive track record. When we consistently do a great job and exceed other people's expectations, we acquire a track record for excellence which others notice. People begin to trust us to deliver what we promise. As a result, they give us important assignments and more responsibility. Bob Schieffer, anchor/moderator for the television show *Face the Nation*, worked as a reporter for a Fort Worth newspaper after completing college. The big story at that time was Viet Nam and Bob wanted to cover it. The paper was initially reluctant to send him to Viet Nam but he finally convinced his boss to send him for four months. His assignment was to find and interview soldiers from Texas. During his time in Viet Nam, Bob was relentless in tracking down Texas soldiers. He would hitch rides on transport planes out of Saigon and then beg rides on helicopters and smaller planes that flew to more remote outposts. After five to ten days in the field he would return to Saigon and write his stories. At the end of the four months he had found and reported on 235 soldiers.[27] By the time he returned to Fort Worth, he had shown the paper and others that he could consistently deliver under the most difficult of circumstances, namely war. His track record made him a local celebrity and opened doors that helped him take his career to the next level.

POWERS THAT GET US NOTICED

VISIBILITY Doing things in ways that attract the attention of decision makers and influential people. This can include potential customers or senior people in an organization. Visibility makes others aware of what we have to offer.

EXAMPLE Once Donny Deutsch decided to build his father's advertising agency into a media power, he used visibility to acquire the Pontiac Dealers Association account for the New York-New Jersey-Connecticut tri-state area. To get the attention of Bob Conway, the person choosing the advertising agency for the association, Donny sent Bob a different car part every hour during a twelve-hour period. Bob received a headlight with a tag that read, "We'll give you bright ideas." He received a fender with the tag, "We'll protect your rear end." This deluge of car parts got Donny and the agency noticed and ultimately, the agency was awarded the account.[29]

RELEVANCE Performing activities or accomplishing things that are highly valuable to other people or closely related to an organization's main objectives.

EXAMPLE Oprah Winfrey's show has been one of television's longest running shows. It has value to women viewers because she addresses topics that relate to their lives. The show's enormous popularity has also made it highly profitable for ABC which makes Oprah extremely relevant in the eyes of ABC executives.

TRACK RECORD A long-term pattern of consistently producing great results, going the extra mile, and making important contributions to a business, organization or other people.

EXAMPLE Lee Iacocca built his career at Ford by establishing a track record for creative problem solving. In 1956 while he was assistant sales manager for the Philadelphia district, he introduced the idea of selling cars using installment plans. Sales increased so dramatically that he was moved to Ford's national headquarters as manager of national truck marketing. He later was instrumental in developing the popular Ford Mustang which further built his track record at Ford and helped put him on the fast track to becoming president.[28]

Build a Strong Power Base

A large crowd gathers for the Wizard and Dorothy's departure for Kansas in the Wizard's hot air balloon. The Scarecrow, the Tin Man, and the Lion stand holding the ropes of the balloon as the Wizard and Dorothy with Toto in her arms climb into the basket. Just as they are about to leave, Toto jumps out of Dorothy's arms and races after a cat. Dorothy follows in hot pursuit. Dropping the ropes the Scarecrow and the Lion rush to help. Freed, the balloon slowly floats away with the Wizard. Watching the balloon leave, Dorothy sees her chances of ever returning to Kansas fade. This despair changes to joy when Glinda arrives waving her wand, and reveals to Dorothy that she can return home by just clicking her heels.

When Dorothy arrives in Oz, she is alone and powerless, but by the time that she is ready to leave in the Wizard's hot air balloon, she has built a strong power base that provides her with access to important resources. The Scarecrow, the Tin Man, and the Lion are always available to help her. The Wizard willingly shares his resources with her after the group kills the Wicked Witch. In fact, it is his hot air balloon which is to take Dorothy home to Kansas. Glinda is an invaluable source of expert information. After the Wizard floats away in his balloon, it is Glinda who tells Dorothy that to return home all she needs to do is tap the heels of her ruby slippers together three times.

Superstars similarly achieve their goals by building strong power bases. Historically, the primary type of power that people sought was formal authority, like the Wizard had. Today there are many other valuable types of power that we can acquire which don't depend on us being at the top of an organizational heap. These powers provide us with the ability to mobilize others and get things done without formal authority. Two of the most important are centrality and autonomy.[30]

Centrality, as its name implies, involves being at the center of formal and informal networks of people who can provide us with the resources and information that we need to accomplish things. At the heart of centrality are the relationships that we form with people who can either directly help us or link us to other people who can. Personal contact is one of the best ways to develop these relationships but the Internet is also useful. Today, many people have virtual networks as well as personal ones.

The value of centrality is that with it we can accomplish important things without having to rely on formal authority.

Research has found that people who position themselves at the center of networks of people are more successful than those who remain isolated or on the periphery.[31] This is because many problems that we face in the workplace require resources and people that are beyond the reach of our formal authority. Knowing a manager in another department who can lend us an expert to fix quirky software or a person in purchasing who can get us materials overnight can make the difference between failing and succeeding. Centrality also extends outside the boundaries of organizations. When The Body Shop began to rapidly expand, Anita Roddick put added demands on the manufacturers who supplied her products. They kept pace with her increased needs because she had good relationships with them.[32]

Superstars focus on placing themselves at the center of networks. When Madeleine Albright went to work for President Carter's National Security advisor, Zbigniew Brzezinski, she made sure to position herself where she would have the maximum opportunity to build relationships with major players in the Carter administration. Instead of taking a large office with a marble fireplace in the Old Executive Office Building, she opted for a small closet-like office in the basement of the White House where the real action was.[33]

A major source of Bill Clinton's rise to superstar status lies in the vast number of people with whom he has maintained personal contact during his career. These include people from his childhood in Arkansas, from Georgetown University, and from Yale Law School as well as people whom he has met in the course of his working life and political career. As a result, whenever he faces a special problem, he has a large and disparate network of people on whom he can call for advice and help.[34]

We can also acquire centrality by placing ourselves at the center of critical flows of resources, information, or work. Warren Buffett pursues an investment strategy that puts him at the center of companies' financial health. Most investment firms try to dilute risk by putting small amounts of money in a large number of companies. Warren Buffett instead picks a few companies, which he perceives as having the potential to provide strong long-term returns, and invests heavily in them. The size of his investments places him at the center of these companies' financial flows which gives him a voice in major decisions, despite his lack of formal authority. After Buffett bought a substantial portion of *Washington Post* stock, he became an important advisor to Katharine Graham, the president of the company.[35] When a bond trading scandal hit Salomon Brothers, in which he had $700 million invested, the company asked Buffett to step in as interim chairman to help minimize the damage. This Buffett ably did.[36]

Another valuable source of power is autonomy. Superstars strive for autonomy because it gives them freedom to innovate, exercise initiative, and make quick decisions. They avoid positions with narrow rules and cumbersome procedures because such rules and procedures limit the scope of what they can accomplish. Moreover, they aren't afraid to exercise autonomy even if they lack the formal authority to make decisions. When Lance Armstrong first started racing professionally, he chafed under the fact that his coaches would not let him ride his own race. Bicycle racing is a team sport. Designated team members ride in front of the rider making the final sprint to reduce wind resistance and help him preserve his energy by drafting off them. Experienced sprinters know when to break from the pack. As a young rider, Lance was instructed to stay behind the lead riders until signaled to begin sprinting. Lance didn't always wait for the signal before he broke out of the pack. At times, this proved to be a misjudgment because he faded well before the finish line but at other times he won.[37] Lance's initiative showed his coaches that even though he didn't yet fully understand bicycle racing, he had the potential to be great.

In professional sports, coaches regularly fight with owners and general managers for the autonomy to choose the players for their teams. Without this autonomy they know they will be restricted in their ability to build a championship team.

Phil Jackson, the legendary National Basketball Association coach, frequently clashed with the Los Angeles Lakers' owner and management because he wanted the power to pick personnel and run his own show. In 2006, when he was considering whether to return to the Los Angeles Lakers as head coach, negotiations purportedly became stuck over personnel issues and the amount of autonomy Jackson would have.[38]

Richard Branson also has always viewed autonomy as essential to his ability to succeed. In 1986 when he took Virgin public, he quickly discovered that the price of that move was a loss of autonomy. He could no longer call the shots. The London stock exchange required that he have outside directors on his board and institute formal procedures for board meetings. Many of Richard's past successes had been due to his ability to meet quickly with his top people and decide whether to go forward with a deal. Now he found himself thwarted. He couldn't act until a formal board meeting was held which could sometimes take weeks. Frustrated by his loss of autonomy, Richard bought Virgin's shares back at their original offering price, making Virgin again a private company.[39]

Both centrality and autonomy can be important considerations when we are deciding whether to accept a job. We tend to consider jobs with formal authority more prestigious, but often having centrality and autonomy will give us a greater opportunity to shine. After Kevin Simpson, now COO of Thermogenesis, graduated from Harvard Business School, he took a job as assistant to the president of Haemonetics. This job had little formal authority, but it gave him the opportunity to build a strong power base using centrality and autonomy. One of his initial assignments was to make a video for the company's forthcoming public offering. Kevin at first dismissed this part of his job. It didn't seem like the type of task that would use the skills and knowledge that he had acquired at Harvard Business School. Contrary to his expectations, making the video turned out to be the best part of his job. The president was extremely busy and gave Kevin complete autonomy over making the video. Through the interviews that Kevin did for the video with core members of Haemonetics, he built a solid network of relationships with people through-out the company. Moreover, in listening to people talk about their work, he gained valuable information about the com-pany and how it operated.

The video was a grand success. When first shown to the investors, it received a standing ovation. Soon afterward Kevin was made manager of the commercial plasma section even though he had only been at the company for six months. The centrality and information that he had acquired while making the video gave him a head start at succeeding in this new posi-tion and in a little over three years he became of vice president of commercial plasma.[40]

POSITIONAL POWERS

CENTRALITY Being part of formal or informal networks that give us access to the people, resources, and informa-tion that we need to build power and get things done.

EXAMPLE When President Lyndon Johnson first came to Washington in 1933, he was a lowly congressional aide. To acquire centrality he first set out to be elected speaker of a relatively insignificant organization called the Little Congress. It had originally been created to provide Congressional staff with experience in Congressional debate and parliamentary procedures but had deteriorated into a social club. Once he was elected speaker, Johnson used this organization to put himself at the center of what was hap-pening in Washington. He organized serious debates of bills currently before the real Congress. During debates, aides for Congressmen would take the same positions as the Congressmen for whom they worked. Thus, the votes at the end of a debate were a good indicator of what would happen in the actual Congress. Johnson was quick to make the press aware of these debates, and they began to closely cover them. This, in turn, attracted famous political figures who knew that when they spoke before the Little Congress, they would receive valuable press coverage. This allowed Johnson to cultivate relationships with some of the most powerful men in Washington and put him at the center of what was happening.[42]

AUTONOMY Being able to make our own decisions without needing someone else's approval or agreement.

EXAMPLE After leaving college Donny Deutsch went to work for the prestigious advertising firm, Ogilvy and Mather. Soon after he started he was told, "Don't talk. Don't say anything. Just listen and learn."[41] When Donny did try to take initiative, he was quickly squelched. The lack of autonomy in his job made it impossible for him to thrive and display his creative talents which were one of his greatest strengths. In contrast, when Donny went to work at his father's advertising agency developing new business, his father gave him free rein. Donny could pursue whatever accounts he wished and use his creative talents to devise innovative strategies for attracting clients. The autonomy that he had was a key factor in his building the agency into a major advertising power.

Know How to Motivate Others

As Dorothy, the Scarecrow, the Tin Man, and the Lion come around a bend on the Yellow Brick Road, they see the Emerald City glimmering in the distance across a large poppy field. Excited, they run across the field toward the city. Part way across, Dorothy is struck by a wave of tiredness. The Scarecrow and the Tin Man grab her hands and urge her forward. Slowly she sinks to the field and falls asleep. The Scarecrow and the Tin Man frantically try to pick her up and carry her but they can't move her.

Dorothy is extremely good at motivating others to work for her goals. When she meets the Scarecrow and the Tin Man, their lives are at a dead end. Dorothy motivates them to help her by offering them the opportunity to be engaged in meaningful work, namely saving her from the Wicked Witch and finding a way for her return to Kansas. The Scarecrow and the Tin Man eagerly embrace this work because it gives purpose and meaning to their lives. It appeals to their inner need to feel useful and valued by others. As a result, they are highly motivated to see that Dorothy succeeds. When Dorothy falls asleep in the poppy field, they do everything in their power to keep her awake. They even try to carry her to the Emerald City.

We need to be able to motivate others if we want to become a superstar. No matter how much power we acquire, we can't fully utilize it if we don't know how to motivate others to work hard at helping us achieve our goals. We may be the manager and make the decisions but if we can't get others to implement our decisions, this power is useless. Professor Linda Hill at Harvard Business School has pointed out that many new managers fail because they don't know how to motivate others. They assume that their position alone will cause people to follow their instructions. They soon discover that moving people to action is far more complex. It requires that we understand how to motivate them.[43]

Superstars motivate others by fulfilling important deep inner needs that they have. They are aware that trying to force people to do things just doesn't work. As Lee Iacocca has commented, "You don't succeed for very long by kicking people around."[44] Superstars also realize that money is a short-term motivator that only works if people lack the basic essentials needed to live. It suffers from the "dog biscuit problem" that Frederick Herzog vividly described in his famous *Harvard Business Review* article, "One More Time: How Do You Motivate Employees?" Herzog relates that when he took his dog to obedience training, he learned to dangle a dog biscuit in front of his dog's nose to make him move. Herzog found that this worked well, but he went on to ask, "Who is motivated? Is it the dog or is it me?" He concluded that he was the one who wanted the dog to move, not the dog. The dog only moved because he wanted a dog biscuit.[45]

Money operates the same way as a dog biscuit. It is a reward. It moves people to act when it is dangled in front of their noses but it only works in the short-term. It lacks the long-term power of motivators that appeal to people's deep inner needs. When we fulfill people's inner needs, monetary rewards become less important to them. Moreover, we don't have to monitor their every move. Like Dorothy, we can fall asleep in a poppy field and still be reassured that they will work hard to help us achieve our goals.

The famous psychologist, Abraham Maslow, identified two key types of deep inner needs that motivate people. They are the need for love and belonging and the need for self esteem. The need for love and belonging includes the desire for family and friends and to be identified as a member of groups and organizations. The need for self-esteem involves a desire to be recognized and appreciated. This need to feel important and valued by others is why people seek meaningful work that they feel contributes to something bigger than themselves. These needs are very different from basic needs for food, shelter, and safety which diminish once they are fulfilled. The needs for love and belonging and self-esteem become stronger once they are activated and persist even after they have been fulfilled. They are like a sweet nectar that people never get tired of drinking.[46]

Superstars focus on motivating people by fulfilling these deeper needs. This is what Dorothy did. She appealed to the Scarecrow's, the Tin Man's, and the Lion's deep inner needs. She inspired them to help her by telling them how important it was for her to return to Kansas because Auntie Em was sick. In addition, she treated them like family and made them feel appreciated. As a consequence, they were highly motivated to help her succeed.

In building his advertising agency, Donny Deutsch similarly motivated his employees by satisfying their deep inner needs. He made appreciation a core principle of his management philosophy. He has commented, "If your people feel their win means something to you—that you get actual joy from it—they will walk through fire for you."[47] If we forget to appreciate people and acknowledge their value, they can quickly become discouraged. Donny Deutsch relates how he once failed to show his employees how much he appreciated them after they won a large account. They soon appeared in his office steeped in gloom. When he asked them what was wrong, they replied, "You didn't even tell us 'Great job.' "[48]

As Donny Deutsch shows, appreciation doesn't have to be elaborate. It can be a simple "thanks" or a word of praise. Bill Clinton's success rests, in part, on the fact that he never forgets to say "thank you." His autobiography is packed full of "thank you's" to all of the people who have helped him along the way. Sam Walton similarly considered praise to be key in motivating people. At Wal-Mart he encouraged managers to look for the things that employees were doing right rather than just what they were doing wrong.[49]

An equally important way of showing people your appreciation is by expressing interest in their personal lives and concerns. In Nigeria's traditional tribal culture, people greeted each other by saying, "I see you." Today we rarely "see" people. Donny Deutsch made it a point while running his advertising agency to see the people who worked for him. He would take time to informally chat with them about what was happening in their lives. He understood that by doing this, he made people feel valued.[50] Moreover, people often value sharing their joys, worries, and fears with us as much and even possibly more than receiving an impersonal white envelope with a bonus check inside at the end of the year.

At Wal-Mart, Sam Walton was always open to seeing his employees even after Wal-Mart became a $50 billion company. Hourly associates were welcome to stop by his office and talk about their problems. One of Sam's managers has commented,

> If you've ever spent any time around Wal-Mart, you may have noticed that it's not unusual for somebody in Philadelphia, Mississippi, to get in his pick-up on the spur of the moment and drive to Bentonville, where you can find him sitting in the lobby waiting patiently to see the chairman.[51]

Another important motivator that superstars use is making people feel that they belong and are accepted for who they are. Many of us have felt the discomfort of entering a room full of people where we know no one and are completely ignored. The person who comes over and talks to us is like a life preserver in a churning sea. Anita Roddick strives hard to make her employees feel that they are part of The Body Shop family. She encourages them to act like real family members by openly voicing their concerns and suggesting how things can be done better.[52]

At Wal-Mart, Sam Walton always treated his employees as if they were one large family. His Saturday morning meetings began with a large cheer in which everyone participated. At these meetings people were urged to bring problems forward so they could all solve them together. In describing the meetings Sam Walton has written, "We make our people feel part of a family in which no one is too important or too puffed up to lead a cheer or be the butt of a joke. . . ."[53]

Providing people with meaningful work is another potent motivator used by superstars. Most people want the opportunity to do work that makes a difference and contributes to something greater than themselves. At Merck Research Laboratories, Roy Vagelos motivated scientists to give up projects that had little hope of success by offering them the opportunity to work on promising new projects that had the potential of leading to life-saving drugs.[54] Stan Shih, head of Acer, motivates his employees by using inspiring slogans which emphasize Acer's grand vision. These slogans remind employees that they are part of a great company that is achieving amazing feats. When Acer expanded beyond Taiwan and Asia into the European and American markets, he created the slogan, "The Rampaging Dragon Goes International."[55]

People also find work more meaningful when they have ownership of how they do their work. Warren Buffett motivates his managers by giving them free rein over their investment choices and decisions. He follows the philosophy of Teddy Roosevelt who commented, "The best executive is one who has sense enough to pick good people to do what he wants done, and the self-restraint to keep from meddling with them while they do it."[56] Richard Branson has taken a similar approach in his business. When Patrick Zelnick proposed starting what became Virgin's highly profitable Paris Megastore, Richard let Patrick take the lead and stayed in the background as an advisor.[57] Google also gives its employees ownership of their work by letting them spend time on projects that they propose. They are encouraged to submit their ideas for projects to a review board. If an idea is approved, the employee can then spend up to 20% of his or her time working on it. Google's famous Gmail was the outgrowth of one of its employee's self-initiated projects.[58]

In choosing a motivational strategy to use with people, it is important to remember that "one size doesn't fit all." There is great variation in what motivates people. One way to discover what motivates a particular individual is to listen to what brings a sparkle to their eye. Another approach, if you have plenty of resources, is to appeal to multiple deep inner needs. Google does this extremely well. It starts by making people feel needed and appreciated. Jeff Levick, Google's director of vertical markets, has commented, "The way to keep people challenged and motivated is by making them understand how core they are to the business."[59] In accordance with this approach, Google's founders hold large open weekly meetings for employees at which they show them how their work is contributing to Google's success. Google also strives hard to make people feel like family. Employees eat together in large dining halls that have wide selections of food from around the world. Adjacent to each work area are snack centers where people can gather. Exercise centers throughout the Google complex let employees sweat together. On each floor of the Google complex, there are free tee shirts with Google emblazoned on the front that employees can wear to show that they belong to the Google family. Finally, Google tries to make employees' work meaningful by providing them with opportunities to pursue projects which they personally believe are important.

TAKE A MOMENT TO REFLECT

What powers are you currently using to build your career? What additional powers do you need to acquire?

On the page below, list the powers you are currently using and the ones that you need to acquire to be more successful.

Know How to Create
Your Personal Success Syndrome

Before Dorothy sets out for the Emerald City, Glinda explains that it is a long journey. She asks Dorothy, "Did you bring your broomstick?" Dorothy laments, "No, I'm afraid I didn't." Glinda replies, "Well, then you will have to walk to the Emerald City."[1] Like Dorothy, most superstars start their journey by walking. They begin with effort, but effort alone is not enough. To become a superstar, we must use effort wisely and purposefully to create what Professor John Kotter of Harvard Business School has termed our personal "success syndrome."[2]

To create our personal success syndrome, we must systematically invest the powers that we currently have in projects which, when successful, will result in us acquiring more powers. When we do this well, we create a success cycle that feeds on itself. Each time one of our projects succeeds, we increase the powers that we have. We can then use these powers to invest in more ambitious projects which in turn will bring us even greater powers and, as a result, more success.

Professor Kotter has found that an important factor distinguishing superstars from people who are less successful is that superstars start creating a personal success syndrome early in their careers. They actively look for opportunities to increase their powers. They carefully evaluate the powers that they

89

have and strategically calculate how they can use these powers to acquire more powers. Based on their analysis, they pursue projects that they can successfully complete with their present powers and avoid ones that they can't complete.[3] Richard Branson did this in building his Virgin empire. He first started small businesses that fit with his limited powers. When they succeeded, he used his increased powers to start larger businesses. By slowly and steadily increasing his power base, he created a highly effective personal success syndrome.

There is no fixed formula for creating our personal success syndrome. Depending on where we are going, we don't need to use or acquire all the powers that were described in Step Three. Superstars typically start by using effort and expertise to get on the playing field and to develop a solid track record. Many then employ visibility to make sure that people notice what they've accomplished. Those who work in organizations often seek to be involved in jobs and projects that are critical to the organization's success and thus, will increase their relevance and visibility. Finally, most rely on attractiveness to expand their personal networks and increase their centrality.

The following stories show how four superstars built their personal success syndromes. They feature Jack Welch, former CEO of General Electric; Dr. Ben Carson, one of the foremost pediatric neurosurgeons in the world; Margaret Thatcher, Great Britain's first and to-date only female Prime Minister; and Bill Gallagher, founder of A D S Financial Services Solutions (ADS), one of the foremost providers of technological services to the banking industry. Their stories show that there are many different ways to build the powers that lead to becoming a superstar. Each person created their success syndrome by following their own unique route. Jack Welch relied heavily on effort to build a positive track record. This increased his relevance at General Electric and resulted in him being promoted to higher and higher positions within the company. Dr. Ben Carson used effort to build expertise. This then led to his acquiring the autonomy that has allowed him to develop the groundbreaking surgical procedures that have saved children's lives and made him a legend in his field. Margaret Thatcher repeatedly used effort combined with visibility and relevance to make herself a valued defender of the Conservative Party's positions in Parliament. Her success at doing this led to her being elected head of her party and ultimately Prime Minister. Bill Gallagher combined attractiveness with expertise and effort to build ADS's track record and make it a major provider of technological services to financial institutions.

Jack Welch, CEO of General Electric

During his tenure as CEO, Jack Welch transformed General Electric (GE) from a slow moving bureaucracy to an innovative high growth company. His climb to the top of General Electric shows how one can use effort, attractiveness, visibility, relevance and a positive track record to acquire one of the ultimate types of formal authority in business, the position of CEO of a Fortune 500 company.

Like Dorothy, Jack Welch began building his personal success syndrome by using effort. He grew up in Salem, Massachusetts, which is just north of Boston. His father was a conductor on a Boston commuter line. After high school Jack entered the University of Massachusetts where he obtained an undergraduate degree in chemical engineering. Jack wasn't a brilliant student but he made the dean's list each year by working hard. His effort reaped rewards. During his senior year he was offered a fellowship to pursue a doctorate in the University of Illinois's highly ranked chemical engineering program.[4] There Jack again relied on effort rather than genius. He lived in the lab, arriving at eight each morning and leaving at eleven in the evening. Through his extraordinary effort, he completed his Ph.D. in a record three years.[5]

The expertise that Jack acquired with his Ph.D. led to a job at General Electric in Pittsfield, Massachusetts, in a research

91

group developing new plastics.[6] When he arrived at Pittsfield, Jack expected the same red carpet treatment that he had received during the recruitment process. He was sadly disappointed. Instead, he was placed in a small office in a warehouse with three other men. Jack chafed at this type of treatment. When at the end of his first year he received the same standard $1,000 raise that everyone was given, he felt that this was the last straw. He walked into his boss's office and quit.[7]

Jack's career at General Electric would have ended at this point, but earlier in the year he had attracted the attention of Reuben Gutoff, his boss's boss. Gutoff had asked Jack to do a basic cost and physical property analysis of a new plastic that General Electric was developing. Rather than simply giving Gutoff the analysis that he requested, Jack went the extra mile. He also compared the plastic with major competing products. Jack commented:

> What I was trying to do was "get out of the pile." If I had just answered [Gutoff's] questions, it would have been tough to get noticed. . . . To set myself apart from the crowd, I thought I had to think bigger than the questions posed. I wanted to provide not only the answer, but an unexpected fresh perspective.[8]

Jack's extra effort made an impression on Gutoff. When he learned that Jack had quit, he called him and invited him and his wife to dinner. For four hours Gutoff tried to convince Jack to stay. He offered him a larger raise, more responsibility and promised to protect him from the bureaucracy. Finally Jack relented and agreed to stay.[9]

Jack continued to expend great effort to build a positive track record. This led to a steady stream of promotions. With each promotion Jack acquired more autonomy. In 1968 he was made general manager of GE's plastic business.[10] This provided him with the power to take a novel approach to promoting General Electric's plastics. He had a series of entertaining television and radio commercials made which advertised GE's plastic in the same way as laundry detergent. One commercial portrayed a bull wreaking havoc in a china shop while GE's plastic remained unbroken. Jack even staged a publicity event in which a professional baseball player hurled fastballs at a piece of plastic that he was holding. While some people at General Electric didn't like his unorthodox approaches, he acquired a great deal of visibility and gained relevance because his approach worked. He doubled General Electric's plastics' business in three years.[11]

While Jack steadily built his personal success syndrome and moved up the corporate ladder, he had a problem. He was not on the succession list to become the next CEO. In 1974 there were nineteen people on the list of people to succeed CEO, Reg Jones. Jack was not one of them. In 1975 the list was reduced to ten and Jack was still not on it. Jack's bosses and most people with whom he worked closely liked and respected him, but the head of Human Resources who made up the list had reservations about putting Jack on the list. He thought that he was too young and that he at times pushed the people who worked for him too hard for results. Jack was saved by Reg Jones who decided that given Jack's great track record for delivering profits, he should at least be given a chance to compete to be CEO. At Reg's insistence Jack was put on the succession list.[12]

In 1977 Jack moved to corporate headquarters where he was one of seven men being considered to be the next CEO.[13] There, Jack's attractiveness played an important role in his selection. Reg Jones and the board, who were the decision makers, liked him. They enjoyed socializing and playing golf with him and considered him one of them. In addition, his style of work and background closely matched that of Reg. Both were self-made men from working-class backgrounds with similar working styles.[14]

> We both loved numbers and analyses. We both did our homework and showed little tolerance for anyone who didn't.[15]

In 1980 Jack was chosen as General Electric's new CEO.[16]

Dr. Ben Carson, Pediatric Neurosurgeon

Dr. Ben Carson is a true American success story. He grew up in a poor African-American community in Detroit. When he was eight, his father left his mother, who had only a third-grade education, to single-handedly raise Ben and his brother Curtis. At age 33, Dr. Carson became Director of Pediatric Neurosurgery at Johns Hopkins Medical Institutions, the youngest physician to ever head a major division at Johns Hopkins. Today he still holds this position as well as a professorship in neurosurgery, oncology, plastic surgery, and pediatrics. His position at Johns Hopkins has given him the opportunity to develop groundbreaking surgical procedures that now make it possible for children with formerly life-threatening brain injuries and pathologies to survive and live relatively normal lives. Dr. Carson catapulted to fame in 1987 with his successful separation of the Binder conjoined twins who were joined at the back of the head.[17]

Dr. Carson began building his personal success syndrome in the 5th grade. He was doing so poorly in school that his classmates called him a "dummy." Even he thought that he was stupid. His mother was deeply upset by his failure in school. After much thought and prayer, she decreed that Ben and his brother, who was also doing badly, could only watch three television programs a week and must read two books each week. At the end of the week they were to submit written book reports to her. Ben was at first opposed to this regimen but soon he discovered that he liked to read. He started with stories about animals and then moved to more serious scientific books on plants, animals and rocks.[18] One day, Mr. Jake, the science teacher, brought a rock to class and asked students if they could identify it. The only student who knew the rock's name was Ben. The class was flabbergasted that the "class dummy" had identified the rock.[19] By becoming an expert on rocks, Ben had taken his first step in building his personal success syndrome.

Recognizing Ben's potential, Mr. Jake invited Ben to stop by his science laboratory after school so they could start a rock collection for him. Ben relates:

> And from there on, I started going to the laboratory every day, getting involved with feeding the red squirrel named Maynard. There was a tarantula, a crayfish, a Jack Dempsey fish, and I got involved in all this stuff, and there was a microscope. I started looking at water specimens and learned all about paramecium and volvox and amoebas, and it was just incredible. And that really was what started me on my way.[20]

By seventh grade Ben was the top student in his class. Students no longer called him a "dummy." They came to him when they couldn't solve a problem.[21] He had acquired a very positive type of visibility.

Ben's success in school led to a scholarship to Yale University. After graduating from Yale, he entered medical school at the University of Michigan. In medical school, Ben continued to use expertise to acquire visibility. In his fourth year he became intrigued with neurosurgery. He read everything that he could find and soon became an expert. His newfound expertise was not lost on his professors. They quickly noticed that Ben, only a fourth year medical student, knew more about neurosurgery than interns and residents who had already completed medical school. During neurological surgery grand rounds, professors would turn to Ben when interns and residents couldn't answer a question and say, "Carson, suppose you tell them."[22]

During his final year in medical school, Ben applied for an internship in neurological surgery at Johns Hopkins. Internships at Johns Hopkins were highly competitive. Out of a pool of 125 applicants only two interns were chosen.[23] Ben's good grades, high national board scores, and strong recommendations from his professors made him competitive, but it was his expertise in an entirely different area that helped him be chosen for the internship. In high school Ben had discovered classical music when his older brother, Curtis, brought home a record of Schubert's *Eighth Symphony (Unfinished)*. Even though Ben thought it was weird, he soon found himself humming the *Eighth Symphony* during the day. This began his love of classical music. By attending concerts and reading books on classical music, he quickly became an expert.[24]

Based on his grades and recommendations, Ben made it to the final stage of the selection process at Johns Hopkins. He was invited for an interview with Dr. Udvarhelyi, head of the Neurological Surgery Training Program. Ben arrived feeling apprehensive, but his anxiety quickly evaporated. He and Dr. Udvarhelyi discovered that they had attended the same classical music concert the previous night. Like Ben, Dr. Udvarhelyi was a great classical music aficionado. They spent the interview in animated conversation about the concert. Years later Dr. Udvarhelyi told Ben that he had strongly recommended him.[25] Ben's expertise in classical music had made him a highly attractive candidate to Dr. Udvarhelyi. Like most of us, Dr. Udvarhelyi wanted to work with an intern whom he liked and who shared his enthusiasms.

After completing his internship, Dr. Carson was invited to spend a year as Senior Registrar in Neurosurgery at the Sir Charles Gardiner Hospital, Queen Elizabeth II Medical Center in Western Australia. Having already been offered a faculty position at Johns Hopkins, Dr. Carson and his wife agonized over whether to go to Australia, but finally decided to accept the challenge.[26] This turned out to be a great opportunity for Dr. Carson to build expertise and a superb track record. In the less competitive arena of Western Australia, Dr. Carson was given lots of autonomy. This allowed him to experiment with new techniques and take challenging cases that forced him to expand his skills. He also did more surgery than many American doctors do in a lifetime.[27] He related:

> In my one year there I got so much surgical experience that my skills were honed tremendously, and I felt remarkably capable and comfortable working on the brain.[28]

Dr. Carson returned to Johns Hopkins with extensive surgical expertise and a spectacular track record for someone so young. He was soon performing most of the pediatric neurosurgeries at Johns Hopkins. A few months after he returned he became Johns Hopkins' youngest Chief of Pediatric Neurosurgery.[29]

Dr. Carson's position as Chief of Pediatric Neurosurgery did not markedly increase his formal authority, but it did increase his centrality. It put him in an excellent position to attract top people from other areas of the hospital to work on his surgical and support teams. His ability to acquire talented people to work with him on complex and difficult operations was an important resource and critical to his further building his personal success syndrome.

The other advantage to his position was that it gave him more autonomy to accept difficult cases and try controversial procedures.[30] One such case was Maranda, a four-year-old girl who had Rasmussen encephalitis. This incurable disease causes inflammation of the brain which progressively leads to paralysis, mental retardation, and eventually death.[31] In an act of desperation, Maranda's parents brought her to Johns Hopkins after being told by other doctors that there was nothing that could be done. Since the disease was confined to the left side of her brain, Dr. Freeman, Dr. Carson's mentor, suggested that removing that side of her brain might save her. The operation, which is called a hemispherectomy, was rarely done at that time because of high mortality rates and severe side effects. After much research and thought Dr. Carson decided to perform the operation despite the low likelihood of success. He knew that without it, Maranda faced certain death. For over eight hours he slowly and carefully cut away Maranda's inflamed hemisphere. Beating all odds, Maranda made a complete recovery with only a few minor side effects.[32]

Dr. Carson's success in operating on Maranda showcased his extraordinary expertise as a neurosurgeon. It significantly increased his visibility and relevance. Patients came from across the country to see him when other doctors couldn't help them.

As a result, Dr. Carson created an ever-expanding personal success syndrome. His track record and visibility brought him increasingly difficult cases. His success with them further increased his track record, visibility and, relevance. These successes led to his being asked to separate the Binder Siamese twins who were joined at the head. His successful separation of them further helped cement his reputation as one of the foremost pediatric neurosurgeons in the world. Working on these seemingly hopeless cases also increased his expertise. The challenges that they represented provided him with the opportunity to develop and perfect the innovative technologies and procedures that have now made him a medical legend.

Margaret Thatcher, British Prime Minister

In 1975, Margaret Thatcher was elected leader of the Conservative Party. Four years later when the Conservative Party gained a majority in the House of Commons, Margaret became the first woman Prime Minister of the United Kingdom of Great Britain and Northern Ireland. As Prime Minister, Thatcher pursued her brand of conservatism which became known as "Thatcherism." She introduced bills to limit the role of the government and moved the United Kingdom toward a more open free-market economy. She reduced the size of the civil service, cut social programs, and privatized many state-owned companies, significantly changing the relationship between the British people and their government. Her combative style, battles with trade unions, and strong commitment to fiscal rigor and individual responsibility made her a larger than life public figure in Britain.[33]

Margaret Thatcher was born in Grantham, Lincolnshire. Her father, a grocer, was heavily involved in local politics which exposed Margaret to politics at an early age.[34] By the time Margaret entered Oxford University, she wanted to become a Member of Parliament (MP). To build her personal success syndrome Margaret relied heavily on effort and visibility. During her first term at Oxford, she joined the Oxford University Conservative Association (OUCA). Its political counterpart, the Labour Club, was far more popular, but Margaret considered the OUCA's lack of popularity to be to her advantage. In the OUCA she could more easily acquire visibility and build a power base because she had less competition.[35]

Margaret Thatcher wasn't particularly popular at the OUCA. Many found her bossy and dowdy, but this didn't deter Margaret. She set out to use effort, not attractiveness, to make herself invaluable at the OUCA. She sold tickets to OUCA balls, organized events, and collaborated on policy papers. Through her efforts she built a positive track record for getting things done. One member of the OUCA recalls that when Margaret organized events, they never ran out of food or drink and the events were well attended. Based on her hard work, in her third year at Oxford she was elected secretary and then treasurer of the OUCA. During her final year she was elected President in Michaelmas.[36]

Margaret used her position as President in Michaelmas of the OUCA to further her goal of being elected to Parliament. She began developing relationships with important members of the Conservative Party by inviting them to speak at the OUCA. An impressive number accepted. She wrote in her autobiography,

> It was there [at Oxford] that I first rubbed shoulders with the great figures of the [Conservative] Party—and, in fact, I kept in touch with many of them over the years.[37]

In addition to her activities within the OUCA, Margaret also increased her visibility in the Conservative Party by working for candidates running for election. She canvassed for them, and when home in Grantham, she was a warm-up speaker for the district's Conservative candidate. Some evenings she would speak at half a dozen meetings.[38] She not only managed to attract the attention of the party but also of the press which reported on many of her speeches.[39]

After Margaret graduated from Oxford, she continued to build her personal success syndrome by using visibility and effort to increase the network of people whom she knew within the Conservative Party. She joined the Young Conservatives in Colchester, where she lived, and became the principal speaker for their debating team. She attended weekend party conferences and constantly sought opportunities to speak for the party. Her intense involvement in party affairs and the increasingly large network of people in the party with whom she was acquainted led to her being introduced to the Chairman of the Dartford Conservative Association. Dartford, a Labour stronghold, was looking for a candidate to run in their district. Impressed with Margaret, the chairman asked her to put her name forward.[40]

During the Dartford selection process, Margaret reassured the committee that she would fight for the Dartford seat with "all the energy at my disposal. . . ." After she was selected, she remained true to her word. She gave speeches, debated her opponent, visited factories, and went door-to-door meeting her constituents. When it rained heavily, she used a car with a loudspeaker to reach out to potential voters.[41] She also began to work at making herself attractive. After attending a Conservative Party program on how to dress during campaigns, she transformed herself into a well-dressed attractive woman in a smart black suit and hat who charmed the press and public.[42] The attention that she paid to her clothes and personal appearance became one of her trademarks throughout her career.

During the Dartford campaign, Margaret exhibited an uncanny flair for getting noticed. She was a master at getting press coverage. Women were still a novelty in politics and Margaret capitalized on it. She delighted the press by dancing with her opponent at one political event. To meet male constituents she signed on as a barmaid at a club in Dartford that only admitted men. This resulted in an article in the *Daily Mail* with a picture of her pulling pints. Wherever she went,

the press loved her. The *Daily Mail* wrote, "She is easy
at, soft-voiced, feminine, charming and clear-headed."[43]

Through her tireless efforts campaigning and her skill for
acquiring visibility, Margaret made an impressive showing at
Dartford. While she did not win, she cut the Labour majority
by a third. Moreover, the positive publicity that she generated
for the party helped Conservative candidates win in surrounding districts. As a result, she increased her centrality. Alfred
Bossum, the Chairman of the Kent Members of Parliament,
began inviting her to his lavish eve-of-session parties for MPs
and attempted to find a winnable seat for her.[44]

In 1951 Margaret again ran for the Dartford seat and lost,
but she again reduced the Labour Party's advantage.[45] Her
long hours of vigorous campaigning and her ability to attract
votes further increased her visibility and relevance to the party.
Members began to realize that she could win for the party.

Margaret's efforts were rewarded in 1959 when she was
given the opportunity to run for the Finchley seat which was
a Conservative Party stronghold. She won by a huge majority and finally achieved her goal of becoming a Member of
Parliament (MP). Margaret immediately set out to get noticed
in her new venue. She alerted the press of the time when she, the
youngest MP, would be arriving on the first day of Parliament.
The next day her picture appeared in all the papers.[46] For her
maiden speech she introduced a bill that favored the press.
The speech was on a Friday afternoon when most MPs had left
for the weekend. To increase attendance Margaret used effort.
She hand-wrote notes to each of the 250 MPs alerting them of
her speech. In her autobiography Margaret wrote:

> In the end, however, there is no substitute for one's own efforts. I
> wanted to get as many MPs as possible to the House on a Friday (when
> most MPs have returned to their constituency) for the Bill's Second
> Reading-this was the great hurdle. I have always believed in the impact
> of a personal handwritten letter-even from someone you barely know.
> So just before the Second Reading I wrote 250 letters to Government
> backbenchers asking them to attend and vote for my measure.[47]

101

urnout for her speech and received rave
The *Daily Express* wrote, "A new star was
She appeared on television and was inter-
crew at her home.[48]

was masterful at making herself visible to
ess, she had to get the attention of senior
party memb__ ɔ advance within the Conservative Party. To
do this, Margaret again relied on effort. Before her speeches in
the House of Commons, she would spend hours in the library
collecting statistics and facts that supported her points. On
one occasion, she worked so hard that she collapsed at her
desk and was sent home to rest. In her speeches she would
bombard her opponents with endless numbers, statistics and
facts. This made her Labour Party opponents reluctant to
attack her because they usually weren't as well prepared as she
was. Moreover, when they did attack her, Margaret corrected
their facts, which further added to their trepidation.[49]

Members of the Conservative Party were quick to notice
Margaret's value. After being in Parliament for only two years,
she was offered a junior post in the Ministry of Pensions and
National Insurance. Despite the fact that Margaret was a
mother with young twins at home, she knew that in politics
"when you're offered a job you either accept it or you're out."[50]
From pensions, she moved to ever-higher ministry positions
within the Conservative Party. In these positions she became
renowned for the enormous effort that she expended. When
she was asked to argue a position for the party in the House
of Commons, she would review every relevant document and
statistic that she could find. When in 1966 she made her first
speech as a member of the Treasury ministry, she announced
that she had read every Budget speech since 1946![51] In addition, she became renowned for her expertise as a debater and
for a lack of reservations in engaging in the rough and tumble
jousting that occurs on the floor of the House of Commons.
Writing about her performance in a debate on rising prices,
the *Daily Telegraph* reported:

> Mrs. Thatcher gave a dazzling performance, firing salvo after salvo of devastating statistics into the Labour benches like a cannon firing grapeshot into a crowd.
>
> It is always rash to take on Mrs. Thatcher where facts and figures are concerned. Tonight, Labour references to the deficit they had inherited had clearly riled her and she decided to give the Socialists a statistical bombardment they would not forget in a hurry.[52]

This willingness to be the party attack dog and the effort that she put into developing expertise in any area she was assigned steadily increased her track record and relevance to the Conservative Party.

In October of 1974 the Conservative Party lost its majority in the House of Commons and returned to being the opposition party. After this defeat, the party's spirits were low and their confidence in Edward Heath, the current leader of the party, waned. At the time Margaret was highly visible. She was brilliantly leading the Conservative Party's opposition to the Labour Party's finance bill on the House floor. Her success made her a highly attractive candidate to replace Heath. Several MPs asked her to challenge him. Initially reluctant, Margaret finally agreed.[53]

Margaret's uncanny ability to get noticed was instrumental in her being elected. Two weeks before the vote she debated Denis Healy, a leading member of the Labour Party, on the House floor. Healy was renowned for his skill as a debater but Margaret took him on and soundly beat him. The publicity and acclaim that she received carried her to victory in the balloting and she became the first woman to lead the Conservative Party. Once more she had skillfully combined effort with visibility to create her personal success syndrome.[54]

Bill Gallagher, Entrepreneur

Bill Gallagher[55] began his journey to becoming a superstar as a bank messenger. Today, he sits at the top of his own company, A D S Financial Services Solutions (ADS) that he founded with Robert Howe in 1980. ADS initially designed and built computer systems for banks. As the computer industry has changed, ADS has grown into a consulting firm that now helps banks capitalize on technological innovation and change. Over a 25-year period Bill, with his partner, has built ADS from a company of four employees to a company of over 100 employees with revenues exceeding eighteen million dollars. In 2004, ADS was named to the FinTech 100, a list of the top 100 providers of technology to financial institutions.

Bill grew up in Boston. When he was four, his mother left his alcoholic father and moved into government subsidized housing where she struggled to raise Bill and his three siblings on her own. Money was so scarce that at the age of fourteen Bill took a full-time job in a drugstore. After graduating from high school, he became a bank messenger because he couldn't afford to attend college.

Bill began building his personal success syndrome at the bank almost immediately by using attractiveness to acquire banking expertise. During slow periods between delivering documents to other banks, Bill waited in the Treasurer's office where he often encountered the bank CEO. Curious about why the documents that he curried between banks were so valuable that his briefcase had to be handcuffed to his wrist, he started asking the CEO questions about the documents. The CEO was a gruff man who was not easy to approach, but Bill's engaging manner and genuine interest in banking broke down his reserve. He began to teach Bill about banking. Bill would ask, "What does the Federal Reserve do?" After the CEO finished explaining, Bill would translate what he said into pictures and diagrams that showed the relationships between the different bank processes. This became a game that they both enjoyed. Through these informal teaching sessions, Bill acquired expertise in bank processes, as well as visibility at the highest levels of the bank.

Bill soon added computer expertise to his banking knowledge. The bank where he worked was one of the first in Boston to purchase a large IBM mainframe computer. At that time, computers were new and very few people knew how to operate them. As part of installing computers for customers, IBM gave their employees a computer aptitude test to identify which employees would be good at running the computer. Bill took the test with the rest of the bank's employees and received one of the highest scores ever recorded on the test. IBM urged the bank to put Bill in charge of running the computer, despite his lack of a college degree. Bill's case was helped by the fact that he was not merely a faceless messenger, but a highly visible one whom the CEO who knew and liked. Bill was given the job and IBM trained him. In a year and a half, he had moved from being a messenger with expertise in bank processes to being the bank's computer expert.

After serving as the bank's computer expert for five years, Bill's job ended when the bank decided to no longer have its own computer. Instead it joined a consortium of 28 banks that were forming a company to provide centralized computer services for its members. Bill applied for a job with this new company. Based on his expertise and positive track record at the bank, he was hired as the most junior member of a nine-member technical group whose job was to computerize bank processes.

The group was headed by the company's chief technology officer, a brilliant technician from MIT's Computer Lab. Bill's job within the group was to design bank forms. He quickly realized that none of the other members of the group, including the chief technology officer, knew anything about bank processes. Using the knowledge that he had acquired while a bank messenger, Bill quickly established himself as the group expert on banking. At meetings, he would instruct other members on how to computerize financial transactions and advise them on appropriate timelines. He would point out, "That's not how you calculate accruals. This is how you do it," or "You

105

have a month to do this? This looks like a week to me." His expertise gave him relevance and centrality within the group and soon the chief technology officer was turning to Bill for advice and assigning him important projects.

Bill's expertise, relevance and expanding track record also attracted the attention of the president of the company. Recognizing Bill's value, he asked Bill to take over the management of a loan project that had fallen behind schedule. After Bill successfully completed the project, the president assigned him to head another failing project. Within three years of starting at the company, the president made Bill head of technology.

Bill's autonomy and relevance continued to grow with his increasingly important positions. A year after Bill became head of technology, the president decided that he wanted to spend his time on political projects. So he asked Bill and Robert Howe, Bill's future partner, to run the company for him. This further increased Bill's autonomy and provided him with an opportunity to build additional expertise. He became involved in all facets of the business including upgrading hardware, converting additional banks to the system, designing international standards for check processing, developing credit card encryption protocols, and even marketing the company's services.

The personal success syndrome that Bill had built at the company came to a grinding halt, however, when the president resigned. Bill's future was now uncertain. He and Robert ran the company, but their power came from the informal authority delegated to them by the president and not from formal positions. The president recommended to the board that they make either Bill or Robert the new president. The board refused. Bill didn't have a college degree and neither he nor Robert had experience as bank executives. They were just two mavericks who through their expertise and ability to deliver had acquired enormous autonomy, centrality, and relevance. The chairman of the board bluntly told them, "There is no way I can make either of you president. You aren't traditional

Yankee bankers." Faced with the prospect of losing their autonomy and strong power base, Bill and Robert quit. Armed with expertise in banking and computers, they started Atlantic Data Services (ADS). Bill ran the technical side of the business while his partner managed the sales and financial side.

Bill now faced a new set of challenges. In an organization we build our success syndrome by steadily acquiring more personal autonomy, centrality, relevance, and formal authority. As an entrepreneur, we already have these powers. Instead, we must focus on building our company's personal success syndrome. We must get our company noticed by establishing a sound track record for it, making it visible to potential customers, and providing customers with products and services that they consider valuable. To do this, we must use effort, expertise and attractiveness.

Bill began to build his personal success syndrome by using the same attractiveness that had helped him launch his career at the bank. He soon discovered that he also needed to teach his employees to be attractive when dealing with clients. One of ADS's first major contracts was to computerize a general ledger system for a bank. When the system was completed, the client refused to let Bill test it by running the new system in parallel with the old system. The client said, "We want to go live immediately. Convert us." Bill attempted to convince the client to change his mind but the client was adamant that he wanted to "go live." When Bill told his technicians who were working with him, they were outraged. They complained loudly, "We can't do that. This is stupid." Bank employees who were working in the area froze, and all ears became focused on Bill and his technicians. Realizing that they were the center of attention, Bill took his employees into a private room. He said,

> Listen. Sometimes we will be able to convince our clients to do things the right way, but sometimes they will want to do stupid things. We must protect ourselves. When a client wants to do something stupid, we are going down the rapids with them. Whether they want to do it the right way or the wrong way, we are going with them.

107

> As good as you are, I will have to fire you if you ever again behave unprofessionally in front of a client. We can discuss our professional opinions privately but ultimately it is the client's decision. Our job is just to support them professionally. You can say whatever you want to me, but you can never say these things in front of a client.

Bill's technicians learned this lesson quickly, and they never again complained in front of a client.

This same general ledger client subsequently further tested Bill's commitment to attractiveness. Two months after ADS completed the general ledger, the treasurer at the bank discovered that the old manual system and the new computerized system were not in agreement. The new system had an investment balance that was $500,000 greater than the manual system. The treasurer was livid. He told Bill, "You have to figure this out. This is unacceptable." Bill responded with concern. He checked the computer system that they had installed and found that it was running perfectly. He then offered to check the old system. There he found the problem. ADS had updated the value of the bank's investments to current market values while installing the general ledger system, whereas the bank had failed to keep the value of their investments up-to-date. By quietly solving the problem without making the client wrong, Bill created good will for ADS and added to its track record.

The other power that Bill heavily relied on in building ADS was effort. In the early years of the company, resources were scarce. This meant that Bill often had to do the work of two people. When a new employee that he had hired to write a sophisticated computer settlement system for a Boston bank proved incapable of doing the job, Bill stepped in and did it. Every day for three months, he left home at 6:00 am and drove 70 miles to a client site where he spent the day installing a computer system. At 5:00 pm he left and drove an hour to the Boston bank, where he worked late into the night writing the settlement system. The president of the Boston bank's computer services subsidiary was so impressed by Bill's effort that he hired ADS to build all of their computer systems for the next eleven years.

Bill also went the extra mile to make sure that his employees succeeded. One Friday evening at a firm social gathering, one of his best technicians told him that he was having trouble completing a credit approval system that was due on Monday. The technician decided at the end of the evening to go back to work to see if he could figure out the problem. When Bill left, he also didn't go home. Instead, he turned his car south and drove 80 miles to the client site where the technician was working and spent the night helping him solve the problem. When the client arrived Monday morning, the system was up and running.[56]

While Bill didn't hesitate to expend effort in building ADS' track record, he also carefully calculated where his effort combined with his expertise would bring the most return. A major problem that ADS faced when it started was that it had no visibility. Potential clients were unaware of ADS or the value that it could add to their businesses. One of Bill's strategies was to take financially and professionally risky jobs which if successful would give ADS visibility and increase its track record. He employed this strategy with National Cash Register (NCR), a major provider of bank teller machines, ATMs and other peripheral equipment. IBM had just introduced competing peripheral banking equipment that could send information directly to IBM mainframe computers. This threatened NCR's market because its peripheral equipment couldn't do this and most customers used IBM mainframes.

Bill saw the problem that NCR faced as an opportunity for ADS to acquire lucrative contracts from them and increase its visibility within the banking industry. He approached NCR and asked if they would be interested in ADS writing software for them that would let their peripheral equipment send information directly to IBM computers. NCR replied, "That would be unbelievable. Of course we are interested."

Bill said, "Send me your equipment. We'll do it for $2,500, but if it works, you have to pay me a lot more money. The other part of the deal is that if we finish it by October, you feature us at your booth at the National Bank Automation Show."

Bill and his employees frantically started designing an interface. The protocol used by IBM was so complex that ADS' first attempts failed. As the days went by, they weren't sure that they could make it work. Each extra hour that they spent cost them more money. Four months after they began, they finally succeeded. They met the October deadline for the National Bank Automation Show and were featured at NCR's booth where they demonstrated the interface. It was a big hit. They had done what many considered impossible.

NCR significantly increased sales of its peripheral equipment and became an important ADS client. The visibility that ADS acquired and their connection with NCR was a turning point for ADS. It brought them many new clients as well as establishing a track record for ADS as a company that could solve the difficult problems involved in integrating technology and bank services.

Effort, a Major Ingredient
for Becoming a Superstar

Once Dorothy decides to go to the Emerald City to ask the Wizard for help, she moves quickly. Even though she stops to help the Scarecrow, the Tin Man, and the Lion, she never lingers long before she is back on the Yellow Brick Road. When she finally sees the Emerald City on the horizon, she urges the group forward crying, "Let's run."[57]

Dorothy wastes no time trying to find a way back to Kansas. Once she decides to go to see the Wizard, she focuses all her efforts on reaching the Emerald City. Each person in this chapter similarly expended great effort in pursuing their goals. To become a superstar, we too must use effort, but we must use it wisely. No matter how hard we work, there are only twenty-four hours in a day and the amount of effort that we have is finite. Thus, we must make sure that we strategically use our effort in ways that will help us acquire more power because raw effort is not enough.

Bill Gallagher used his effort wisely and strategically in building ADS into a highly successful company. He looked for jobs that would increase ADS' revenues and give it visibility. When Jack Welch first arrived at General Electric, he put extra effort into a market analysis requested by a high level manager because he knew that this would give him visibility and build his track record. Margaret Thatcher worked tirelessly to increase the Conservative vote in her first run for Parliament even though she had no hope of winning. By putting forth such an extraordinary effort, she gained party attention and proved that she could deliver votes. In his fourth year in medical school, Dr. Carson spent hours reading every journal article and book that he could find on neuroscience and the brain. The expertise that he acquired was an important factor in his obtaining a prized internship at Johns Hopkins.

If we are to fully capitalize on our effort and create an effective personal success syndrome, we must also align our effort with our mini-strengths. Trying to be a superstar when we are not using our mini-strengths is like trying to move a large boulder with brute force. If we lack basic arm strength, no matter how hard and long we push, it won't budge. We can, however, often move such boulders by aligning our effort with our mini-strengths. This is the underlying principle behind the lever, one of the inventions that helped man make the gigantic leap from caves to our current technologically sophisticated world.

The superstars in this chapter moved the heavy boulders that they encountered in their careers by using their mini-strengths as levers. Margaret Thatcher knew that she wouldn't gain admittance to the "old boys" club in the House of Commons on the basis of simply working hard. First, she was a woman. Second, people didn't naturally warm to her.

Third, she came from a different social background than most Members of Parliament. She did know, however, that she was a good debater and that it would be hard for party leaders to turn their back on her when they saw that she could win debates on the floor of the House of Commons. Bill Gallagher's empathy and skill at handling difficult situations helped ADS attract and retain clients. When at one point an employee stole money from a client, he used these strengths to reassure the client that ADS was not directly involved, thereby saving ADS's reputation. The long hours that Jack Welch spent reviewing the operational effectiveness of the plants that he managed was critical to his establishing a track record at GE as a person who delivered results. Dr. Ben Carson's gifted hands have been as important to his becoming a superstar as the effort and time that he has invested in becoming an expert in neurosurgery.

The other factor that we must align with effort is passion. Effort is like an old steam engine chugging up a hill. It moves us slowly up the hill one chug at a time. Without passion, it is hard to keep this effort up long enough to get up the hill. The four people whose careers were examined in this chapter had great passion for what they were doing. Dr. Carson was intrigued by the brain from the time he began studying it in medical school. Jack Welch was deeply committed to increasing efficiency and eliminating bureaucracy at General Electric. Bill Gallagher loved solving computer problems and developing new business. Margaret Thatcher relished demolishing opponents on the floor of the House of Commons. As their successes demonstrate, when we use effort strategically and align it with our strengths and passion, we can create a powerful personal success syndrome.

TAKE A MOMENT TO REFLECT

What is your personal success syndrome? How can you expand it?

On the page below, describe your personal success syndrome and ways in which you can make it more powerful.

Know How to Get and Give Help

Dorothy would never have become a superstar without the
help of the Scarecrow, the Tin Man, the Lion, and Glinda,
the friendly witch. Each time the Wicked Witch of the West
attacked her on her way to the Emerald City, one of these four
stepped forward and saved her. After Dorothy was imprisoned
in the Wicked Witch's castle, the Scarecrow, the Tin Man, and
the Lion rushed to her rescue. In return, Dorothy helped each
of them achieve their dreams.

Like Dorothy, knowing how to get and give help is critical
to our becoming a superstar. We share this world with many
people, and if we don't have some of them on our side, we are
unlikely to go far. When we look at the careers of superstars,
there are always people behind the scenes who have helped
them succeed. Superstars also help others. In building Wal-
Mart, Sam Walton made employees at the lowest levels of the
business richer than they ever imagined. As Oprah has noted,
"Nobody gets through this life alone."[1]

Don't Be Too Proud to Ask for Help

After Dorothy first encounters the Wicked Witch of the West, she turns
to Glinda and says, "Oh, I'd give anything to get out of Oz altogether; but
which is the way back to Kansas?"[2]

115

Dorothy begins asking for help as soon as she arrives in Oz. The purpose of her trip to the Emerald City is to ask the Wizard of Oz for help. Unlike Dorothy, we sometimes don't ask for help because we believe that our ability to become a superstar depends solely on our own efforts. American culture reinforces this idea. As children we grow up hearing stories of how Abraham Lincoln built his own log cabin and Daniel Boone settled the West. Movies and television feature larger-than-life heroes who single-handedly save the day. Schools reward individual rather than group achievement. Children who receive all "A's" or play first string on the school team are the ones who are considered superstars. As a result of living in a world where the individual is king, we can end up believing that asking for help is a weakness. True heroes, like "Superman," conquer the world on their own.

Superstars recognize that they can't do it alone and ask for help. They have the confidence to say, "I'm stuck. I don't know how to move forward." Dr. Ben Carson uses the mantra, "I can do anything, and if I can't do it, I know how to get help."[3] The well-known television talk show host, Larry King, wasn't afraid to ask for help in pursuing his dream of being on the radio. Larry's father died when he was nine, forcing his mother to rely on welfare to support the family. Lacking the money to attend college, Larry took a job as a mail clerk for Associated Merchandising Corporation. The company was located on the third floor of a large building in New York City and on the twenty-second floor was the WOR radio station. Larry used to pretend that he worked at WOR. Five or six times a day he would ride the elevator to the twenty-second floor and then back down to the first floor, imagining that he was on his way out to lunch after doing his radio show.[4] One day he met James Sirmons, a staff announcer at CBS. Larry immediately asked him for advice. He said, "Mr. Sirmons, I've always wanted to be in radio. You got any suggestions?" Mr. Sirmons replied,

> Well kid, I'd go down to Miami. They've got a lot of stations, non-union, don't pay a lot. So, they've got to get very young guys, or old guys who are hanging it up on the way out, alcoholics. Go down there and knock on doors.[5]

Larry quit his job and moved to Miami where he slept on his uncle's couch. Each day he knocked on radio station doors asking for a job. At a small station across from a police station, he received his big break. Marshall Simmonds, the general manager, gave him a "mike test." He said,

> You sound very good. I'll tell you what, I'm going to give you a suggestion. I don't have any openings, but a lot of people come and go here, we're a very small station. Why don't you hang around? You can clean up the place. We'll give you a little money every week, and the first guy that quits, you've got the job.[6]

Larry was at the station day and night sweeping floors and learning how to rip and read. One day an announcer quit. True to his word, Marshall gave Larry the job. Larry's request for help in New York had led him to Miami, where he finally fulfilled his childhood dream of being on the radio.[7]

Asking for help is critical when, like Larry King, we are struggling to get on the playing field. At such times we are sometimes too embarrassed to ask for help because we feel like a failure or don't want to call attention to our situation. What we don't realize is that people like to help. By asking people for help, we acknowledge their power and good will. Studies have found that charitable organizations are more successful at raising money and getting people to volunteer their time when they tell people that they really need their help. Organizations and businesses similarly want to help their employees. Most have elaborate systems to provide failing employees with second chances. My research on workplace performance confirms this. In a study of over 200 managers, I found that most managers dislike firing people and will go to extraordinary lengths to bring a person's performance up to an acceptable level. When they are unable to do this, managers themselves often feel a deep sense of failure.[8]

Ben Richardson, an African-American and Vice Chairman and Chief of Operations at Gant Electronics, discovered the value of asking for help the hard way. When he arrived at Cornell as a freshman, he set out to be a "Renaissance man." In the '70s and '80s being a "Renaissance man or woman" was highly admired. It meant that, like Leonardo De Vinci, the brilliant Renaissance artist and inventor, you were highly talented in many areas. In pursuit of this image, Ben played football and basketball, took extra courses and became involved in fraternity life. He was a man on campus who could do it all. During his sophomore year he realized that he was in over his head. He was failing his courses and his vision of being a "Renaissance man" was unraveling. Not knowing how to ask for help, he dropped out of Cornell. Reflecting later on his naiveté, he remarked:

> I realized that some [white] students understood things that I didn't. They learned from their fraternities about how the power structure worked. They learned how to maneuver around the institution. I learned it the hard way because I didn't maneuver. I remember talking to one of my professors, I hadn't done well in his course, and he told me, "If I had known you were getting into trouble, you could have come to me and talked about it." I didn't know that. I didn't know that was part of the rules. . . . I realized that whatever explicit rules there are in the institution, there are also unspoken rules.[9]

Ben used this lesson to climb the corporate ladder at Gant Electronics. He and other African-American sales representatives formed a self-help group. In the group, they used their accumulated knowledge and experience to help each other navigate the corporate system and deal with problems that they encountered in their jobs. It was through the help of this group that Ben eventually became Vice Chairman and Chief of Operations at Gant.[10]

Get Others to Join You

By the time that Dorothy approaches the Emerald City, she has the Scarecrow, the Tin Man and the Lion helping her. Together they skip toward the Emerald City.

In The Wizard of Oz, Dorothy and Toto start down the Yellow Brick Road alone, but they soon have the help of the Scarecrow, the Tin Man and the Lion. Without them, Dorothy and Toto would not have succeeded in reaching the Emerald City. Like Dorothy and Toto, superstars get others to join them on their journey. While the media may portray them as being the sole source of their climb to the top, most owe their success to a host of silent people behind the scenes who helped them.

Superstars are aware that most tasks in this world are just too big to do alone. As Sam Walton commented, "One person seeking glory doesn't accomplish much. . . ."[11] Richard Branson is the first to admit that he did not create the Virgin enterprises by himself. He has stated, "As far as I was concerned, the Virgin staff were the most important thing about Virgin."[12] Dr. Ben Carson attributes his high success rate in performing complicated brain surgeries to the superb teams of people who support him in the operating room and the staff who care for the patients once they leave the operating room.[13] Sam Walton has repeatedly acknowledged that Wal-Mart could not have succeeded without the help of his family and Wal-Mart's employees.

Steve Jobs similarly attributes his success to the teams of people who have helped him. He relates,

> My model for business is The Beatles: They were four guys who kept each other's negative tendencies in check. They balanced each other. And the total was greater than the sum of the parts. That's how I see business. Great things in business are never done by one person, they are done by a team of people.[14]

Superstars not only know that they need to recruit others to share their dreams, but they are adept at getting others to join them. Richard Branson genuinely likes other people. He sees the best in them and easily forms relationships. Most importantly, he exudes a positive energy that others like to be around. Psychologists have found that we literally catch each other's moods. If we are around someone who is depressed, we can become tired and listless. In contrast, we are energized by being around positive enthusiastic people.[15] Richard Branson's positive energy is the reason why he has never had trouble attracting talented people to work at Virgin. Even in Virgin's earliest days when all his employees were paid 20 pounds a week, plenty of young people wanted to work for Richard.[16]

Richard is also good at establishing relationships with others because he has enormous empathy for people and does not judge them. In 1979 he went to Paris to find someone to set up a French subsidiary for Virgin. There he met Patrick Zelnick at a lunch with the French head of Polygram. Richard immediately saw that Patrick, despite his wild distracted Woody Allen look, would be a good person to run Virgin's French subsidiary. After lunch, Patrick couldn't remember where he had parked his car. Rather than rush off to another meeting, Richard spent four hours helping Patrick search the narrow Paris streets for his car. Before they parted, he suggested that Patrick come and see him the next time that he was in London. A month later, Patrick showed up in London and agreed to run Virgin's French subsidiary.[17]

As the story of Richard helping Patrick find his car illustrates, when we show other people that we are aware of their needs and interests, they become eager to join us. Stan Shih, Acer's founder, stresses how important it is to put the interests of other people first if we want them to make a long-term commitment to helping us, but he notes how difficult it is to do. No matter how hard we try to be unselfish, we still tend to think of our own interests first. This, however, is counterproductive because putting the interests of others first is actually in our own interest in the long run. Shih has commented:

> If I do not care for others' interests, they will not trust me anymore once their interests are exploited. They will either cease to generate any contributions or take malicious revenge towards the company. This way, I will never enjoy any more benefits in the future. Therefore, placing my personal interest behind others ensures a safer and long-term benefit for myself.[18]

Dr. Ben Carson understood early in his career the power of putting other people's interests first. Following his freshman year at Yale, he got a summer job as a supervisor of a highway crew of inner-city students who picked up trash along the interstate highways around Detroit. While Ben liked his job as supervisor, he soon ran into problems. Picking up trash was hot dirty work. The students on his crew questioned why they should do it at all because people would just litter the highway again the next day. The other supervisors were only able to get their crews of five or six students to fill 12 trash bags during an eight-hour day. Ben took an approach with his crew that spoke to their interests. He made a deal with them. If they would start at 6:00 am each morning when it was cool, they could go home as soon as they filled 150 bags and still earn a full day's pay. The crew loved the idea. They soon learned to clean a stretch of highway in two or three hours. As the other crews arrived for work, they would be on their way home. The supervisors in the Department of Public Works were amazed. They asked Ben, "How come your guys can get so much work done?" Ben would reply, "Oh, I have my little secrets."[19]

Sam Walton was initially slow to learn that others are more willing to help us if we take their interests into consideration. When he first started Wal-Mart, he paid his employees as little as possible. He later regretted paying them so little because he realized that sharing the company's profits with employees actually made good business sense. He subsequently noted,

"The larger truth that I failed to see . . . is: the more you share your profits with your associates—whether it's in salaries or incentives or bonuses or stock discounts—the more profit will accrue to the company."[20]

Know Where You Need Help

As the Scarecrow and Dorothy oil the Tin Man, he gives them directions, "Oh, oil my arms, please! Oil my elbows!"[21]

When Dorothy, the Scarecrow, and Toto come across the Tin Man, he is stuck in one position. He desperately needs to be oiled or he will remain frozen forever in the same position. We all need other people to help oil us when we get stuck. One of the things that distinguishes superstars is that they recognize when they need help and, like the Tin Man, they also know where they need to be oiled. Soon after Richard Branson started Virgin, he realized that he needed help managing money. Under his financial management, Virgin was teetering on the edge of financial disaster. This knowledge caused Richard to bring in his childhood friend, Nik, who was a master at managing money. Nik was just what Virgin needed. He helped transform it into a profitable enterprise.[22]

Anita Roddick also didn't hesitate to acknowledge her financial naiveté and need for expert help when she started the Body Shop. Needing capital to finance her first store, she went to see the local bank manager wearing a "Bob Dylan" T-shirt with her two daughters in tow. She enthusiastically described her vision for the Body Shop to the manager, but he wasn't impressed. He flatly turned her down. Instead of giving up, Anita realized that she needed expert advice. She enlisted the help of her husband, Gordon, who was more sophisticated in these matters than she was. Gordon had an accountant draw up a professional business plan with projected profits and instructed Anita to buy a suit. A week later Anita, dressed in a suit, marched into the bank with Gordon and a business plan in hand. The bank manager immediately authorized the loan.[23]

Warren Buffett decided several decades ago to leave his billions to charity, but he has always been aware that he would need help to do this well. Giving away money is not as easy as it looks. Before foundations make grants, they must carefully review proposals and investigate the groups applying for money. Once they give money to a group, they must then monitor how the group uses it. Warren Buffett knew that he didn't have the expertise to do this. So, in 2006 he gave $30 billion to the Bill & Melinda Gates Foundation because he knew that they were experts at distributing money in ways that would do the most good.[24] By knowing where he needed help, Warren Buffett now has more time to devote to investing which is what he enjoys and does well.

Get the Most Talented People to Help You

When the Wicked Witch of the West realizes that Dorothy won't give her the ruby slippers, she threatens to kill her. Frightened, Dorothy decides to leave Oz as soon as possible. Glinda tells her that the person most likely to know how she can get back to Kansas is the "wonderful Wizard of Oz." Dorothy immediately determines to ask him for help.[25]

Dorothy travels to the Emerald City to ask the Wizard of Oz for help once she learns that he is the most knowledgeable person in Oz. Superstars understand how important it is to seek the help of the most talented people that they can find. Jack Welch considered his ability to find talent critical to his success at General Electric.

> From my first days in plastics, I understood the importance of getting the right people. It was clear that when I found someone great, it made all the difference in the world.[26]

Bill Gates' success is, in part, due to his ability to recognize excellence in others and go after it. The DOS software that

123

put Microsoft at the forefront of the burgeoning computer industry in the seventies was written by a graduate student at Harvard. Bill Gates saw its potential. He purchased it, refined it, and then built a huge company around it by attracting talented software developers to work with him.

In sports, many world-class athletes owe their success to the talented coaches and trainers who work with them. These athletes know that their raw athletic ability is not enough. Without talented coaches and trainers to shape and develop it, they will remain like an unused lump of clay on a shelf in an artisan's workshop. In 2005, when Justine Henin-Hardenne won the French Open tennis tournament for the second time, she dedicated it to Carlos Rodriguez, her coach of nine years.[27]

In team sports it is even more critical to be surrounded by talented people. Corey Dillon, a professional running back, spent seven years playing football for the Cincinnati Bengals football team. He broke most of the Bengals' rushing records but despite how hard he worked, the team didn't win. Discouraged, he asked to be traded to a winning team. In 2004, he joined the New England Patriots. There, he was surrounded by a cadre of highly talented players. With their support, he not only had the opportunity to become a winner, but also to cap his career with a Super Bowl ring.[28]

Superstars not only seek talent in others but they also aren't intimidated by people who are smarter and more capable than they are. They want the best and brightest on their team. Michael Eisner, Disney's former Chairman of the Board and CEO has commented,

> I love surrounding myself with people who are better than I am. That's the key. It makes you look good. It doesn't make you look weak to have strong people around you.[29]

Ben Richardson, Vice Chairman and Chief of Operations at Gant Electronics, agrees.

> You can't be afraid to have smart people around you. You need them. You have to have the self-confidence not to feel threatened by it. . . .

> The decision I made early on [was] to go for the really smart people and get them on my side. . . .[30]

Oprah also likes to have smart people around her. She sees it as an opportunity to grow. She states, "I feel best in surroundings where other people are smarter than I am because I feel like I can always learn something from it."[31]

Because superstars value talent, they are always on the lookout for it. Richard Branson has a good eye for talent. When he meets someone new, he is quick to notice his special talents. In 1971 when Virgin was struggling to make its record business profitable, Richard's cousin Simon, whom Richard had never met, stopped by his offices. Simon was obsessed with music and at lunch Richard discovered that he "knew more about music than anyone he had ever met."[32]

He knew all the current popular bands and who had influenced their music. He could even predict which new bands would eventually make it. Richard immediately saw Simon's value and convinced him to become a buyer for Virgin's record shops. Simon proved invaluable in this capacity. With his ability to spot fledgling bands that would soon become popular, Virgin became a store where you could go and find the records of bands that were about to become famous.[33]

Roy Vagelos, CEO of Merck, understood that talent was vital for the company's success. On Saturday mornings, he would walk around the laboratories and stop to chat with researchers who were working on the weekend. This was how he discovered Dr. Arthur Pachett, who had been banished to a peripheral peptide project after failing as a project manager. In speaking with Dr. Pachett and observing his work, Roy realized that he was a brilliant chemist whose talents were being wasted. He moved him to one of Merck's key research projects where he helped develop a new treatment for high blood pressure.[34]

Listen to Those Who Know More Than You

Dorothy listens attentively as Glinda tells her that the Wizard of Oz might help her. She then asks for directions. When Glinda tells her to follow the Yellow Brick Road, Dorothy starts down the road.

Dorothy is aware that she is a stranger to Oz and knows nothing about how things operate there. She listens carefully to Glinda's advice because Glinda, as a native of Oz, knows much more about Oz than she does. Superstars recognize when others are wiser than themselves and actively listen to what they have to say. It's easy to think that we know it all and to lose our openness to the world. This is particularly true when we are young. At eighteen, I thought that I knew it all. When my parents attempted to give me advice, I dismissed it. Older people who didn't embrace my youthful optimism were "sticks-in-the-mud." Jeffrey Bezos, who founded Amazon, recalls how self-assured he felt when he graduated from Princeton.

> One of the things that it's very hard to believe when you're 22 or 23 years old is that you don't already know everything. It turns out-people learn more and more as they get older. . . . [As you get older you] realize that you know less and less as every year goes by. I can only imagine that by the time I'm 70 I will realize that I know nothing.[35]

To be a superstar, it is essential to acknowledge that other people have valuable information that can help us reach our destinations more easily and quickly. Sam Walton continually sought out others who had expert information on retailing that he could use to make Wal-Mart better. He was never afraid to acknowledge that he didn't know it all. Moreover, he often used his lack of sophistication and knowledge as a way to gain entrée to people who could provide him with expert information. He would walk into the headquarters of discounters and introduce himself saying that he had a few stores in Arkansas and ask to see the head of the company. Once he gained access to the head of the company he would ask him endless questions about every aspect of his business.[36]

One of the people Sam approached for expert information in 1967 was Kurt Barnard, Executive Vice President of the National Mass Retailers' Institute, in New York. Kurt describes how Sam Walton arrived at his office one day and asked if he could speak with to him for a few minutes. He recalls:

> . . . he proceeds to extract every piece of information in your possession. He always makes little notes. And he pushes on and on. After two and a half hours, he left, and I was totally drained. [37]

It is also just as important to listen to the people below us in organizational and social hierarchies as those above us. They often have valuable information that we miss by only speaking to people at the top. Regardless of a person's job or status, they are an expert on their special corner of the world. After Jack Welch became CEO of GE, he discovered that GE was a lumbering bureaucracy with enormous layers of upper management. It was only while chatting with some employees in the boiler room of a jet engine factory that he realized that this problem of too many management layers also extended to the lowest levels of the company.[38]

When Kevin Simpson, currently COO of ThermoGenesis, was trying to decide what job offer to accept after he graduated from Harvard Business School, he talked to everyone at the companies that he visited.

> I talked to a variety of people in each of the organizations. Not only did I speak to the people at the top, but I also talked to the people working in the cafeterias or people sweeping the floors. It is important to find out how they feel about the company and they are more likely to tell you what they think than a VP or someone. [39]

Richard Branson always listens to customers when he visits one of Virgin's businesses. He walks around and talks to people and asks for their feedback. If someone has a good idea, he implements it. He also asks staff for suggestions and even

127

experiments with doing their jobs. He once tried delivering meals on a Virgin Air flight using one of their trolleys. Seeing how difficult it was, he then worked with the staff to find a better way. [40, 41]

To take full advantage of the useful information that other people have, we must actively listen to them. Research shows that most of us are bad listeners. We only hear about one-fourth of what is said to us.[42] When people stop and ask me for directions, I am always struck by how many appear to listen attentively but then walk off in the wrong direction. Other people don't even pretend to listen. In my family, it was a standing joke that Auntie Helen, who moved through the world like lightning, would ask you a question and be gone before you opened your mouth to answer.

Given that we are such poor listeners, we must train ourselves to focus on what people are telling us or, like Sam Walton and Richard Branson, take notes. In addition, we must guard against putting our own interpretation on what is said. Studies show that we tend to filter what we hear through our preexisting beliefs, ideas and assumptions.[43] To overcome this, we must wipe our minds clear and approach the world with the wonder of a small child who is encountering the information for the first time. When we are able to do this, we begin to see dimensions of the world that we didn't know existed. The end result is that we make better decisions.

Stan Shih, CEO of Acer, has mastered this art of always listening to the world anew. When he is invited to speak at conferences, he carefully listens to the other speakers and comments on what they have said. He believes that even if a speaker doesn't seem to have anything new or interesting to say, we can still learn something from him. In some cases, it may just be a realization that what he is saying is incorrect or not of value. Shih notes, "Even though the opinions of others are so meaningless, at least we can learn to avoid making the same mistakes in the future."[44] In other cases, this open receptivity can keep us from missing important information that can help us avoid disastrous outcomes. All of us have witnessed or been involved in situations that could have been avoided by people listening to each other. Often at such times, one of the parties involved will say to the others, "Why didn't you tell me?" Someone will pipe up, "I did. You just didn't hear me."

Find Mentors

Soon after Dorothy lands in Oz, Glinda arrives floating through the air in a beautiful bubble. Throughout Dorothy's journey through Oz, Glinda magically appears to help her when she is in trouble. Glinda transfers the ruby slippers to Dorothy's feet, tells her about the Wizard, rescues her from the poppy field, and when the Wizard's balloon floats away without Dorothy and Toto, she tells Dorothy how to return home.

Glinda is the type of mentor that we would all like to have. Whenever Dorothy flounders, Glinda steps in and helps her solve the problem. Superstars seek mentors, like Glinda, to help them navigate the novel and rocky terrain that they encounter on the road to becoming a superstar. Mentors provide us ongoing personal guidance. Jack Welch attributes his ability to complete his undergraduate degree in chemical engineering at the University of Massachusetts and his doctorate at the University of Illinois to the mentors that he had at each institution. Dr. Ben Carson's first mentor was his fifth grade science teacher. Throughout the early years of his career, he continued to have other valuable mentors who helped show him how to build his personal success syndrome. Now, he mentors others.

Mentors, however, do not magically arrive on our doorstep. We have to be on the look out for them and once we find them, we must be ready to learn from them. One reason Jack Welch had mentors was that he was aware of how important they are. He accepted the job at GE in plastics after completing his doctorate because he felt that Dr. Dan Fox, who was in charge of new chemical concepts, would be a good mentor.

Like my earlier professors, Fox struck me as someone who was smart and whom I could trust. In Fox, I saw a coach and role model who brought out the best in everyone who worked with him.[45]

Finding a mentor is particularly important if we are female or members of minority groups. Mentors can increase our credibility and show us the ropes. Soon after Charles Ogletree, the well-known Harvard law professor, arrived at Stanford as an undergraduate, he sought out Dr. Sinclair Drake, a professor in the African-American Studies Department who was known to mentor African-American students. Charles, whose parents had never completed high school, knew that he would need help to navigate this strange new world.[46]

When Madeleine Albright, President Clinton's Secretary of State, resumed her professional life after having three children, she also realized that she needed mentors and began actively seeking them. She stayed in touch with Zbigniew Brzezinski, a professor of hers at Columbia University, and developed a friendship with him. When he came to Washington to be President Carter's national security advisor, she helped him find a place to live. After she went to work for him at the White House, he not only taught her how foreign policy is made, but he also instructed her in the subtle expectations that are part of any job. Following her first meeting in the Cabinet Room in the White House with President Carter and other members of his inner circle, Brzezinski asked Madeleine to look up in her notes the precise words that the President had used in his comment about selling jets to moderate Arab countries. Dismayed, Madeleine looked at the sketchy notes that she had taken and told him that she had not written down the President's comment. Afraid that she might be fired, she decided to take the offensive. As a modern professional woman she wanted to make sure that he didn't think of her as a secretary. She went to his office when he was free. She began:

"I was not aware I had been hired as a secretary."

Without raising his voice, Brzezinski said he didn't know what I was talking about. "Did you look around at who was in the Cabinet Room?"

"Of course."

"Were you not the most junior person there?"

"Without a doubt."

"Well, there's your answer. You're not a secretary, just the most junior person in a high level meeting, and that's your job."[47]

Mentors can also transform us from outsiders to insiders. J. Paul Getty, the oil tycoon, went to work in the oil fields of his father's highly successful company when he was only fifteen. As the son of the owner, he was a definite outsider. He only became an insider by being mentored by Grizzle, the tool dresser or "toolie." Toolies were critical to the success of drilling operations. As highly specialized blacksmiths, they sharpened and shaped the drilling bits to make sure that they didn't break.

> I decided I wanted to learn the tool-dresser's craft-more an art, if the truth is to be told. I did-thanks to the patience and efforts of a leathery, veteran toolie who agreed to take me under his wing and be my mentor. I regret that I am unable to remember his Christian name, but I can never forget his surname, Grizzle. While accurately suggesting his physical appearance, its connotations were at sharp odds with his helpful and outgoing nature and personality. Grizzle taught me all he knew, not only about dressing and maintaining the drilling tools, but about virtually every phase of field operations-and his knowledge of these was encyclopedic. Such was his reputation in the fields that when he pronounced that he considered me a qualified toolie, it carried more weight than any dozen university diplomas.[48]

The mentoring that Getty received from Grizzle later helped him make his own oil business a success. Top drillers wanted to work for him because they considered him an "Honest to Gawd" oilman. In the early years, he worked alongside the men in the oil fields. Their respect for him and his ability to be involved in the drilling process resulted in men working harder and doing a better job for him than they did for others. He recalls that as long as "I abided by oilfield codes of fairness and (sometimes elemental) justice, employee morale and efficiency soared."[49]

When we find a potential mentor like Grizzle, we must also communicate our respect for him and our willingness to learn from him. No one wants to mentor a person who thinks that he knows it all or is not willing to listen and work hard. After Roy Vagelos completed his medical residency, he went to the National Institutes of Health to work in Earl Stadtman's laboratory. Earl Stadtman, a world-famous biochemist, was skeptical of Roy's commitment and ability to become a serious biochemist. Roy had taken only one basic course in biochemistry during medical school. However, Roy's willingness to learn and work hard to master biochemistry soon convinced Earl that he was worth mentoring. Under Earl's guidance, Roy became a leading researcher in the area of fatty acid synthesis. This expertise was the springboard that ultimately helped him become CEO of Merck.[50]

We also need emotional mentors. The journey to becoming a superstar can be long and hard. It is difficult to travel the road alone. Men, like Roy Vagelos and Jack Welch, recognize the important role that their wives' emotional support played in their success. Roy Vagelos viewed his wife Diana as his partner. When he was building his career at the National Institutes of Health, she helped him maintain the frantic pace that he needed to be successful.

> It would have been impossible to maintain this pace without Diana's enthusiastic support. She somehow kept all of us going because she fully understood the importance of my work to me as well as the critical nature of the competition. We functioned as a team then and throughout our lives.[51]

132

STEP FIVE: KNOW HOW TO GET AND GIVE HELP

Similarly Jack Welch looked to his first wife, Carolyn, to bolster his spirits when the pressures at GE became too intense. After becoming CEO, Jack faced intense criticism for the large cuts that he made in the workforce. The press called him "Neutron Jack." Despite being portrayed as heartless, Jack was deeply troubled by having to lay off people, but he saw no other way to maintain GE's position in an increasingly competitive business climate. At such times his wife, Carolyn, was there to emotionally support him and reassure him that he was making the best decision for everyone involved.[52]

While most of us would like wives like these to emotionally mentor us, they are a dying breed and if we are women, we often don't qualify for a wife. We can still, however, have people in our lives who provide us with this type of support. My extended family has always been a rock in my life. No matter how badly the world has treated me, they are always on my side. When I call my mother-in-law and relate how I've failed to get a client that I wanted, she always booms out in her deep powerful voice, "Well it's their loss. They don't know what they are missing."

Another option is to form support groups with our colleagues and peers. The support group formed by Ben Richardson at Gant Electronics provided emotional as well as professional mentoring to its members. In this capacity, it was critical in helping members of the group overcome the periodic struggles and challenges that they encountered in their careers.[53]

The Giving Help Principle

As Dorothy zips down the Yellow Brick Road on her way to the Emerald City, she stops and cuts the Scarecrow down from his pole, oils the Tin Man, and listens to the Lion's fears. She tells each of them about the Wizard and encourages them to ask him for help.

The Scarecrow, the Tin Man, and the Lion eagerly help Dorothy because she has helped each of them to move forward with their lives. Moreover, she genuinely cares about their problems which is why she suggests to each of them that the Wizard of Oz might help them achieve their dreams. By helping them, Dorothy ends up helping herself. The Scarecrow, the Tin Man, and the Lion join forces with her and become her staunch allies.

Giving help to others helps us become superstars. Vanessa Wu, a former student of mine from Taiwan, has taught me this lesson. During the past year we have each been engaged in starting new businesses. Vanessa is always ready to help and encourage me and I, in turn, do the same for her. As we seek clients and financing, we keep our eyes open for opportunities for each other. Vanessa's attitude is that my success is her success and I have learned to think of her success as my own. By helping each other, we have made far greater progress than we would have achieved alone.

Giving help is at the heart of great successes. It is part of the universal principle of exchange that is present in all cultures. If we provide people with products and services that they deeply need or desire, they will gladly compensate us. Sam Walton's success in building Wal-Mart into a mega-company lay in the fact that he helped people save money. He accomplished this by finding cheaper ways to buy the merchandise that he sold and then passed these savings on to his customers. As a result, people flocked to Wal-Mart because they could buy more for less and improve their standard of living.

Bill Gates, founder of Microsoft, has helped people by designing software that makes computers easy to use. When computers were initially developed, they were so complicated that only highly trained technicians could understand and use them. Now even small children can use computers. Dr. Ben Carson helps people who would otherwise die or be severely disabled to live relatively normal lives. With his gifted hands he performs delicate brain surgeries that others can't do. People come to him as a last resort when no one else can help them. Oprah's popularity is due to the fact that she helps people deal with crushing problems in their personal lives. The guests that she has on her show provide information that viewers can use to constructively tackle their own problems and lead psychologically healthier lives. Each of these superstars' careers is based on giving help to others by providing them with something that they can't obtain elsewhere. While we may be able to build short-term successes without using the principle of exchange, becoming a superstar and achieving lasting success depends on finding ways to help others. Moreover, it is personally satisfying to know that through our actions we are making other people's lives better.

The principle of exchange also applies when we work for someone else. Becoming a superstar at our job, depends on helping our boss. In 1980, John Garbarro and John Kotter published a landmark paper titled "Managing Your Boss" which is still required reading for Harvard Business School students. It points out that our boss needs help just like anyone else. He is just as dependent on us for his success as we are on him. As Garbarro and Kotter explain, we must view our relationship with our boss as one of *"mutual dependence* between two *fallible* human beings."[54]

To be superstar at our job, we must actively manage our relationship with our boss and determine how we can best help him. The first step in building a positive relationship with our boss is to understand what he needs to do his job well and the pressures that he faces.[55] This is difficult to do if we look at our boss as a demanding authority figure who will punish us if we don't do what he wants. One afternoon I tried to explain this idea to the UPS man. He complained that he was having trouble with his boss who felt that he was taking too long to deliver the packages on his route. I explained that his boss was probably under pressure from his manager to keep the hours spent on deliveries to a minimum. Despite my efforts, the UPS man was unable to let go of his view of his boss as an authority figure. From his perspective, his boss was trying to hurt him by cutting his hours. When, like the UPS man, we fail to see our boss's pressures, we sabotage ourselves and miss valuable opportunities to succeed because we become a victim of our boss rather than becoming his ally. If the UPS man had focused on making his boss look good by delivering packages more rapidly, he would have advanced his career at UPS rather than put himself in a position to be laid-off.

Once we recognize that we have a symbiotic relationship with our boss, we need to collect data on how to most effectively help him. We must closely observe how he works. When does he need help? What types of requests does he make? What are his strengths and weaknesses?[56] Zbigniew Brzezinski's request that Madeleine Albright provide him with the precise words that President Carter used during their meeting on selling jets to Arab countries provided her with a valuable clue about the type of help that he needed. His request showed that he paid close attention to what people said during meetings and wanted to have an exact written record to which he could later refer. This meant that Madeleine could help him by writing down each word that was said in meetings.

Brzezinski's request also indicated that he liked written information. This is not true of all bosses. Some prefer that we communicate with them using brief email messages. Others want detailed written memos that they can review. Still others like oral reports either by phone or in person.[57] In contrast to Brzezinski, Richard Branson prefers information to be delivered by phone or in person and is not as interested in minor details. Since he has dyslexia, it makes sense that he would prefer auditory to written information. Jack Welch likes to talk directly to people. He also wants to know every relevant detail. At GE he would fly to plants and interrogate his managers for hours in order to get all the facts.

It is also important to find out what our boss's expectations are with regard to work products and performance. We often think that it is up to our boss to tell us exactly what he wants, but Garbarro and Kotter have found that many bosses fail to communicate their expectations. In some cases, they themselves don't know what is possible or what they want. In other cases, they are too busy to focus on what needs to be done, or they assume that we know what they have in mind. Superstar employees make sure that they know exactly what their boss needs and wants. They initiate a dialogue with him, talk to others who have worked for him, or institute formal planning systems that help get their boss to clearly define the outcome that he wants.[58]

In addition to knowing what our boss expects, we also need to be aware of the degree to which he wants to be involved in day-to-day decisions. Some bosses prefer to be consulted about every decision no matter how minor, whereas others only want to be involved in major decisions or when problems arise.[59] Richard Branson likes to turn over the running of entire divisions of his company to others. He doesn't intervene unless there is a serious problem. Sam Walton, on the other hand, was always extremely involved in everything his managers were doing. Each Saturday morning, he would meet with them to review every aspect of the business.[60]

While the idea of managing our boss appears simple, it is not easy at times to let go of our preferred ways of doing things. We all have a tendency to try to impose our way of doing things on our boss. For example, students in my classes like to communicate with me by email. I ask them to call me because I can answer their questions quicker in a telephone conversation than by exchanging multiple emails with them. Despite explicitly telling them this, my request often falls on deaf ears because students are wedded to using email. They are unable to abandon their way of contacting professors.

To become a superstar, we need to be able to see and hear what our boss wants and put aside our ways of doing things. When we are able to step out of our own preconceived ideas and begin to see the world through our boss's eyes, we will be more highly valued by our boss. Every boss wants an employee who anticipates what they need and delivers it without their having to describe in detail what they want. If we are good at doing this, others will also notice how valuable we are. President George W. Bush's former personal aide, Blake Gottesman, was renowned for his ability to anticipate President Bush's needs. Joe Hagin, the White House Deputy of Staff, commented that Blake was like Radar O'Reilly, the clerk in the television series *M*A*S*H* who always knew ahead of time what the colonel was going to say. Blake acquired such a reputation for understanding and managing his boss that when people wanted to see President Bush, they first asked Blake if it was a good time to speak with him about a particular issue.[61]

Acknowledge Others

After the Wicked Witch appears and warns the Scarecrow and the Tin Man to stay away from Dorothy, the Scarecrow declares that he isn't afraid of the Witch and will see that Dorothy safely reaches the Wizard. The Tin Man seconds this. Dorothy responds, "Oh, you're the best friends anybody ever had."[62]

Like Dorothy, superstars readily acknowledge the contributions that others make to their success. After Margaret Thatcher was elected to the House of Commons, she handwrote thank-you notes to the 700 party members who worked on her campaign.[63] When Carly Fiorina was at Lucent Technologies, she gave employees on her team balloons and flowers when they landed a big contract.[64] In 1972 people were surprised to see J. Paul Getty, one of the world's richest men, appear in a television commercial for the brokerage firm, E. F. Hutton & Company. When asked why he did it, Getty explained that E. F. Hutton had helped him gain control of Tidewater Associated Oil Company. During Getty's two-decade fight to buy a controlling interest in the company, E. F. Hutton had at times provided him with loans to buy shares in Tidewater even though he lacked sufficient collateral to cover the loans. Getty's appearance in the E. F. Hutton commercial was his small way of acknowledging its help.[65]

Another way superstars acknowledge others is by recognizing their importance. John Wooden is one of college basketball's greatest coaches. At UCLA his teams won the national collegiate championship ten times. Coach Wooden always loved and cherished each of his players including those who weren't considered superstars. His recognition of each player's importance to his teams was a keystone of his coaching style from the start of his career. In his first year of college coaching at Indiana State, he refused an invitation to take his team to the National NAIA Tournament because they didn't allow African-Americans to play. Coach Wooden had one African-American player on his team and even though he wasn't a starter and didn't play often, Coach Wooden's attitude was that every member of his team counted. If this player couldn't play, then the team wouldn't play. As a result of Coach Wooden's considering each of his players to be equally important, everyone on his team always gave him their best. Even when his teams were not as big and strong or as naturally talented as their opponents, they still found a way to win for him.[66]

TAKE A MOMENT TO REFLECT

Do you regularly ask others for help and advice when you face a problem?

On the page below, write down your thoughts about asking others for help and advice.

STEP SIX

Know How to Use
the Power of Your Emotions

The Lion in *The Wizard of Oz* is a continuous tangle of emotions. Dorothy, the Tin Man, and the Scarecrow constantly have to encourage and push him to take action. After the group reaches the Emerald City and is finally admitted to see the Wizard of Oz, the Lion is so terrified that he decides that he really doesn't want to see the Wizard. Dorothy says, "Don't you know the Wizard's going to give you some courage?" The Lion replies, "I'd be too scared to ask him."[1] Whether we acknowledge it or not, we, like the Lion, also brim with emotions but most of us probably don't wear them on our sleeve. Emotions are powerful tools. We can use them to help us perform at our highest levels and become superstars or, as in the case of the Lion, let them interfere with our ability to succeed.

Learning how to manage our emotions and use their power is essential to our becoming superstars because our lives are filled with a kaleidoscope of events and interactions with others that trigger our emotions. Some of these incidents cause us to feel upbeat and positive while others unleash a torrent of negative emotions. When we become overwhelmed with negative emotions, it is difficult for us to act in our best interests and perform well. We can become paralyzed by anxiety or even strike out in anger.

People who become superstars don't let life's vicissitudes throw them off their stride. They manage their negative emotions and transform them into positive constructive forces that move them forward towards their goals. Richard Branson is a master at this. He never panics or loses his temper when things fall apart. Instead, he channels his emotional energy into finding solutions. Dr. Ben Carson, by his very profession as a pediatric neurosurgeon, lives in an uncertain world, where at any moment during an operation complications can arise that trigger fear and worry. His ability to manage his emotions and remain calm ensures that those fears and worries don't interfere with his flawless execution of the fine motor movements that are essential to being a superstar surgeon.

Manage Your In-the-Moment Anxiety

After the Wicked Witch of the West captures Dorothy, she locks her in a room at the top of the castle. Before the Witch leaves the room, she picks up a large hourglass, turns it over and says to Dorothy, "Do you see that? That's how much longer you've got to be alive! And it isn't long my pretty! It isn't long!" As Dorothy sits alone in the room, her anxiety builds as she watches the sand slowly drain out of the hourglass. Bursting into tears she calls for Auntie Em.[2]

Like Dorothy, we all experience times when our anxieties reach a fever pitch and we feel trapped in a situation that we perceive can only end badly. At the root of such anxiety is fear that we will suffer some type of harm or be unable to do what is needed or expected of us. Superstars find ways to conquer their anxieties and underlying fears. In some cases, they even use their anxieties and fears to drive their performances to higher levels.

Knowing how to manage our in-the-moment anxiety is essential because anxiety kills performance. Moderate amounts of anxiety can help us perform better, but once our anxiety levels go beyond a certain point they paralyze us. Psychologists have found that anxiety can make us so tense that our cognitive abilities deteriorate, our social skills diminish, and our muscles freeze.[3] When Larry King finally had an opportunity to fulfill his dream of being on the radio at a small station in Miami, he became so anxious that he couldn't speak.

> I go in, I sit down, cue my record up—Les Elgart, "Swinging Down the Lane"—and my hands are shaking. . . . And I'm really scared. Now I start the theme music and [try to speak] but nothing comes out. Nothing. I turn off the microphone, I turn up the record, and in that one minute all you're hearing at home is that record being faded, I'm realizing that I don't have the guts. In other words, I have everything else I wanted, but I don't have the chutzpah to say, "I'm a broadcaster." This is a pipe dream, and I really in that minute saw everything go away.[4]

Dr. Ben Carson was similarly overcome with anxiety when he was a senior resident at Baltimore City Hospital and paramedics brought in a man who had been severely beaten on the head with a baseball bat. The hospital faculty were away at a meeting and he couldn't reach the senior faculty person at Johns Hopkins who was providing telephone coverage. As Dr. Carson watched the man rapidly deteriorate, Dr. Carson's anxiety grew more intense. He continued to frantically call the senior faculty person but still couldn't reach him. He became more anxious by the minute as he realized that the only way to save the man was to perform a lobectomy but if he did, he would be violating the law, which didn't permit residents to operate without an attending surgeon present. He thought:

> What happens if I get in there and run into bleeding I can't control? I thought. Or if I come up against another problem I don't know how to handle? If anything goes wrong, I'll have other people second guessing my actions and asking, "Why did you do it?"[5]

In both these situations Larry King and Dr. Ben Carson were flooded with anxiety because they were afraid that they couldn't do the task that lay in front of them. Larry King overcame his anxiety by acknowledging his fears and forging ahead determined to do the best that he could. He started by announcing on the air that he was afraid.

> I did something then, almost 40 years ago, only 22 years old, that I still do now. I decided I had nothing to lose, so I was just myself.
>
> I turned on the microphone, turned down the record and I said, "Good morning, this my first day ever on the radio. All my life I wanted to be in radio. I prayed for this moment. I was just given a new name. My name is Larry King. It's the first time I've ever said my name and I am scared to death. But the general manager just opened the door and said that this is a communication business. So bear with me, I'm going to try to communicate.[6]

As Dr. Ben Carson pondered whether to operate on the man who had been hit with a baseball bat, he realized that he was spending his time worrying about what would happen to him if he botched the lobectomy. Instead, he should concentrate on the man before him who would definitely die if he did nothing. He put his fears aside and began to focus on performing the lobectomy to the best of his abilities.

> Once I made the decision to go ahead, a calmness came over me. I had to do the surgery, and I would do the best that I could.[7]

When we are gripped by the type of anxiety that Larry King and Dr. Ben Carson experienced, it is hard to act. Not acting is attractive because we then don't have to directly confront our inability to handle the situation. In such situations, superstars, like Larry King and Dr. Ben Carson, are not afraid to address and articulate their fears. They accept their fears and acknowledge what they are able to do. This process helps them shift their focus from themselves to the task at hand. They stop worrying about how they will look and put their attention on what needs to be done.

The strategies used by Larry King and Dr. Ben Carson were cognitive. They used the power of their minds to overcome their anxiety. In such situations, we can also use our physical bodies to calm our minds. Top athletes and professional performers frequently employ breathing techniques to reduce their anxiety. These techniques work because there is a close symbiotic relationship between our minds and bodies. When we become anxious, our bodies, as well as our minds, become agitated. Our heart rate increases, our breathing becomes short and rapid, and we tense our muscles. For actors and athletes these physiological components of anxiety literally threaten their ability to perform. Actors can't deliver their lines and singers can't sing if the muscles of their diaphragm, which controls breathing, become too tense. When athletes' muscles tense, their reaction time slows and their coordination is impaired. Breathing techniques both minimize these physiological effects and also calm our minds.

Two simple breathing techniques that can be done anywhere are the "full breath" and "sighing." The full breath involves taking a long slow breath in which you completely fill your lungs. You first fill the lower part of your lungs by forcing out your abdomen, then your middle chest cavity, and finally the upper part of your lungs by slightly raising your chest and shoulders. Once your lungs are full, you hold your breath for a few seconds and then slowly empty your lungs by pulling in your abdomen and lowering your chest and shoulders. You can make this technique even more powerful by filling your lungs to a count of four and emptying them to a count of eight.

Sighing is another valuable technique for releasing tension and anxiety. With sighing, the focus is on emptying your lungs. To receive its full benefits, you slowly expel all the air in your lungs. If you are a vocal person, you can sing or hum as you sigh. When your lungs are empty, it is important to stop and savor the magical moment of silence that ensues before you begin to refill your lungs. This is a quiet time in which you can let all your worries and fears spill out and vanish into the ether. These are two simple easy-to-learn techniques but there are many other ones that you can use. Yogis have known the power of the breath for centuries and books on yoga include a multitude of breathing techniques for releasing tension and anxiety.

Athletes and performers use these breathing techniques before they perform as well as while they are performing. A deep breath can restore and center us when we are in the midst of struggling to do something. Richard Branson describes how at a critical moment when he was trying to learn to swim and was close to drowning, he stopped and took a deep breath. He recalls, "The breath steadied me, and I relaxed."[8] It was after this breath that he was finally able to swim. Most of us, however, don't instinctively breathe when we are in a tight situation. Like elite athletes and performers we need to practice breathing techniques until they become an automatic response when anxiety strikes.

Use Anxiety as a First Alert System

When Dorothy arrives in Oz, she is bewildered and confused as she looks out her front door at the Munchkin village. Holding Toto in her arms she says, "Toto, I've a feeling that we're not in Kansas anymore." She soon discovers that no one in Oz has heard of Kansas. When she asks the way back to Kansas, the Munchkins all shake their heads.[9]

After Dorothy learns that no one in Oz has ever heard of Kansas, she begins to worry that she will never be able to return home. During her travels through Oz, this worry never leaves her. Dorothy's worrying is also a form of anxiety. Its effect is not as intense as the in-the-moment anxiety that Larry King and Dr. Ben Carson experienced, and this type of anxiety doesn't paralyze us. Instead it produces a nagging sense of unease that something is wrong. It can pursue us through our days and keep us awake at night. Its precise source at times is somewhat hazy and the best way to resolve it is not always clear. Superstars welcome this type of anxiety because it alerts them that they have a problem and pushes them to address it.

Jeffrey Bezos, founder of Amazon, sees it as a sign that he is failing to pay attention to something that he shouldn't ignore.

> So if I find that some particular thing is causing me to have stress, that's a warning flag for me. What it means is there's something that I haven't completely identified perhaps in my unconscious mind, that is bothering me, and I haven't yet taken any action on it. I find that as soon as I identify it, and make the first phone call, or send off the first e-mail message, or whatever it is that we're going to do to start to address the situation—even if it's not solved—the mere fact that we are addressing it dramatically reduces any stress that might come from it.[10]

George Soros in his early years managing the Quantum Fund similarly used his anxiety as a first alert system.

> When you are a serious risk taker, you need to be disciplined. The discipline that I used was a profound sense of insecurity, which helped to alert me to problems before they got out of hand.[11]

By acknowledging and listening to our underlying anxieties, we can, like George Soros, identify a problem before it derails us on our journey to becoming a superstar. Jack Welch knows the value of anxiety as a first alert system. When he became CEO of General Electric, he actively worked to generate anxiety in managers of GE businesses that were in trouble and needed to change course. GE's nuclear power division was a classic example of a division whose managers had turned off their anxiety meters. After the Three Mile Island nuclear power accident, the managers of the division continued to believe that they could sell three nuclear power reactors a year. This optimism was unrealistic because people now were afraid of nuclear power and were not placing orders. Moreover, the managers had ignored solid evidence that they had a problem. They had received no new orders for reactors in the last two years and their reactor business was projected to lose twenty-seven million dollars in the current year. By pointing this out, Jack

Welch raised their anxiety levels about whether they could survive by selling nuclear reactors. It pushed them to address the problem and find alternate sources of revenue. The result was that the managers of the division transformed it into a fuel and services business that regularly showed a profit.[12]

Use the Power of Your Anxiety to Do Great Things

Dorothy's anxiety over returning to Kansas drives her to walk to the Emerald City to see the Wizard of Oz.

If Dorothy had not been so anxious about returning to Kansas, she would have remained in Munchkinland as a national heroine, basking in the adulation of the Munchkins and never gone to see the Wizard. Superstars, like Dorothy, use their anxiety to motivate themselves. They view anxiety as a powerful force that drives them to elevate their performance and accomplish more. As former Olympic basketball coach Jack Donahue has aptly commented, "It's not a case of getting rid of the butterflies, it's a question of getting them to fly in formation."[13] Studies of elite athletes show that they feed off their feelings of anxiety. An Olympic swimmer views his anxiety as essential to turning in a top performance.

> You have to get nervous to swim well. . . . If you're not bothered by it, you are not going to swim well. . . . I think the nerves bring out the best in you and I soon realized that I wanted to feel this way.[14]

Larry Ellison, founder of Oracle, similarly views anxiety as a key contributing factor to his becoming a superstar.

> It drives me to work very hard. It drives me to make sure that my life is very orderly, that I'm in control of my company, . . . so that I'm not at risk of failure.[15]

To effectively use our anxiety, however, we must know how to control and manage its intensity. Psychologists have found that each of us has our own optimal level of anxiety where our "butterflies fly in formation" and we perform at our best. When we exceed this optimal level, our performance deteriorates. On the other hand, when our anxiety levels fall below our optimal level, we don't produce our best performances. Instead we become complacent and lose our edge.[16]

Operating at our optimal anxiety levels depends on choosing challenges that are the right level of difficulty for us. If we select a challenge that is too great a reach for us, our anxiety levels skyrocket and cause our performance to plummet. George Soros, the investor, discovered this in the early '80s when the Quantum Fund that he started grew so rapidly that he could no longer conduct the research that he needed to make good investment decisions.

> While the Fund grew from $100 million to $400 million, I felt that the controls were slipping from my hands. I knew less about the situations that I entered than about the ones that I exited. I realized that I could not keep it up much longer because I would need a lot more ideas to feed a $400 million fund than I had needed at the beginning of this wild ride. The pressure became really almost too much to bear.[17]

Conversely, if we choose a challenge that is too easy or ultimately no challenge at all, we lose interest and become bored. We fail to generate the anxiety that we need to deliver a great performance. Instead our performance is lack-luster and mediocre. George Soros warns that this can happen when we become so successful that we no longer have the anxieties and worries that drove us to the top.

> Once you take your success for granted, you let down your guard. When you are in trouble, you just sit back; you know you are successful and you will always get out of trouble somehow. That's when you have lost your ability to get out of trouble.[18]

Identifying the types of challenges that produce our optimal anxiety levels is not easy. It requires that we be a good judge of our abilities and be willing to accurately and honestly assess what we are capable of doing. Psychologists have found that people aren't particularly good at this. They tend to either overestimate or underestimate their capabilities. Moreover, men and women differ in terms of the direction in which they err. Women tend to underestimate their capabilities and men overestimate them.

Madeleine Albright, who became President Clinton's Secretary of State, committed the error of underestimation. She never envisioned attaining such a high-level position. She believed that it was beyond her capabilities. Reflecting on being chosen to be Secretary of State, she has commented:

> When I was named Secretary of State, some people said I had been plotting to get the job all my adult life. That's not so. For most of that time I could not even have imagined it. . . . The women I most admired were exceptional in all senses of the word; I couldn't expect to follow them.[19]

In contrast, when Richard Branson was extremely young and had first started his magazine, *Student*, he committed the male error of overestimating his capabilities by agreeing to speak on individual rights before a large group at University College in London. Speaking before large groups had never been one of his strengths. At public school, the boys were required once a year to memorize a long poem and recite it in front of the entire school. Richard was notoriously bad at this. He typically forgot the poem and was gonged off the stage.[20]

Despite his past failures in this area, Richard didn't hesitate to accept the invitation to speak. On the day of his speech he became increasingly anxious as he stood in the crowd waiting while the other speakers delivered brilliant speeches. When he finally walked up to the podium and took the microphone, he panicked, his mouth became dry and all he could do was utter a few incomprehensible words. As he looked at the crowd, he realized that he had been overly optimistic about his capabilities and that his anxiety levels were out of control. There was no way that he could deliver his speech. He recalls:

I gave a final inarticulate mumble, somewhere between a cough and a vomit, dropped the microphone, leaped off the podium and disappeared into the safety of the crowd.[21]

This experience made Richard come to terms with the fact that public speaking is a type of challenge that quickly pushes his anxiety levels beyond their optimal levels. He now sticks to challenges, like starting new businesses, which generate just the right level of anxiety that he needs to perform at his best.

Like Richard, superstars learn how to accurately assess what they can do and to choose challenges that trigger their optimal anxiety levels for peak performance. Sam Walton was particularly good at doing this. He was always keenly attuned to the amount of anxiety that he could tolerate. Although he loved the challenge of opening new stores and entering new markets, he limited Wal-Mart's growth to a pace that never exceeded his abilities or elevated his anxiety to unmanageable levels. He was aware, however, that incurring large amounts of debt was essential to building the Wal-Mart empire. He has written, "I was never really comfortable with debt. But I recognized it as a necessity of doing business. . . ."[22]

One way he managed his anxieties about incurring this debt was to delegate purchasing decisions to his managers. His managers would then play a little game with him whereby they would hide new equipment they had bought when they knew he was visiting a facility. This way, even though Walton knew what they were doing, he didn't have to directly confront the physical evidence of their spending which might have further triggered his anxieties about incurring too much debt [23]

Another strategy that Sam Walton used to manage his anxiety levels was to increase his knowledge and expertise when he faced a new challenge that exceeded his present capabilities. Often when our anxiety levels skyrocket, it is because we are operating at the outer limits of our competence. Sam Walton was quick to anticipate when he was moving out of his comfort range. When he decided to compete directly with Kmart by putting a Wal-Mart store in the same town as a Kmart store, he knew that he faced a daunting challenge. At this time in the early seventies, Kmart was a much larger and more sophisticated retail operation than Wal-Mart. To prevent this challenge from overwhelming him, Sam spent hours in Kmart's stores speaking to their people and intensively studying every detail of their operations.[24] By increasing his retail knowledge and expertise, Sam kept his anxiety at optimal levels and in the end, it was Wal-Mart that surpassed Kmart.

When we are able to operate at our optimal anxiety levels, it is exhilarating and self-affirming. Richard Branson savors the experience of starting new businesses. At this point in his career he knows how to do it and it is the type of challenge that brings out the best in him. Explaining his decision to challenge Coke by starting Virgin Cola, he commented:

> I love stirring the pot. I love giving big companies a run for their money—especially if they're offering expensive, poor-quality products.[25]

Larry Ellison similarly loves riding the edge between success and failure.

> I certainly feel a little stress, if I just bought a jet fighter and I'm flying it for the very first time and doing aerobatics very low to the ground. I wouldn't call it fear, but it's a little bit of a rush. That gets the adrenaline going, and I thrive on it. I don't really call that fear. That's a somewhat pleasant experience for me. Extreme fear is awful, but out-on-the-edge a little bit, where you have a mild sensation of apprehension and concern, is something I actually enjoy.[26]

By learning how to operate at our optimal anxiety levels we get in touch with the best part of ourselves. When we successfully walk the tightrope between too much or too little anxiety and perform at our peak, it is personally satisfying and builds our self-confidence. Early in his career a colleague challenged Dr. Ben Carson's decision to perform a highly risky hemispherectomy. Despite the colleague's objections, Dr. Carson went ahead with the surgery. The successful completion of this operation affirmed his faith in his abilities and belief in his own judgment.

> It confirmed in me that when people know their capabilities, and they know their material (or job), it doesn't matter who opposes them. Regardless of the reputation of the critics or their popularity, power, or how much they think that they know, their opinions become irrelevant.[27]

Like these superstars, we must accept that we will feel anxious at times but be confident that if we choose the right challenges for ourselves, we can use the power of our anxiety to fuel our journey to becoming a superstar.

Know How to Manage Your Anger

After the Scarecrow suggests that the Apple Tree has "little green worms," the Tree becomes extremely angry and throws its apples at Dorothy.[28]

Anger is a powerful emotion. When, like the apple tree, we become enraged, we are easily manipulated and do foolish things that are not in our best interest and can endanger our ability to become a superstar. At such times, we surrender power to the person who made us angry. We let that person dictate how we behave. Superstars know the dangers of anger and learn how to manage their anger and use its energy in constructive ways.

Dr. Ben Carson discovered at an early age how anger can destroy our dreams and hopes before we even leave the starting gate. As a child, he had a fierce temper. Small insignificant incidents would throw him into a rage. In the ninth grade he almost killed his best friend after he made a derogatory comment about Ben's choice of music. Ben became so angry that he pulled out his camping knife and thrust it into his friend's stomach. Dr. Carson was lucky. The knife hit his friend's belt buckle, broke in two, and dropped to the floor. This incident made Dr. Carson aware that he must learn to control his anger or he would never

153

fulfill his dream of becoming a doctor. At home he locked himself in the bathroom and spent days praying and thinking about how he could control his temper.[29] These efforts paid off. In the years since this incident, he has weathered unfair treatment, racism and personal attacks without responding with anger.

Roy Vagelos also learned the dangers of giving vent to one's anger when he was a young doctor at the National Institutes of Health. He almost destroyed his career by acting in a fit of anger. Roy had asked for a neurologist at the Institute to provide a second opinion on a patient because Roy was puzzled by the admitting physician's diagnosis that the patient had grand mal seizures and a heart condition. Based on his examination of the patient, Roy could find no evidence of either condition.

The neurologist arrived with an entourage of foreign visitors. After looking at the patient's X-rays, he pointed to an area of the X-ray that looked normal to Roy and declared that the patient had a brain lesion. He then read Roy's report and demanded to know who wrote it. Roy replied that he had. The neurologist responded, "You could be guilty of malpractice for missing this diagnosis!"[30] Roy pointed out that he couldn't see the lesion on the X rays that the neurologist claimed was present. The neurologist then turned to the foreign visitors and explained that Roy was new on the case and incompetent.

Furious and humiliated by how he had been treated, Roy wrote an angry note to the neurologist questioning his diagnosis and expressing outrage at the manner in which he had treated him. The neurologist immediately went to the director and demanded that Roy be court-martialed for insubordination.[31] Roy found a way to save his career by showing that his diagnosis was right, but he learned how dangerous anger can be to our careers, particularly when it is directed at someone who has far more power than we do.

Anger not only endangers our ability to become a superstar, but it directly affects our ability to perform at our highest levels because it is distracting. When we become angry, we shift our attention to the source of our anger and stop concentrating on what we are doing. Basketball players know this. They often use what is termed "trash talk" to make players on the opposing team angry. Whenever play stops, they deluge a targeted player with all sorts of denigrating comments that are specifically designed to make him angry. They know that if the player takes these comments seriously and becomes angry, it will cause his performance to drop and give them an edge. John Wooden, one of college basketball's most successful coaches, always taught his players that they must focus on their own game and not what others on the court are doing or saying. His message was:

> If you get too engrossed in things over which you have no control, it
> is going to adversely affect the things over which you have control.[32]

Like top basketball players, we must keep our attention on what we need to do and can control. When we fail to do this and become angry, we lose our ability to perform well.

In addition to learning how to control our anger and walk away from insults and slurs on our character, we also must learn how to deal with the anger of others. When someone becomes furious with us, it is easy to respond with anger. This is because, at such times, we tend to feel unjustly attacked and believe that we must defend ourselves. Superstars know that when someone becomes excessively angry with them, it is not about them. It is because the other person is currently in the grip of their own personal fears and anxieties. We are just a convenient target who has inadvertently strolled onto their shooting range. Michael Eisner, former head of Disney, has spent most of his career managing highly volatile creative people who are quick to anger. He has reflected that we can't take the anger of people whom we manage personally.

> You really have to deal with people who have a lot of things going
> on in their life that don't relate to what you think they're relating to.
> When somebody gets mad in the workplace, or somebody yells at

you, or blames you for something, maybe they're dealing with their own frustrations, their own sense of failure.[33]

As an African-American, Dr. Carson has had to deal with angry attacks based on racism. When he was a young intern, he was verbally attacked by a chief resident who found it difficult to accept having a African-American intern. The man ranted at Dr. Carson:

You really do think you're something because you've had an early acceptance into the neurosurgery department, don't you? Everybody is always talking about how good you are, but I don't think you're worth the salt on the earth. As a matter of fact, I think you're lousy.[34]

Dr. Carson was able to calmly walk away from this incident because he knew that the resident's anger was not due to his performance but was a result of the resident's ignorance and lack of exposure to African-American doctors. If Dr. Carson had expressed his anger in this situation, he would have given power to the chief resident. Other people hearing about the incident would have labeled Dr. Carson as a person who was unable to control his temper under stress, despite the fact that his anger was justified.

When superstars do become angry, they don't wallow in it or strike out at others. They channel it into positive action. Dr. Roy Vagelos' anger over being threatened with a court martial ultimately drove him to find out what was really wrong with his patient.

Even more incensed by this threat [of a court martial], I decided to do everything possible to confirm my conclusions about the patient. First, I needed to observe one of the seizures, which always occurred at night. The patient's room was just across from the nurse's station, and I arranged to leave the door slightly ajar so I could see what happened. I sat up all night at the nurses' desk, peering in through the cracked door. The patient experienced periodic pain, had a "seizure," and asked for morphine. Once the nurses administered the drug, the "seizure" stopped.

This was my tip-off. People having seizures do not request morphine, a potent but addictive analgesic. They usually have no pain.[35]

After calling several city hospitals Dr. Vagelos discovered that the patient was a notorious drug addict who periodically faked seizures at Washington city hospitals in order to get morphine.

Carly Fiorina is also known for using anger constructively. When AT&T was only awarded a small part of an important government contract whose procurement she had spearheaded, she didn't waste time reacting to what she felt was an injustice. She leapt into action. She hired an investigator to determine whether the contract had been awarded fairly. As evidence of favoritism emerged, she began leaking this information to the press. A lawyer on her team at AT&T has commented:

When Carly gets really mad, she doesn't let go a load of expletives. She gets more determined that she's not going to let someone get away with it.[36]

By putting her anger aside and taking action, Carly got the award rescinded. When the new contract was awarded, AT&T received the primary share.[37] When we learn, like Carly, to manage our anger, we can use it to help us become a superstar.

Avoid Toxic People

After the Wicked Witch of the West learns that Dorothy has killed her sister, she becomes enraged. Despite Dorothy's protests that it was an accident, the Wicked Witch tells her, "Accident, eh. Well, my little pretty. I can create accidents too. . . ." Before she leaves, she menacingly says, "I'll get you, my pretty, and your little dog too." After the Witch disappears in a puff of red smoke, Glinda wrinkles her nose and says, "Pooh—what a smell of sulfur."[38]

Certain people are like the Wicked Witch of the West. They leave a bad smell in our lives. After being around them we feel tired and disheartened. Superstars learn to avoid toxic people because it is easy to catch their bad moods and fears. Somerset Maugham, the famous author, describes catching Henry James' fear of riding streetcars. As they stood waiting for a streetcar, James warned Maugham of the dangers of American streetcars.

> [James] urged Maugham to jump on with the greatest agility of which he was capable, and warned him if he were not careful he would be dragged along, and if not killed, at least mangled and dismembered. Maugham informed him that he was quite accustomed to boarding streetcars. Not American streetcars, James said. They were of a savagery and ruthlessness beyond conception. James' anxiety was contagious, and when the car pulled up Maugham jumped on, and felt that he had miraculously escaped serious injury.[39]

Other negative emotions are equally contagious. We can catch people's anger, discouragement, unhappiness or even depression. In a study at Florida State University, psychologists found that students who were assigned to share rooms with mildly depressed students soon became depressed themselves.[40]

Superstars act quickly to remove toxic people from their lives and work environments. Richard Branson has always been closely attuned to the emotions of the people around him and their effect on himself and others. He originally started Virgin Air with Randolph Fields but he soon discovered that Fields was a transmitter of toxic emotions. The first warning sign occurred during a meeting with the Civil Aviation Authority when Fields endangered their chances of getting permission to fly because he became angry at being questioned about Virgin Air's capacity to be a viable airline. A few months later Richard received complaints from workers in the ticketing office that Fields was poisoning the work environment by his behavior and treatment of them. When Fields' verbally abusive behavior led to a key person at the New York office calling Richard to resign, Richard acted immediately and removed Randolph from his airline business.[41]

During the early years of the Quantum Fund, George Soros had a similar experience with his junior partner, Jim Rogers, who was a superb analyst and "did the work of six."[42] Soros and Rogers worked well together but when it became necessary to bring in other analysts, the working environment took a negative turn. Rogers didn't mind being criticized by Soros, but he couldn't tolerate this from analysts whom he had trained. Soros relates, "… he couldn't stand his disciples criticizing him or disagreeing with him, so as soon as they became really productive, he would go out of his way to destroy them, which created a very unpleasant atmosphere."[43] Even though Soros initially had a positive experience working with Rogers, the toxic atmosphere that he now created affected the entire team making it difficult for them to work effectively and keep up with the fund's rapid expansion. Soros determined that he had no choice but to part company with Rogers.

One way that we can protect ourselves from toxic people is by testing our mood after we spend time with people whom we think might be toxic. Do they leave us tired, disheartened, angry, anxious, or depressed? When we find that a person has one of these toxic effects on us, the simplest approach is to avoid them, but life is usually too complicated to just banish a person from our lives. Instead, we must learn to reach into who we are to tune out their bad emotional energy. Wynonna Judd, even as a young singer, insulated herself from the negative emotions of people around her while preparing for performances by totally absorbing herself in her singing. By doing this, she created an inner psychological space where she was protected from the emotional storms of those around her.[44]

Another approach that we can use is to assume the role of a scientist studying a new species. We can carefully observe what situations trigger the person's toxic behavior and seek to minimize them. We can also observe how changing our own behavior affects the other person's behavior. I once had a boss who was given to periodic rages. To disengage myself, I decided to experiment with different ways of interacting with him. I observed which of my behaviors put him in a positive frame of mind and which seemed to elicit anger. I soon discovered that asking questions or proposing new ways to approach projects caused him to become extremely irritated. In contrast, when I was positive about the work we were doing, it put him in such a good mood that he was open to my suggestions about different approaches. Instead of being a victim of his toxic moods, I controlled them.

Surround Yourself with Positive People

After the Lion decides to join Dorothy, the Scarecrow and the Tin Man, they all link arms and skip down the Yellow Brick Road.

In contrast to the Wicked Witch of the West who leaves a bad smell, people like Dorothy are a source of positive emotions and energy. When Dorothy finds the Scarecrow, the Tin Man, and the Lion, each is unhappy and depressed. After being around Dorothy for only a short time, they are dancing and singing down the Yellow Brick Road. Just as we catch people's negative emotions, we also catch their positive emotions. People who emit positive emotions can give us a lift and help us move forward when we encounter roadblocks on our journey to becoming a superstar.

Superstars find positive people to work with them. Lee Iacocca was instrumental in developing the Ford Mustang, one of Ford's biggest moneymakers. He did this by putting together a team of people who energized each other. Iacocca recalls that period of time as one of his best times at Ford.

My years as general manager of the Ford Division were the happiest period of my life. For my colleagues and me, this was a fire-in-the-belly time. We were high from smoking our own brand—a combination of hard work and big dreams.

In those days, I couldn't wait to get to work in the morning. At night I didn't want to leave. We were continually playing with new ideas and trying out models on the test track. We were young and cocky. We saw ourselves as artists, about to produce the finest masterpieces the world had ever seen.[45]

This same type of synergy also existed between Bill Hewlett and Dave Packard, founders of the famous computer-printing giant. They were best friends who fed off each other, even finishing each other's sentences. One of the reasons that they created Hewlett-Packard was because they enjoyed working together.[46] In building Wal-Mart Sam Walton similarly made sure to surround himself with people who created positive emotions within himself and others. His autobiography is filled with glowing descriptions of the people with whom he worked. He considered them essential to his becoming a superstar. Describing Wal-Mart's phenomenal growth during the seventies, he writes,

It was the retail equivalent of a real gusher: . . . We were all working untold hours, and we were tremendously excited about what was going on.[47]

Just as superstars surround themselves with positive people, they also are aware of how important it is to be a source of positive emotional energy for those around them. When we exude positive emotional energy, others want to work with us in pursuing our dreams. Richard Branson has always been a beacon of positive emotional energy. Throughout his business career people have wanted to work for him. When he started his first business, the magazine titled *Student*, he had no money to pay people but people eagerly joined him. They lived off what was in his fridge and they all went out for "cheap curries."[48] This trend has continued throughout his business career. He has always been able to attract top people to come and work for Virgin.

At Wal-Mart Sam Walton purposely worked to create a climate filled with positive emotional energy. His Saturday morning 7:30 a.m. meetings for executives, management, and

161

associates began with a cheer. Walton's attitude was that even though they worked extremely hard, they should still have fun. He called it his "whistle while you work philosophy." He related, "we not only have a heck of a good time with it, we work better because of it."[49]

When one of his stores was struggling with low morale and losing large amounts of money, he had department managers from the store spend a weekend meeting with successful positive managers from other stores. These managers' positive upbeat emotional energy rubbed off on the managers from the failing store. They returned to their store and transformed it into a profitable enterprise.[50]

Part of Bill Clinton's enormous success and popularity is attributable to the positive emotional energy that he exudes. In a recent editorial in The New York Times, Nora Ephron bemoaned how she "fell out of love" with Bill Clinton during his presidency because of his policies. Her feelings changed, however, when she recently watched Bill on television discussing a conference that he held on global warming and poverty. She found it hard to avoid falling in love with him again.

> When Bill described the conference, it was riveting. I could see how much he cared; and of course, I could see how smart he is. It was so refreshing. It was practically moving. To my amazement I could see why I loved the guy in the first place.[51]

When we are able to create this type of positive emotional energy in others, we are like the Pied Piper who stole all of the children of Hamelin because he played a tune that the children could not resist.[52] Others will eagerly join us on our journey to becoming a superstar.

TAKE A MOMENT TO REFLECT

Do you acknowledge your anxieties and then take steps to actively manage them?

On the page below, write down anxieties you often have and how you can manage them better.

Know How to
Manage Your Performance

In *The Wizard of Oz* the Scarecrow, Tin Man, and the Lion accomplish amazing feats in their efforts to rescue Dorothy from the Wicked Witch of the West which, given their bumbling ways, we would not have thought possible. When Dorothy is captured by the Winged Monkeys and imprisoned in the Wicked Witch's castle, they rush to the castle and devise a way to get in by donning guard uniforms and boldly marching into the castle with the guards. Once inside, they dash through the castle's winding passages carefully avoiding the guards while they search for Dorothy. When they finally find her, they chop down the door and rescue her. Each one of them elevates his performance to a higher level. On our journey to becoming a superstar, we too face such pivotal moments in which we must know how to produce our best performances.

Recognize Pivotal Moments

As Dorothy, the Scarecrow, the Tin Man and the Lion apprehensively walk through the Enchanted Forest to the Wicked Witch's castle, Winged Monkeys swoop down from the sky. They grab Dorothy and Toto and fly away with them to the castle. Other Winged Monkeys attack the Scarecrow, pulling out his straw and scattering pieces of him along the ground. The Tin Man, and the Lion rush to his rescue. As they stand looking down at him, he yells, "Don't stand there talking. Put me together! We've got to find Dorothy."[1]

The Scarecrow recognizes that they face a pivotal moment. Dorothy has been captured by the Wicked Witch and they must act quickly to find her. Superstars recognize pivotal moments when their actions have a heightened level of importance. At such times, they spring into action and perform at their highest levels.

Richard Branson knew instantly that he was facing a pivotal moment when on the morning of Mike Oldfield's "Tubular Bells" concert, Mike arrived at his door and told him, "I can't go through with this concert tonight."[2] The tickets for the concert were sold and television coverage was arranged. Moreover, the concert was critical to Virgin's fledgling record business. Mike Oldfield's "Tubular Bells" album had received rave reviews, but a successful concert would generate the publicity needed to send the album to the top of the charts. A best-selling album would establish Virgin as a record label and help them sign other recording stars.

Richard was also aware that it would be extremely difficult to persuade Mike to go on with the concert. The child of an alcoholic mother, Mike was psychologically fragile and shunned public appearances. Confrontation and appeals to his sense of obligation would never work. The only trump card that Richard had was his vintage Bentley. He had recently received it as a wedding present and he knew Mike coveted it. Casually, he suggested that they go for a drive in the car. He first tried a soothing drive to the concert hall. Observing how rigidly Mike continued to sit in his seat, he stopped at the concert hall and suggested to Mike that he drive. As Mike navigated the car through London's streets, Richard asked if he would like the car as a present. Mike protested that the Bentley was Richard's wedding present. Richard responded that the car would be his if he would just go on stage that night and perform. After a long silence, Mike finally said, "It's a deal."[3]

By recognizing how critical it was for Mike to perform and then finding a way to get him to perform, Richard made Virgin a player in the recording business. Mike Oldfield's Tubular Bells album skyrocketed to the top of the charts and Mike became an international star. His popularity also had long-term consequences for Virgin that Richard could never have anticipated. During the next fifteen years, revenues from the sale of Mike's albums helped Virgin survive during times when it desperately needed funds to keep expanding.[4]

Most pivotal moments aren't as dramatic as the one faced by Richard Branson, and we usually do not have to give away a prized possession. We must, however, learn to identify situations that constitute pivotal moments on our journey to becoming a superstar. Situations when our actions are highly visible to others are almost always pivotal moments. Margaret Thatcher was keenly attuned to this fact. From her first days as a Member of Parliament she knew that when she gave a speech before the House, her colleagues and the press would be watching closely. As a consequence, she spent long hours preparing each speech that she made. She meticulously researched every issue and supported her positions with massive arrays of details and statistics that she committed to memory. Her consistently outstanding performances as a speaker were essential to her being selected for ministry positions within the Conservative Party. Her brilliant performance during a debate with one of the opposition's most impressive members was instrumental in helping her win enough votes to be elected head of the Conservative Party and ultimately Prime Minister when the party regained power.[5]

Other types of critical moments are more subtle and we sometimes underestimate their importance. Simple actions, such as spending extra time on a report to be read by a senior manager, promptly returning a phone call, or showing up for a meeting, can affect our rise to superstar status. When Jack Welch was made a group executive at GE, he asked his boss if he could stay in Pittsfield, Massachusetts, rather than move to

167

the corporate headquarters in New York. His boss agreed, but he required Jack to attend monthly meetings at headquarters. Jack never missed a meeting. When snow inundated Pittsfield closing the airport, he would hop into his car and frantically drive to New York.[6] At such times, it would have been easy for Jack to claim that it was impossible for him to attend a meeting due to bad weather, but he never did. He knew that failing to show up for a meeting would damage his chances for promotion. He would not only let his boss down, but he would do so in a highly visible manner. Fellow managers would notice his absence, thus making it difficult for his boss to subsequently justify promoting him.

Starting something new is another type of pivotal moment. Psychologists have found that people give greater weight to their first impressions of a person than to their later ones.[7] Superstars are aware of this and put forth extra effort to impress others when they start something new. During the first week that J. Paul Getty worked as a roustabout in his father's oil fields, he didn't let the blisters that he developed on his hands stop him. He showed the men that despite being a rich man's son who had lived a soft life, he could do the work.[8] When Roy Vagelos began his post-doctoral fellowship at the National Institutes of Health (NIH) under Dr. Earl Stadtman, he worked extremely hard to show him that he had the right stuff. He gave presentations at Dr. Stadtman's biweekly journal club even though he was uncomfortable speaking before groups. To prepare, he used "brute force." This involved reading not only the article that he was presenting but also extensive background material on the topic to make sure that he understood every facet of the article that he was presenting. When Dr. Stadtman asked him if he would teach his microbial biochemistry course at NIH, he took on the challenge even though it added extra hours to his long days.[9]

Part of recognizing pivotal moments also involves being able to anticipate them and knowing when to avoid them. If we are unable to perform at the level needed to succeed during a pivotal moment, then it is better not to put ourselves on the line. Just as people often make judgments about us based on their first impression of us, people have long memories for our poor performances and situations in which we failed to deliver what we had promised. Determining which pivotal moments to avoid requires a willingness to acknowledge when we are unprepared and also an honest assessment of whether a situation plays to our strengths. While a student at Columbia University's College of Physicians and Surgeons, Roy Vagelos painfully learned this lesson. One of his professors during his third year was Dr. Robert E. Loeb whose book on medicine was considered a bible by faculty and students. A brilliant diagnostician, Dr. Loeb was renowned for terrorizing students during medical rounds. He rapidly fired questions at students as they moved from patient to patient and humiliated them if they didn't instantly produce the correct answer. One day during his fourth year when he was no longer a student of Dr. Loeb's, Roy had some time on his hands and decided to join Dr. Loeb's medical rounds. During the rounds Dr. Loeb stopped at the bed of a patient who had inflammation of the kidneys and asked students the incubation period of the disease. When none of the third-year students could answer, he turned to Roy and said, "Vagelos, tell these third-year students what *every* P&S student should know!"[10] When Roy responded that he too couldn't remember, Dr. Loeb publicly berated him. Roy recalls:

> To illuminate just how disappointed he was, he told the group that he had selected me as one of the two P&S students to receive a choice internship at Boston's Massachusetts General Hospital. I was stunned—stunned to learn about my internship, stunned by the manner in which I was told, and stunned by my foolishness in putting myself on Loeb's firing line so casually. Later that day I walked past Dr. Loeb and his wife and heard him telling her how disappointed he was in me: "This is the person I was telling you about," he said.[11]

169

Roy didn't lose his internship, but he learned how important it is to anticipate pivotal moments and only expose ourselves to them when we are ready to perform at our best.

Know How to Focus

In their search for Dorothy, the Scarecrow, the Tin Man and the Lion follow Toto up the stairs of the castle. Toto stops in front of a heavy wooden door and scratches on it. The Scarecrow calls, "Dorothy, are you in there?" Dorothy replies, "Yes, it's me! She's locked me in." The three rush forward and push on the door but it won't budge.

Inside the room, Dorothy watches the hourglass empty. She pleads, "Oh, hurry! Please hurry!" The Tin Man steps forward with his ax and says to the others, "Stand back." He then quickly and efficiently chops down the door.[12]

To perform at our highest levels, we need to be able, like the Tin Man, to put everything else out of our minds and intensely focus our attention on what we need to accomplish in the moment, because the ability to focus is one of the cornerstones of great performances. Superstars know how to focus. Lee Iacocca considered his ability to focus as a key factor in his becoming a superstar. He commented in his autobiography:

> The ability to concentrate and use your time well is everything if you want to succeed in business—or anywhere else for that matter.
>
> By the time I got to college I knew how to concentrate and study without a radio or other distraction.[13]

Sam Walton was known for his ability to focus. Even as a college student, when he was involved in multiple projects, he was able to concentrate when it counted. His former manager at the Columbia *Missourian* newspaper recalls that he was sometimes scatterbrained but "when he focused on something, that was it."[14]

As a student Jack Welch was also good at focusing. To pass the language requirement for his Ph.D., he studied French and German day and night for three straight months. Looking back, he has commented, "Despite not being the smartest, I did have the focus to get the work done."[15]

People who are good at focusing learn to fully fix their attention on what they are doing and put extraneous thoughts out of their mind. Lance Armstrong, seven-time winner of the Tour de France, has often been asked after the three-week race what he thought about while spending six to seven hours a day on his bike.

> I get that question all the time and it's not a very exciting answer. I thought about cycling. My mind didn't wander. I didn't daydream. I thought about the techniques of the various stages. I told myself over and over that this was the kind of race in which I had to always push if I wanted to stay ahead. I worried about my lead. I kept a close watch on my competitors, in case one of them tried a breakaway. I stayed alert to what was around me, wary of a crash.[16]

Richard Branson's intense ability to focus saved his and Per Lindstrand's lives after they accidentally dropped two of their fuel tanks into the Pacific Ocean during their landmark crossing in a helium balloon. This left them with only three fuel tanks which was too little fuel to make the journey across the Pacific. When they made contact with their flight center, they learned that a fierce storm with 50 foot waves was raging below them making ditching in the ocean impossible. Their only hope was to position the balloon directly in the center of the jet stream and use its power to carry them across the Pacific. Through a long harrowing night, Richard's laser-like focus on the controls kept the balloon in the center of the jet stream, saving them from certain death and making them the first team to successfully cross the Pacific in a helium balloon. Richard relates, "I put all thoughts of death out of my head and for the next ten hours concentrated intently on the dials."[17]

This same ability to focus has helped Richard pull through a number of crises at Virgin. When the Bank of Nova Scotia refused to provide a promised 25 million dollar loan less than twenty-four hours before Virgin Music was to sign an 11 million dollar contract with pop singer Janet Jackson, Richard put everything else in his life aside. He spent the next fifteen hours on the phone exploring every possible option for raising the money. His total absorption in the problem helped Virgin find a way to deliver the money to Janet Jackson's lawyers only moments before the agreement was to expire.[18]

Given how important focus is to optimal performance, top athletes actively work at improving their focus.[19] Coach John Wooden, UCLA's famous basketball coach, drilled his players to focus on the basketball and not what opposing players, officials or the crowd were doing because, as he stressed to his teams, if you don't have the basketball, you can't score. Rod Laver, one of tennis's greats, describes how he improved his ability to focus.

> If your mind is going to wander during practice, it is going to do the same thing in a match. When we were all growing up in Australia, we had to work as hard mentally as we did physically in practice. If you weren't alert, you could get a ball hit off the side of your head. What I used to do was force myself to concentrate more as soon as I'd find myself getting tired because that's usually when your concentration starts to fail you. If I'd find myself getting tired in practice, I'd force myself to work much harder for an extra ten or fifteen minutes, and I always felt as though I got more out of those extra minutes than I did out of the entire practice.[20]

Developing our ability to focus can give us an edge and rapidly move our careers forward. As a fledgling neurosurgeon, Dr. Ben Carson learned how to maintain his focus and combat fatigue during long complicated brain surgeries by watching his mentor at Johns Hopkins who was a master at this. By learning how to focus, Dr. Carson was able to carry a much larger surgical load than other residents at his level. As a result, he quickly gained the experience that is key to becoming a top surgeon and soon surpassed his peers. We too can put ourselves on the fast track to becoming a superstar by developing the ability to fully focus all our attention on what we are doing in the moment.[21]

Seek Feedback

After the Tin Man frees Dorothy from the castle room, the group rushes to the front entrance of the castle. Just as they arrive the huge doors swing shut. Trapped, they look up to see the Wicked Witch descending the stairs. She says,"Going so soon? I wouldn't hear of it. Why my little party's just beginning." As she speaks, the Winkie Guards advance towards the group with their spears drawn. The Scarecrow looks about, seizes the Tin Man's axe, and cuts the rope holding the candelabra. It crashes to the floor onto the Winkies. As the Winkies struggle to disentangle themselves, the group runs out of the hall with the Wicked Witch and Winkies following in hot pursuit. They duck into a recess in the wall and watch as the Wicked Witch and Winkies rush past. They then run back to the front door but realize that there is no way to open it. Hearing the Wicked Witch and Winkies returning, they dart up the stairs and along the battlement towards the second tower. Suddenly a group of Winkies comes up the stairs. Another group approaches from the second tower. They stop trapped on the battlement between the two groups of Winkies.

The Wicked Witch approaches smiling. She chants, "Well, a ring around the rosy, a pocket full of spears! Thought you'd be pretty foxy, didn't you? Well, I'm going to start in on you right here—one after another!" She takes her broomstick and lights it using the torch on the wall. Turning to the Scarecrow, she sets his arm on fire. Dorothy screams. She picks up a bucket of water and throws it toward the Scarecrow. The water instead hits the Wicked Witch in the face and she slowly begins to melt.[22]

This scene keeps us on the edge of our seats because it has constant action and feedback. Each time Dorothy and her companions attempt to escape, they are thwarted by the Wicked Witch and her Winkies. The negative feedback that they receive forces them to try something else. Finally, Dorothy hits on the winning move and ends the Wicked Witch's reign of terror.

Feedback is essential to delivering top performances because it continually lets us know how we are doing. It gives us an opportunity to make adjustments and try a different approach. Great performances don't come from doing something perfectly the first time, but rather from our ability to use the information from our failures to find a better way to do something.

Superstars actively seek feedback. When Jack Welch was chosen as one of five possible successors to Reg Jones, he was transferred to General Electric headquarters. The atmosphere at headquarters was tense as each of the five strove to be General Electric's next CEO. Jack Welch knew that his performance was critical to his being selected. He continually collected feedback on how he was doing. When he had to inform the board that he had changed his mind about making an acquisition that he had previously recommended, he worried that this might put him out of the running. During a golf game with board members later in the afternoon, he paid close attention to how they treated him. When one of them joked with him, he received the feedback he sought. He knew that he had not hurt his chances to be CEO.[23]

Superstars also like feedback because it prevents them from making mistakes and provides them with the information that they need to make adjustments when they do make mistakes. Larry Ellison, founder of Oracle, encourages his employees to tell him if he is going in the wrong direction.

> I love it when people point out I'm wrong and explain to me why I'm wrong. That's great. I don't want to be wrong. I would love to be right. If I'm wrong, I love it when people stop me.[24]

When Bill Clinton ran for governor of Arkansas, Dick Morris was his pollster. While some people in Arkansas found Dick Morris' abrasive style offensive, Clinton liked him because he wasn't afraid to give him feedback that he didn't want to hear.[25] The feedback that Madeleine Albright received from her boss

Zbigniew Brzezinski when he called her on the carpet for not taking notes in a meeting with President Carter helped her raise her performance to acceptable levels in her new job.[26] Larry King got critical feedback from his manager, Marshall Simmonds, as he sat before the microphone unable to speak at the start of his first radio show. Larry relates:

> Marshall kicked open the door to the control room and screamed, "This is a communications business! Communicate!" [27]

This feedback jolted Larry King into action.

When we avoid feedback or fail to listen to it, we can run into trouble. Simple problems can turn into giant ones. Peter Meyers, a superstar mediator and founder of the International Academy of Mediators, believes that it is better to find out that we have a problem than to continue blissfully on the road to disaster. His mantra is, "Frequently wrong but never in doubt."[28] Oprah Winfrey similarly stresses how important it is to our success to pay attention to feedback. She observes:

> The universe is always trying to get our attention. Sometimes it starts out as a whisper. By the time it gets to be a storm, you've had a pebble knock you upside the head; you've had a brick; you've had a brick wall; you've had a house fall down. And before you know it you are in the eye of the storm. But long before you are in the eye of the storm, you've had many warnings, little clues.[29]

Lee Iacocca suffered the consequences of failing to listen to the clues that his job was in jeopardy when he was president of Ford Motor Company. At Ford, he reported to Henry Ford II. Ford was a difficult man to work for and often acted irrationally. He would fire top performers because he didn't like how they dressed or took a sudden dislike to them.[30] Even though Iacocca generally managed to stay away from Ford's more paranoid and vindictive side, he periodically did have serious disagreements with Ford, but he blocked them out of his mind.

In 1975, Ford's behavior became more and more bizarre. Iacocca's secretary told him that records of his phone calls were being sent to Ford's office, and someone was going through the papers on his desk at night. Iacocca discounted these incidents.[31] He optimistically reasoned that things with Ford would have to get better and presumed, despite feedback to the contrary, that Ford would ultimately act rationally. He knew that he was valuable to the company and in his eyes he was more important to the company's success than Henry was.

> In my naïveté, I held out hope that because we were a publicly held company, the best man would win.

> I was also greedy. I enjoyed being president. I liked having the president's perks, the special parking place, the private bathrooms, the white-coated waiters. I was getting soft, seduced by the good life.[32]

At the beginning of 1977, Ford reorganized the top positions in the company, essentially demoting Iacocca to third in command. He reorganized again in June of 1978 and Iacocca's position dropped to fourth in the pecking order. In July of 1978, Ford fired Iacocca.[33] In retrospect, Iacocca realized that he had plenty of warning. He just failed to listen to it.

In addition to providing valuable information that we can use to avoid looming disasters, such as the one Iacocca faced, feedback helps us perform at our highest levels by keeping our minds in the game. Continuous feedback is one of the reasons that we become so absorbed in sports and play computer games over and over again. Games give us instant gratification when we make the right moves. When we make the wrong moves, we get second chances to succeed, just as Dorothy did in her attempts to escape the Wicked Witch. It was this instant gratification that initially drew Larry Ellison to computers.

> I could start writing a program and within several hours I could have a result. Freud defines maturity as the ability to defer gratification. The great thing about programming is you don't have to be mature at all. You don't have to defer gratification for more than a few hours. You get wonderful feedback. It's a lot of fun. The reason why games

and sports are so popular is because you win or lose very quickly. You get immediate feedback. It's a very tight loop, you don't wait hours or days or years before you find out if you are winning or losing. You find out a second and a half after you release the basketball. You know whether it's going in or not.[34]

Instant gratification also energizes us and helps us elevate our performance to new levels. We've all watched a losing team transform itself into a winning one when it suddenly breaks through defeat and scores. The players are empowered by their success and bring a new intensity and focus to their play.

To take advantage of the power of feedback, we need to create personal feedback systems that provide us with ongoing concrete and unbiased information that shows us where we need to make changes. Sam Walton used Wal-Mart's numbers to provide him with feedback. Each week before Wal-Mart's Saturday morning meeting, he would go into the office early in the morning to review the books and see how Wal-Mart was doing. He then used that information in the meeting to propose changes and energize his employees to do better.[35] In a similar manner, after Jack Welch became CEO of General Electric, he created what he called his No. 1 or No. 2 strategy. Jack declared that General Electric businesses that weren't No. 1 or No. 2 in their industry were to be sold or discontinued. This gave managers in each General Electric business hard numbers against which they could measure their performance.[36]

Richard Branson of Virgin is also a big believer in feedback. During visits to his various businesses, he goes out and talks to his customers and asks them how well Virgin is serving them.[37] When we develop similar feedback systems for ourselves, we too can elevate our performances and increase our ability to succeed.

Expect to Win

Dorothy, Toto, the Scarecrow, the Tin Man, and the Lion triumphantly return to the Emerald City with the Wicked Witch of the West's broomstick and present it to the Wizard. The Wizard then confers on the Scarecrow a doctorate in thinkology and presents him with a diploma. He next awards the Lion the Triple Cross for "extraordinary valor [and]conspicuous bravery against wicked witches. . . ." [38] Turning to the Tin Man, he takes a heart shaped watch out of his black bag and presents it to him.

The Scarecrow, the Tin Man and the no-longer cowardly Lion are transformed by the Wizard's presentation of these simple symbols. The Scarecrow now believes that he is smart, the Lion believes that he has courage, and the Tin Man believes that he has become a complete human being with all the accompanying emotions. Their responses illustrate how deeply our beliefs about ourselves and our ability to succeed affect us.

Our beliefs directly impact our ability to perform at our highest levels. When we are unsure about whether we can accomplish something, our attention shifts away from what we need to do and our performance falters. In contrast, if we believe that we can win, we put our full attention on our performance. In 1975, UCLA basketball star Richard Washington made the winning shot in the waning seconds of UCLA's win over Louisville in the NCAA semifinal because he believed that he could make it. When John Wooden, UCLA's coach, was asked how Richard made the shot, he explained:

> [Richard] didn't expect to miss because he's a good shooter. He expected to make that shot. Now, if I had let somebody else shoot that shot, they'd feel they have to make it. If you feel you have to do it, that, I think, hurts your chances of doing it. [39]

Because Richard expected to make the shot, his full attention was on perfectly stroking the basketball. He didn't worry about whether the shot would go in or how the coach and fans would react if he missed. He was fully absorbed in his performance because he expected to win.

Superstars deliver great performances because they have this same belief, that they can make the important shots. When Sam Walton was in high school, he was quarterback of the football team. Even though he was small and slow and didn't throw the ball well, he always found a way to help his team win. During his years as quarterback, his team was undefeated and won the state championship. In looking back he remembers that when they played for the state championship, he expected to win and that this experience has led him to expect to always win at whatever he is doing. In talking about the football game he notes:

> It never occurred to me that I might lose; to me, it was almost as if I had a right to win. Thinking like that often seems to turn into a self-fulfilling prophecy.[40]

Unlike Sam Walton, not all superstars initially start out expecting to win. They have to work at building a winning attitude. This happened to Susan Butcher, a four-time-winner of the Iditarod, the grueling 1,150 mile dog race across the heart of Alaska. Before she won her first Iditarod, she kept coming in second even though she had a powerful team of dogs and knew that she had the potential to win. In order to win, she had to convince *herself* that she could win.

> I would often finish a race an hour or a minute or a split second behind someone else, but I'd have the strongest and fastest team. So in 1986 I learned how to pull it all together. I told myself that not only could I win, but that I deserved to win and that I could win today. I knew before that, that "someday" I would win the Iditarod, but I didn't see myself as a winner today. So I kept failing.[41]

Like Susan Butcher, we often fail to win because in our hearts we don't truly believe that we can win. We embrace what Stan Shih, founder of Acer, calls "negative thinking,"[42] which causes us to hesitate and hold back. When Donny Deutsch, Chairman and CEO of one of the nation's premier advertising agencies, first started working in his father's small boutique advertising agency, he didn't believe that the agency could become a major player in the industry. Donny considered million dollar clients to be out of their league. One of his first hires was a young guy named Richie Kirshenbaum, who had just graduated from college. Richie and Donny worked well together but after two years Richie went to work for a larger agency. Six months later Donny learned that Richie had started his own agency. He dismissed it commenting, "Lot of balls, that kid. Oh yeah, that'll last about a week."[43] The first campaign that Richie did was controversial and wildly successful. Soon Richie was featured in *New York* magazine as having one of the new "hot agencies." At first Donny was jealous but then he began to think, "I'm smarter than this guy and have a lot more experience. How did this happen?" He realized that the problem lay in his beliefs about what was possible for him and the agency.

> I wasn't even dreaming that David Deutsch Associates would get written up in *New York* [magazine]. We had been grinding all along but never thought it was possible. Million-dollar clients? Out of our league. If someone had asked me, "Why shouldn't you have the next hot agency?" I'd have had every answer in the world except the right one. Richie Kirshenbaum showed me I was wrong. Why *couldn't* we do work like what I was reading about? That could be us. That *should* be us. We could pitch anybody.[44]

This experience taught Donny what he calls the "Why not me?" attitude. Why shouldn't he be as successful as the Richie Kirshenbaums of the world? By starting from the belief that he too could compete at the top levels, Donny turned himself and the agency into winners.

Once we believe in ourselves and our ability to win, we unleash our full abilities. Dr. Ben Carson was originally a failure at school but once he began to believe that he was smart, he discovered that he had all sorts of innate abilities.

> Everybody has them, everybody who has a normal brain, because there is no such thing as the average human being. If you have a normal brain, you are superior. There's almost nothing that you can't do.
>
> It's really just a matter of understanding that. Take two baseball players, two rookies that come up. The first day in the Major Leagues the

first one comes up [to bat]. He looks out at the mound and he sees
Nolan Ryan. "On no! He's a legend in his own time. He's got a 95
mile-an-hour fast ball, struck out more men than anybody in the history of baseball, and had more no-hitters. I probably won't even see
the ball." With that mind-set, he's very unlikely to get a hit.

Another rookie comes up with the same talent. He looks out there and
says, "Nolan Ryan, he's an old man. I'm probably going to knock the
cover off his ball." He is going to approach that assignment in a completely different way, and his chance of getting a hit is much greater.[45]

Believing that we can win is challenging. We must find
ways to silence the little negative voices whispering to us, "You
can't do that." One way that superstars drown out these voices
and learn to expect to win is by using visualization. They start
seeing themselves as winners. Susan Butcher won her first
Iditarod by hanging onto her vision of herself as a winner.

In 1986, I lived and breathed the vision of winning the Iditarod for
the full year. I held it eleven days into the Iditarod, where I was neck
and neck with Joe Barnie forty-four miles from the finish line.

I had less than twenty hours sleep in eleven days. I had run up every
hill between Anchorage and Nome, but Joe made a final push and
passed me gaining a two-minute lead.

I was exhausted and demoralized, and said to myself, "Well, I guess second place isn't too bad." But through the blur of fatigue, I remembered
my vision of myself winning the 1986 Iditarod, and I knew this race
could be mine alone. So for the next forty-four miles, I ran, pumped
with one leg or pushed until I passed Joe and won my first Iditarod.[46]

Dr. Ben Carson started visualizing himself as a doctor when
he was still a young child struggling to do well in school.

I can remember we used to sit in the hallways at Detroit City Hospital
or Boston City Hospital for hours and hours because we were on
public assistance, which meant that we had to wait until one of the
interns or residents was free to see us. I didn't mind it at all, because
we were in the hospital. . . . I would listen to the PA system, "Dr.

181

Jones. Dr. Jones to the emergency room," just sounded so fabulous. I would be saying [to myself], "They're going to be saying 'Dr. Carson' one day. . . ." It was just wonderful to have that dream and imagine myself in that setting.[47]

Other superstars actually physically act out their visualizations. As a young child Andre Agassi used to stand on the coffee table in his living room and imitate the tennis players that he saw on television. Larry King would pretend that he was a radio announcer.

> I would go to baseball games and I'd roll up the score card, and I'd sit in the back row, and all my friends would look at me, and I'd broadcast the game to myself.[48]

Superstars also often have people around them who nurture and fortify their belief that they can win. Lance Armstrong called his mother in Texas and asked her to come and stay with him a week before he was to race in his first World Championships in Oslo. He writes, "I didn't want to go through it alone, and [my mother] has always been a source of confidence for me."[49] With her support, Lance became the youngest man to win the World Championships. Dr. Ben Carson's mother had such a strong belief in him and his brother Curtis that Ben had no choice but to believe in himself. He recalls, "She had such faith in us, we didn't dare fail. Her unbounded confidence nudged me to believe in myself."[50]

Jeffrey Bezos's parents' confidence in him was so great that they used a large portion of their life savings to provide him with the money to start Amazon. His father didn't even know what the Internet was but he did expect his son to win.

> My dad's first question was, "What's the Internet?" He wasn't making a bet on this company or this concept. He was making a bet on his son, as was my mother. I told them that I thought that there was a 70 percent chance that they would lose their whole investment, which was a few hundred thousand dollars, but they did it anyway.[51]

Other superstars find this type of support in colleagues and mentors. Bill Hewlett and Dave Packard's strong beliefs in each other formed the core of the Hewlett-Packard company that they founded. Their partnership began with a camping trip to the San Juan Mountains in southwestern Colorado after they graduated from Stanford. In recalling their decision to work together, Hewlett facetiously commented, "We trusted each other not to get lost."[52]

Expecting to win is critical to turning in top performances. When we feel uncertain whether we can do something well, it is like carrying a dead weight on our back. It makes it hard for us to function at our peak. To become a superstar, we must free ourselves from this weight by expecting to win. While, like Susan Butcher, we can do this on our own, having family members, friends, and colleagues who also expect us to win can provide the added boost that we need to rise above our insecurities.

Give One-Hundred and Ten Percent

The Scarecrow, the Tin Man, and the Lion storm the Wicked Witch's castle slipping and falling as they go. They give no thought to their personal safety. They are intent on saving Dorothy. They race through the corridors of the castle looking for Dorothy. When they find her, they chop down the door and race to escape.

The Scarecrow, the Tin Man, and the Lion give one hundred and ten percent in their efforts to rescue Dorothy. Superstars bring this same unbeatable intensity and single-mindedness to their key performances. When Lance Armstrong decided, while still in high school, that he wanted to be one of the world's best bicycle racers, his mother told him, "If you can't give 110 percent, you won't make it."[53] Lance followed his mother's advice so closely that during the early years of his career, he, at times, gave too much too soon. He would start sprinting so early in a race that he ran out of steam before the finish line. Susan Butcher called such intense single-minded striving the "winning spirit." In picking dogs for her team, she looked for this first. She noted, "I'm always looking for the mental athlete when I pick my pups. I don't always pick the best physical specimen if he doesn't have the extra athletic heart."[54]

Lee Iacocca brought a similar intensity to trying to save Chrysler. Soon after he became president of Chrysler, he realized that drastic action was needed to save the company. There was no time to do elaborate studies on how to solve the problem. Rather he had to perform triage on Chrysler, which meant focusing on what could be saved. It was through this single-minded intensity that Lee Iococca was ultimately successful in saving Chrysler.[55]

In giving 110 percent, superstars see no limits on how hard they can try. As a result, they go far beyond what others would do to reach their goals. When Dr. Ben Carson became interested in neurosurgery, nothing else existed for him until he mastered the field.

> [T]he field soon intrigued me so much it became a compulsion. . . .
> *I have to know more*, I'd find myself thinking. Everything available in print on the subject became an article I had to read.[56]

He became so knowledgeable that he soon knew more than interns who had already graduated from medical school.

Andrea Mitchell, a top reporter at NBC, pursued stories so intently as NBC's White House correspondent during the Clinton administration that she was described in a *USA Today* feature article as a "pit bull with a bone."[57] The article described how the National Guard at the airport in Hyde Park, NY, chased Andrea across the tarmac because she broke the unwritten rule that reporters don't ask questions during photo opportunities. Andrea had broken this rule during a photo opportunity by asking President Clinton about gays in the military in order to get a sound bite for the evening news on what was a slow news day. Commenting on the incident, Sam Donaldson, formerly of ABC news, said:

> Andrea has always been aggressive. Tough. Assertive. She's always
> pushed forward, sometimes with her elbows. Cameramen have felt
> the sting.[58]

One reason that superstars give 110 percent is because they
have great passion for what they are doing. Anita Roddick passionately believed in the natural products that she sold at her
first Body Shop.

> I loved to tell people where the ingredients had come from, how they
> were used in their original state and what they could do. . . . I read
> everything that I could lay my hands on about the use of natural
> ingredients for skin and hair care and how to make up your own
> products. I think I probably got every book published on the subject
> and I experimented at home all the time, . . .[59]

At Merck, Roy Vagelos was driven to develop Mevacor,
Merck's groundbreaking drug to lower cholesterol, because
he passionately wanted to save people from heart disease.
Since the early days of his career at the National Institutes
of Health, he and his colleague, Al Alberts, had been looking
for a cholesterol-lowering inhibitor similar to the enzyme in
Mevacor. When Mevacor's safety was questioned and it became
unclear whether the Food and Drug Administration (FDA)
would approve Mevacor, Vagelos didn't give up. Instead he
pushed harder to scientifically demonstrate the drug's safety.
In describing his attitude he has stated, "I had twenty-five
years of intense research riding on that project, and I was still
determined to do everything I could to pull it out of trouble."[60] Through his efforts, the FDA finally approved Mevacor.
A few years later Mevacor and Zocor, a spin-off of Mevacor,
had captured over half of the United States market for cholesterol lowering drugs and were sold in more than thirty countries worldwide.[61]

As these examples illustrate, superstars give 110 percent
when they encounter pivotal moments in their careers. At
such times, they reach inside themselves and find the inten-

sity that they need to win. We too need to generate this same single-minded intensity within ourselves if we are to become superstars. When we are able to do this, we can pull away from the pack like Lance Armstrong and produce amazing results.

Take Time-Outs

When Dorothy, the Scarecrow, the Tin Man and the Lion first arrive at the Emerald City, they stop at the Wash and Brush Up Company to refresh themselves before seeing the Wizard. At the Wash and Brush Up Company, hairdressers fix Dorothy's hair, masseuses fill the Scarecrow with new straw, polishers polish the Tin Man, and manicurists clip the Lion's claws. The group leaves singing, "That's how we laugh the day away in the Merry Old Land of Oz. . . ."[62]

Like Dorothy and the group, we need to take time-outs to revive ourselves on our journey to becoming a superstar. Even machines need fuel and tune-ups to keep running. When we fail to take time-outs, we can become so tired and stressed that our performance plummets.

Research shows that too much stress and not getting enough sleep can have powerful adverse effects on our ability to perform well. In a recent study, Dr. Todd J. Arendt and his colleagues compared medical residents' performance on a driving simulation test when they were rested, but legally drunk, to their performance after they had just completed an intense month long hospital rotation. During hospital rotations, residents typically work nonstop for long hours and get little sleep. A driving simulation test was used because driving requires good motor skills, vigilance, quick reaction times, and the ability to pay attention to the road—all abilities that are needed in caring for patients. Dr. Arendt and his colleagues discovered that the residents did poorly in both test conditions. They had the same difficulties staying in one lane and maintaining a constant speed when they were sleep-deprived and burned-out as when they were legally drunk.[63]

Other researchers have found equally striking effects of stress and sleep deprivation on performance. Harris Lieberman and his colleagues at the U.S. Army Research Institute of Environmental Medicine have studied the cognitive effects of combat on soldiers. While combat can look glorious in movies, it is intensely stressful, and when one is in fear for one's life, one doesn't sleep. During combat, soldiers often report entering a mental twilight zone called the "fog of war" in which they are mentally confused and unable to make good decisions. They have trouble focusing and respond slowly, if at all, to crises. Many of the friendly fire accidents that occur during combat are considered to be due to soldiers being in the "fog of war."

To understand and document the effects of the "fog of war" on cognitive performance, Lieberman and his colleagues tested U.S. Army Rangers and U.S. Navy SEAL trainees during exercises mimicking combat. The U.S. Army Rangers were engaged in a five day exercise similar to high-intensity light infantry combat during which they were under continuous stress and slept only a few hours a night. The Navy SEAL trainees were completing "Hell Week." During Hell Week, trainees are subjected to extreme physical and psychological stressors and are not allowed to sleep at all. Over 50% of the trainees who start Hell Week never complete it.

After being exposed to the combat-like conditions, both the Army Rangers and the Navy SEALs had severe declines in attention, memory, logical reasoning, and their ability to perform simple cognitive tasks quickly and accurately. The Navy SEAL trainees who were exposed to the most severe stress and sleep deprivation had the largest performance drops.[64] These results confirm what most of us already know: the more stressed and tired we become, the harder it is to think straight and do things well. If at such times we don't stop and take time-outs to revive ourselves, the same "fog of war" that soldiers in battle experience can overcome us.

Superstars work to avoid the "fog of war" and keep their performances at high levels by taking time-outs. They build ways to restore themselves into their busy schedules. Sam Walton had a passion for quail hunting. During hunting season he would leave work every day in the afternoon to spend a few hours shooting quail.[65]

Jack Welch always made time to play golf while he was at General Electric. Larry Ellison, of Oracle, races speedboats and flies jet planes. Richard Branson flies hot air balloons, and Dr. Ben Carson is deeply involved in his church.

In addition to finding time for activities that refresh them, many superstars create physical retreats for themselves where they can escape from the demands of work. Soon after Richard Branson started Virgin, he found a houseboat to live in on a canal in the Maida Vale section of London because he had always loved being on the water and around boats.[66] Now, when he has time, Richard escapes to his private island in the Caribbean.

One of the most prized possessions of Michael Steinhardt, one of Wall Street's superstar money managers, is his home outside New York.

> Of all my possessions, the only one that I have a deep emotional attachment to is our home in Bedford. It is here that I have developed a passion for horticulture. . . . Growing apples and other fruit provides a near year-round pleasure for me. . . . In many of the flower beds on the property, I have found tremendous pleasure experimenting with new plants. . . . The Bedford house is also the site of my extensive zoological collection, which gives me endless pleasure.[67]

To create such retreats, we don't have to spend a lot of money. Martha Stewart has lived in the same house for 25 years and made only minor improvements. For her, it is a place where she finds peace and respite from her professional life.

> My tastes have gotten a little better, or a little bit more educated. But still, I always get up and clean out the kitty litter. You know, I make sure everybody is home, all the animals. I go down through

the garden and prune, and pick and do all these things. I keep grounded, and by keeping grounded you can then see very clearly what's happened to you.[68]

To become a superstar in today's world, we must often work long hours and live under constant stress. To minimize the effects of these long hours and the never-ending stress on our performance, we must remember to take time-outs to restore ourselves. To tap into the great potential that lies in all of us, we need to be rested and relaxed.

TAKE A MOMENT TO REFLECT

How well do you focus? How can you structure your work to limit interruptions that break your focus?

On the page below, write down your thoughts about your ability to focus and ways that you can improve your focus.

Know How to Manage Risk and Adversity

Throughout *The Wizard of Oz* Dorothy must take risks and deal with adversity. Even before the tornado scoops up Dorothy and Toto and drops them in Oz, Miss Gulch tries to have Toto destroyed. When Dorothy steps out of her house in Oz, she finds herself in a strange and bewildering land. Before she knows where she is, the Wicked Witch of the West appears and accuses her of killing her sister, the Wicked Witch of the East, and then threatens to kill Dorothy. Dorothy's decision to go to the Emerald City is risky and she encounters new challenges at every turn during her journey. Despite this, Dorothy never falters. She is not afraid to take the risks that are necessary to succeed and she faces every adversity with courage and strength.

The journey to becoming a superstar is always filled with risk and adversity. No one makes the journey unscathed. Lance Armstrong was on the verge of greatness in bicycle racing when he discovered that he had cancer and would probably die. Young, healthy, and at his peak, Lance could never have imagined getting cancer. Before he could become the best bicycle racer in the world, he had to undergo dangerous chemotherapy treatments that could have damaged his ability to ever race again or even killed him. Overcoming such adversity requires courage and grit. To triumph, we must take risks, learn to fail, keep going when it seems hopeless, and believe in ourselves.

191

Be Willing to Take Risks

After Glinda tells Dorothy about the Wizard of Oz, Dorothy asks apprehensively, "Is he good or is he wicked?"

Glinda says, "Oh, very good, but very mysterious. He lives in the Emerald City, and that's a long journey from here." [1]

Dorothy takes a big risk when she decides to go to the Emerald City to see the Wizard of Oz. She must travel through unknown and strange territory and she is unsure of the way. Moreover, she has no assurances that the Wizard will help her once she gets to the Emerald City. Despite the risks and uncertainties, she bravely starts off down the Yellow Brick Road because she passionately wants to return to Kansas.

Risk and uncertainty are part of every superstar's journey. There are no road signs that point out the best route or warn of the dangers ahead. Moreover, to become a superstar we must distinguish ourselves from our competitors. This involves taking risks. When Anita Roddick opened her first Body Shop store in the 1970s, her idea to sell beauty products made from natural ingredients was a novelty. Anita had no marketing reports to reassure her that such an idea would be popular. Similarly, at the time Sam Walton started Wal-Mart in 1962, his strategy of cutting operating costs to a bare minimum in order to provide people with products at discount prices was a new, unproven approach to retailing. As Michael Eisner points out, to be a superstar you must be new, different or unusual, and that involves risk.

> You have to be prepared to be on the edge of risk. First of all, research will tell you, which I do not believe in at all, that people want what they saw yesterday, and that's fallacious. They don't know what they want. They want something new, different and unusual.
>
> When you go from new, different, and unusual, whether it's architecture, or paintings, . . . [or] you have a playwright who's willing to take a risk, versus a playwright who's not, it makes all the difference between success and failure.[2]

Superstars consider taking risks part of the essence of living. Donna Shirley, manager of the Mars Exploration Program that landed the Mars Pathfinder and Sojourner Rover on Mars, is not afraid to take risks because it enriches her life and makes it more meaningful.

> Some people spend their whole lives avoiding risk, so they don't get the pleasure out of life that they could get. Maybe they get a different type of pleasure than I get, but I'm one of these people who wants to be out there making a contribution, doing something nobody's done before. That's an inherently daring kind of thing.[3]

Jeffrey Bezos started Amazon because he didn't want to look back at age 80 and feel that he missed out on living his life to the fullest because he was afraid of risk.

> The framework I found which made the decision incredibly easy was what I call—which only a nerd would call—a "regret minimization framework." I projected myself forward to age 80 and said, "Okay, now I'm looking back on my life. I want to have minimized the number of regrets I have."
>
> I knew that when I was 80 I was not going to regret having tried [to start Amazon.] I was not going to regret trying to participate in this thing called the Internet that I thought was going to be a really big deal. I knew that if I failed I wouldn't regret that, but I knew the one thing I might regret is not having tried. I knew that would haunt me every day, and so when I thought about it that way, it was an incredibly easy decision. . . . [4]

To take risks we must have courage. Superstars find this courage in their passion for what they are doing and in their desire to succeed. This passion is so great that they readily risk their lives, careers, reputations and savings in pursuit of their dreams. Deborah Copaken Kogan was willing to risk her life because she passionately wanted to be a photojournalist. She knew that to become a superstar photojournalist, you must shoot pictures of wars, drugs, and other dangerous activities that ordinary people don't encounter in the course of their daily lives. To get started, she took her meager savings after graduating from college and went to Paris which was a center for photojournalists. There she met a well-known and experienced photojournalist, Pascal, who agreed to take her with him to cover the Soviet Union's war in Afghanistan. Deborah knew that in the Pashtun tribal area where they were going women remained in the shadows, and it would be difficult to actually go into the field and shoot pictures of the war. Pascal's help would provide her with an opportunity to "get inside," as photojournalists called it.

They flew to Peshawar, Pakistan, a city on the edge of Afghanistan where many rebel groups fighting the Soviets had headquarters. Their first week in Peshawar was spent visiting rebel headquarters searching for a group who would take them on one of their missions into Afghanistan. They finally found a group who would take them. On the day that they were to leave, Deborah called Pascal at his hotel only to learn that he had left an hour earlier without her. This didn't stop Deborah. She thought, I'll go in on my own.[5]

> For the next week, I began afresh, visiting one group of mujahideen after the other, drinking one glass of sugary tea after another. I was snubbed, insulted, told to wait outside, made to step off their property, given the runaround, made to beg and fed lies until finally, almost a full week after Pascal's departure, the Harakat-I-Islami group told me to meet them at their headquarters at 6 a.m. the next morning to go inside.[6]

Deborah spent a month traveling with the men, trudging through snowy mountain passes and sleeping in caves. She returned to Peshawar tired, dirty and disheveled after she was hit in the hand by a piece of shrapnel from a landmine, but she had the photos that she needed to jump-start her career and be recognized as a genuine photojournalist.

Dr. Ben Carson is so passionately committed to excellence that he is willing to take risks with his career by making his own rules if it means that he can do a better job. During his summer job supervising a highway crew while he was in college, he was an incredibly successful supervisor because he created special rules for how and when his crew collected trash. He had them come in early when it was cool. Instead of making them put in an eight-hour day, he let them leave as soon as they had collected 150 bags of trash. Dr. Carson's supervisors looked the other way because his crew collected far more trash than any of the other crews.[7] Reflecting on his approach, Dr. Carson has commented:

> "I did it my way." Not because I oppose rules—it would be crazy to do surgery without obeying certain rules—but sometimes regulations hinder and need to be broken or ignored.[8]

Throughout his career as a pediatric neurosurgeon, Dr. Carson has followed this path. He has pioneered life-saving surgical techniques and operated on patients that other doctors refused to take because the chances of success were so low that it might adversely affect their careers if they failed. In such situations, Dr. Carson has never hesitated to operate if in his judgment he had a chance of success and the surgery would give the patient an opportunity to survive and lead a normal life.[9]

Hillary Clinton's opposition to the war in Viet Nam was so strong that she was willing to risk her reputation as she sat on the stage waiting to speak at her graduation from Wellesley College. As she listened, Senator Edward Brooke of Massachusetts, the commencement speaker, gave a long pompous speech calling student protests against the war in Viet Nam "mindless" and self-indulgent. He further insulted the graduates of the all-female college by quoting Al Capp who was currently ridiculing the feminist movement in his "Li'l Abner" cartoon column with his character, "Joaney Phoney." Hillary Clinton was not afraid to challenge Senator Brooke despite the formality of the occasion and the presence of her classmates' more conservative parents. Throwing away her prepared speech, she strode to the podium and gave an impassioned speech opposing the war. Parents were dismayed but the Wellesley graduates gave her a standing ovation.[10]

195

Frederick Smith was willing to take an enormous financial gamble in starting Federal Express because he passionately believed that reliable overnight delivery of documents and packages was the wave of the future. He first conceived of the idea while writing an undergraduate paper at Yale. Even though his professor wasn't convinced of the value of his idea, Smith continued to be intrigued by it. His belief in the need for such a system grew during his four years as a lieutenant in the Marine Corps where he observed the problems that the military had in getting supplies to the right place at the right time. After leaving the military, Smith borrowed $80 million from his family and investors to start Federal Express. The first years of operation were rocky because Federal Express was ahead of its time. The world was moving toward the fast-paced computer age of today but businesses did not yet consider overnight delivery of packages and documents essential for their survival. The first night of operations Federal Express's fleet of 14 jets flew only 186 packages. After two years the company had lost $27 million and it was on the verge of bankruptcy. Only by renegotiating their loans was Smith able to save it. Despite these setbacks, Smith was so committed to his idea that he never really saw it as a risk. During his four years in Viet Nam he had learned that there were far greater tragedies that could befall one than losing money.

> In retrospect it was ridiculous to try to put this system together, which required so much up front money, and required changing a lot of government regulations but I didn't know that at the time. I think probably my experience in the service [was important.] The currency of exchange in FedEx was just money, it wasn't people's arms and legs, or lives. . . . I was willing to take a chance, because losing wasn't the worst thing in the world that could happen to you. I had seen that very clearly.[11]

Katharine Graham was willing to risk the survival of the Washington Post Company which she owned because she deeply believed in the power of journalism and freedom of the press. At the height of the Viet Nam war, she didn't hesitate to give her editors at the *Washington Post* the go-ahead to publish the *Pentagon Papers*, top secret papers prepared by the Defense Department which detailed the United States' involvement in the Viet Nam war. By publishing the papers she exposed her company to possible prosecution under the Espionage Act. If convicted, the company would have lost its licenses to operate its lucrative television stations. In addition, at that time the company was on the verge of going public. Under the terms of their contract, the underwriters could withdraw if the company was prosecuted. Despite these risks, Katharine Graham's commitment to making the *Washington Post* a paper that embodied excellence in journalism prevailed.[12]

As these stories illustrate, superstars aren't afraid to take risks. They don't stay on the sidelines of life. They put themselves in the middle of the playing field where the stakes are high and everyone can see them win or lose. Moreover, their passion for what they are doing is so great that they don't stop to consider the downside of their actions. Like Dorothy dancing down the Yellow Brick Road, they charge ahead without worrying about the risks around the next corner.

Learn to Fail

Dorothy, the Scarecrow, the Tin Man, and the Lion excitedly wait outside the Wizard of Oz's palace while the Guard goes in to announce them. The Scarecrow says, "Did you hear that? He'll announce us at once! I've as good as got my brain!"

The Tin Man replies, "I can fairly hear my heart beating!"

Dorothy responds, "I'll be home for supper!"

The Lion says, "In another hour, I'll be King of the Forest. Long live the King!" and he breaks into song.

A few minutes later, the Guard returns and tells them, "Go on home. The Wizard says go away!"[13]

Dorothy and her companions are devastated when they hear that the Wizard won't see them. They were sure that fulfillment of their dreams was within their reach. Such setbacks are common on the journey to becoming a superstar. Failure strikes everyone. Superstars take wrong turns, run into dead ends, or, like Dorothy and her companions, have success snatched away due to factors beyond their control. George Lucas, writer and director of *Star Wars* and *American Graffiti*, is considered one of Hollywood's greatest filmmakers but sixty percent of his movies fail.

> Sometimes people are surprised to learn that most of the films I've made don't work. They've been released but nobody has ever seen them. Maybe 40% of them are very successful. That's a very high percentage; most people have maybe 10 or 15% of their films work.[14]

Failing is only an impediment to our becoming a superstar if we see it as an end to our hopes and dreams rather than a change in direction. Superstars aren't afraid to fail and make mistakes because they consider it a normal part of the process of becoming successful. It is not the final word on whether they will ultimately become a superstar. Lee Iacocca expected to fail when he first left engineering and went into sales at Ford because he knew nothing about sales. He realized that sales was like any other job. He would need to work at it and he would only become good at it through serious practice and by making lots of mistakes.[15] George Soros, founder of Soros Fund Management, also considers failure to be part of being human. He takes pride in identifying his failures.

> To others, being wrong is a source of shame; to me, recognizing my mistakes is a source of pride. Once we realize that imperfect understanding is the human condition, there is no shame in being wrong, only in failing to correct our mistakes.[16]

Jack Welch looks back and laughs at his hiring failures when he was a young manager at General Electric. He writes, "I learned a lot [about hiring] the hard way—by making some big mistakes. The consistency of my first hires was laughable."[17]

Superstars also realize that their failures help them be more successful. They provide valuable information that lets them make adjustments that improve their performance and ultimately lead to their success. Michael Eisner has stated, "If [people] don't fail, they will probably never succeed."[18] Michael Jordan echoes this sentiment. He believes that the reason he became a basketball player is a result of all of the shots that he missed because with each miss he got feedback that made his next shot better.

> I've missed more than 9,000 shots in my career. I've lost almost 300 games. Twenty-six times I've been trusted to take the game winning shot and missed. I've failed over and over and over again in my life-and that is why I succeed.[19]

Steve Jobs also believed that failure had a positive effect on his success. When he was fired from Apple, the company he cofounded, he was devastated. He recalls, "It was awful tasting medicine." Looking back years later in his famous Stanford graduation speech, he commented that being fired was one of the best things that happened to him.

> The heaviness of being successful was replaced by the lightness of being a beginner again, less sure about everything. It freed me to enter one of the most creative periods of my life.[20]

To become a superstar, we must overcome our fears of failure and learn to fail in a way that lets us grow from our failures and turn them into new beginnings. This involves being ready to quickly recognize and accept our failures and then look for the lessons embedded in them because hidden within each failure is another opportunity to succeed. When we refuse to recognize and accept our failures, they act as a barrier to our becoming a superstar. We become trapped like an insect that flies over and over again into a light bulb, and never sees the open window that would allow it to escape to freedom. For a long time, Fantasia Barrino, the American pop star who launched her career on the television show *American Idol*, couldn't bring herself to admit that she couldn't read or write. Her fear that people would find out even kept her from looking for a job when she was a struggling single mother. She recalls, "I was so ashamed. . . . What will people say about me?" At *American Idol* she hid her illiteracy by memorizing the words to songs while listening to them. In looking back, she realizes that by not accepting that she couldn't read and write, she retreated from life and didn't seize opportunities. She notes, "[It] kept me . . . in a box and I didn't, wouldn't come out."[21]

Speed is of the essence in accepting and recognizing our failures. The longer we wait to acknowledge them, the bigger they will become. Often it is tempting to find ways to rationalize that what we are doing is going as well as can be expected or that things will eventually improve with time. Superstars have the courage to quickly identify their failures and make changes. They know that it is easier to limit the damage if they act immediately and proactively. David Glass, former CEO of Wal-Mart, describes how Sam Walton never hesitated to move on and try a different approach when he failed.

> [H]e is less afraid of being wrong than anyone I've ever known. And once he sees he's wrong, he just shakes it off and heads in another direction.[22]

Anita Roddick also believes in rapidly accepting her failures and changing direction. Before opening the Body Shop, she and her husband started a restaurant in Littlehampton, England, that offered health foods with an Italian twist. In the early 1970s Littlehampton was not ready for gourmet vegetarian dishes. The restaurant was a huge failure. For three weeks they sat in an empty restaurant waiting for customers who never came.

> The reason was quite simple—we had done everything wrong. It was the wrong kind of restaurant in the wrong street in the wrong town, launched at the wrong time. . . .

What saved us, once again, was our willingness to recognize that we were wrong and our ability to move swiftly on to the next idea. "We've got to face up to the fact that this is not working," Gordon said. . . .[23]

Their quick recognition that they were failing and their willingness to try something different curtailed their losses. They changed their menu to steak and chips and their restaurant became one of the most popular in town.

Accepting and recognizing our failures is only the first step. We must then learn from them. Stan Shih, founder of Acer, considers failure life's tuition. It is the price that we pay to learn and grow.

My personal experiences have been accumulated with the payment of a huge tuition. Over the past few years, several of Acer's investments have lost hundreds of millions of dollars, but my management capability has been improved as a result. As long as the money we pay can generate returns for the company in the long run, it is considered an investment fee, not wasted money.[24]

Stan Shih follows this same policy with his employees. When an employee makes a mistake, his manager examines what went wrong and works with the employee to prevent it from happening in the future. This approach has led Acer to discover flaws in its procedures and new ways to increase its bottom line.

J. Paul Getty considers the costly failure of his first drilling enterprise on the Didier Ranch in California to have been a bargain because it taught him the importance of closely supervising drilling projects and paying attention to costs. At the time that he started the drilling at the Didier Ranch, he was too busy to directly supervise it because he was working with his father on other projects. Instead, he hired a drilling contractor. Seven months later he discovered that he had paid the contractor almost $100,000 and the contractor had only drilled down 2,000 feet. At the time, this was an enormously expensive drilling operation. Getty immediately stopped the drilling and gave up the lease. From then on, he became directly involved in his drilling operations.

> My costly experience with the drilling contractor proved a bargain because of the lesson it drove home. During the A.D.—After Didier—period, whether operating in association with my father or on my own account, I acted as my own drilling superintendent.[25]

Anita Roddick had a similar learning experience with the first advertising campaign that she did with Friends of the Earth. The campaign was to alert the public to the dangers of acid rain. She had a poster created showing a dead tree growing out of a decomposed human head with factory chimneys smoking in the background. The heading read "Acid Reigns."

> It was very, very sophisticated: the trouble was that our customers and the public hadn't got a clue what we were getting at. . . . [A]ll we achieved was to mystify everybody.

> We learned from the experience, and we learned very quickly that simple emotive imagery was the key to getting the message across.[26]

Anita Roddick's next poster was direct and simple and as a result it was a success.

Learning to fail takes courage and guts. As children, we are taught to avoid failure at all costs. Often we are punished for our failures. When we fail, few adults say, "Great! What did you learn from this?" To overcome our early training, we must continually remind ourselves that even though failure is extremely painful, it is how we learn. When a student in one of my classes at Harvard says, "Oh, I made a mistake," my reply is, "We don't have mistakes in my class. We only have learning experiences."

Never, Never, Never, Never, Never Give Up

When Dorothy, Toto, the Scarecrow, the Tin Man, and the Lion finally see the Wizard of Oz, he states that he won't help them unless they bring him the Wicked Witch's broomstick. Despondent over having failed to achieve their goals and facing new dangers, the group sets out for the Wicked Witch's castle. As they near the castle, they see the sign, "Haunted Forest, Witches Castle, I mile." Another sign attached to the side says, "I would turn back if I were you." Apprehensively they peer into the dark menacing forest that lies ahead. The trees are twisted and contorted and haunting sounds echo from the forest. Two owls sit on a tree branch. They ominously stare at the group and begin to hoot. The group links arms and enters the forest.[27]

Dorothy and her companions thought that once they arrived at the Emerald City the Wizard would grant their requests. When the Wizard refuses to help them unless they bring him the Wicked Witch's broomstick, the group doesn't give up. They start out for the Wicked Witch's castle only to encounter the dark menacing Enchanted Forest filled with strange and frightening creatures. In the forest they are threatened at every turn by a new danger. Instead of fleeing, they continue to struggle forward.

On the road to becoming a superstar, there are always dark sections of the road where our attempts to make progress appear futile. At such times, superstars refuse to give up. They find the courage to hang onto hope and keep putting one foot in front of the other. Lance Armstrong's mother taught him, "Son, you never quit."[28] During tough races when he felt like giving up, her words would ring in his ears and he would keep pedaling. Johnny Cash fulfilled his dream of singing on the radio by refusing to give up. When he left the Air Force in 1954, he went to Memphis and started knocking on doors of recording studios. Despite being rejected, he kept trying. His mantra, based on Prime Minister Winston Churchill's famous World War II "Never Give Up" speech, was "Never, never, never, never, never give up."[29] His refusal to give up resulted in his finally obtaining a record contract with Sun Records.

> There was a label called Sun Records in Memphis that was pretty hot, with Elvis Presley and two or three locally well-known country acts, and some black blues and gospel singers. When I got out of the

Air Force, I went and knocked on that door and was turned away. I called back for an interview three or four times, was turned away. So one morning I found out what time the man went to work. I went down with my guitar and sat on his steps until he got there and when he got there, I introduced myself and he said, "You're the one that's been calling."

I said, "Yeah." I had to take the chance, he was either going to let me come in, or he was going to run me off. Evidently, he woke up on the right side of the bed that morning.

He said, "Come on in, let's listen."[30]

Two days later, Cash cut his first record.

It takes courage not to give up because the journey to becoming a superstar is difficult. Superstars always go through periods of struggle when it seems that they will never emerge into the light of success. George Lucas, creator of Star Wars, points out that behind every superstar's success lies years of struggle.

No matter how easy it looks on the outside, it's a very, very difficult struggle. You don't see the struggle part of a person's life. You only see the success they have. But I haven't met anybody here at the Academy [of Achievement] or anywhere else who hasn't been able to describe years and years and years of very, very difficult struggle through the whole process of achieving anything whatsoever.[31]

George Lucas experienced this struggle in the years after he left film school. Getting his first film off the ground almost broke his will to succeed.

My first six years in the business were hopeless. There are a lot of times when you sit and say, "Why am I doing this? I'll never make it. It's just not going to happen. I should go out and get a real job, and try to survive." I'd borrowed money from my parents. I'd borrowed money from friends. It didn't look like I was ever going to actually be able to pay anyone back.[32]

Even when you make progress, unexpected events can suddenly yank success away from you. Sam Walton's first

Ben Franklin store was in Newport, Arkansas. He spent five years building the store into the number one Ben Franklin in Arkansas and the surrounding six state region. At the end of the five years, he tried to renew the lease on his store only to discover that the lease did not have an automatic renewal clause and the landlord didn't want to renew his lease. The landlord had observed Sam's success and he wanted to buy his store for his son. Sam had no option but to sell his store to him.

> It was the low point of my business life. I felt sick to my stomach. I couldn't believe it was happening to me. It was really like a nightmare.[33]

Serious setbacks like Sam Walton's can also hit us after years of success and challenge our will to continue. Lee Iacocca was devastated and humiliated when Henry Ford fired him after he had been president for eight years and had worked at Ford for thirty-two years. His career had suddenly imploded and he was now just an unemployed former Ford employee.[34]

He relates, "I really felt like I was coming apart at the seams."[35]Even though he was only fifty-four and still engaged in life, he seriously considered abandoning his business career, but he had always been fighter. Instead he accepted a job as chairman and CEO of Chrysler, where he made a name for himself by saving it from certain bankruptcy and rebuilding it into a serious competitor in the automobile industry.

Superstars survive the dark periods of their journey by hanging onto hope and remaining optimistic. Psychologists have found that optimists are more successful than pessimists. In a study of life insurance agents, Martin Seligman found that the agents who scored in the top ten percent on his optimism scale sold 88 percent more life insurance than the agents who scored in the bottom ten percent.[36] Martha Stewart, who spent five months in prison following her conviction for obstruction of justice and lying to prosecutors, found prison "pretty horrifying," but she managed to maintain a positive attitude.

> I did not allow myself to get depressed. I did not allow myself to get down too much. I faced what I had to face. I lived through it, actually, with flying colors, if you can live through [prison] with flying colors.[37]

George Lucas has survived the black periods in his career by remaining optimistic and hopeful.

> The secret is not to give up hope. It's very hard not to because if you're doing something worthwhile, I think that you will be pushed to the brink of hopelessness before you come through the other side. You just have to hang in through it.[38]

In addition to maintaining a positive and hopeful attitude, superstars survive these difficult and challenging periods by just keeping moving. Stan Shih, founder of Acer, says that the key to surviving bottlenecks and failures is to "stand up again when beaten."[39] Superstars do this. They don't stop and wallow in their setbacks. They get up and continue to try to move forward even if they can only take small steps at a time. Continuing to move forward is essential because when we stop moving, we die. I first discovered this by watching amoebae under a microscope in my high school biology class. Some were a bundle of energy rapidly contracting and extending their pseudopods in search of food. Others were barely moving. When I asked my teacher why, he explained that the ones barely moving were dying.

The link between movement and life was central to Lance Armstrong's decision to return to racing after he had cancer. When he finally completed his treatments and learned that he was cancer-free, Lance struggled with whether to race again. In an effort to convince Lance to return to racing, a friend took him to train in the Appalachian Mountains in North Carolina. While cycling up Beech Mountain, Lance suddenly understood the link between movement and life. He realized that racing again would affirm that he was alive and well.

> It was time to quit stalling, I realized. *Move*, I told myself. *If you can still move, you aren't sick.*[40]

Superstars also know that it is not important how fast we move forward but simply that we keep moving like the tortoise in Aesop's fable. In the fable, the tortoise becomes tired of listening to the hare bragging about how fast he is and challenges him to a race. The hare leaves the starting gate with a burst of energy racing far ahead of the tortoise but he soon becomes tired. Thinking that he can easily win, he stops for a nap. By the time he wakes up, the tortoise has slowly plodded past him and won the race. To win the Tour de France, Lance Armstrong had to give up being a hare. During the early years of his racing career, he was a single-day racer. He recalls, "I would win on adrenaline and anger, chopping off my competitors one by one."[41] As he matured, he realized that being a hare would never let him win the grueling twenty-one day Tour de France. To win he needed to be like the tortoise and just slowly and steadily keep moving through the long difficult mountain climbs that make the Tour de France one of the world's most challenging bike races. He relates, "It was a matter of continuing to ride and ride, no matter how uninspired you felt, when there was no rush of adrenaline left to push you."[42]

George Lucas has similarly always followed the approach of slowly and steadily moving forward during periods of hopelessness. He says, "You simply have to put one foot in front of the other and keep going. Put blinders on and plow right ahead."[43] When Sam Walton lost his store in Newport, Arkansas, he just kept moving.

> I've never been one to dwell on reverses, and I didn't do so then. It's not just a corny saying that you can make a positive out of most any negative if you work at it hard enough. I've always thought of problems as challenges, and this one wasn't any different. . . . I didn't dwell on my disappointment. The challenge at hand was simple enough to figure out: I had to pick myself up and get on with it, do it all over again, only even better this time.[44]

In retrospect, Sam Walton might never have started Wal-Mart if he hadn't been forced to leave Newport and start over again.

Sometimes we can't move forward because we run into roadblocks. When this occurs, superstars keep trying, but instead of using brute force they use their ingenuity and resourcefulness to find a way around the roadblock. Jeong H. Kim's original plan in founding his telecommunications company, Yurie Technologies, was to obtain venture capital financing. For over a year he tried unsuccessfully to interest venture capitalists in his company. He finally realized that the venture capitalists would not give him money because they saw him as a Navy man with no business track record. Kim didn't give up. He just found a way around this roadblock. He refinanced his house and borrowed on his credit cards to raise the money that he needed to move his company forward.

> So I thought about the situation. "What I have is the ability to come up with new product ideas. What I don't have is a track record. I don't have money and I do not have an ongoing business or structure." I thought about the movie *Field of Dreams* with its line, "[If] you build it, they will come." So I approached it differently. "I'm going to build a shell company and I'm going to do whatever I can to generate business and build up a track record, so next time when I try to raise some money, it will be easier."[45]

In 1998, Kim sold his business to Lucent Technologies for over $1 billion.

There are always times on the road to becoming a superstar when things appear hopeless and it seems that we will never fulfill our dreams. At such times, we must find the strength to keep trying. Like the amoeba, we must continue to expand and contract searching for what we need to stay alive and find ways around the roadblocks that all superstars encounter on their journey.

Believe in Yourself

After the Wicked Witch warns the Scarecrow and the Tin Man to stay away from Dorothy, the Scarecrow tells Dorothy, "I'm not afraid of her. I'll see you get safely to the Wizard now, whether I get a brain or not!"

Echoing his comment, the Tin Man says, "I'll see you reach the Wizard, whether I get a heart or not." [46]

The Scarecrow and the Tin Man aren't frightened by the Wicked Witch. They are confident that they can protect Dorothy because they believe in themselves. Their belief in themselves is the psychological armor that gives them the courage to stand up to the Wicked Witch's threats. They are not afraid to accompany Dorothy and Toto to the Emerald City, enter the Enchanted Forest, and storm the Wicked Witch's castle because they believe in themselves.

Superstars know the power of believing in themselves. Dr. Ben Carson states, "In any career, whether it's that of a TV repairman, a musician, a secretary—or a surgeon—an individual must believe in himself and in his abilities." [47]

Jack Welch considers self-confidence and believing in yourself essential to being a top executive because it gives you the courage to take the risks that are often needed to achieve your goals. At General Electric it was a quality that he both sought and worked to develop in the executives whom he managed. [48]

Our belief in ourselves must be unshakable if we are to weather the adversity that we will meet on our journey to becoming a superstar. Unless it rests on a solid foundation, it will quickly crumble when we are challenged or make mistakes. At General Electric, Jack Welch saw highly successful managers self-destruct and fall into what he called the "vortex" because they did not believe in themselves strongly enough to survive the criticism that they received when they made mistakes. [49]

Superstars aren't born believing in themselves. They learn to believe in themselves. Some are lucky enough to have parents who teach them to believe in themselves. Jack Welch has

209

stuttered since he was child. His mother, however, instilled such confidence in him that his stuttering has never fazed him.

> Perhaps the greatest single gift [my mother] gave me was self-confidence. . . .

> [She] served up the perfect excuse for my stuttering. "It's because you're so smart," she would tell me. "No one's tongue could keep up with a brain like yours." For years, in fact, I never worried about my stammer. I believed what she told me: that my mind worked faster than my mouth.[50]

For those of us whose parents primarily focused on what was wrong with us rather than what was right about us, we must build our own beliefs in ourselves brick by brick. Superstars do this by acquiring skills, expertise and other competencies because believing in ourselves ultimately rests on our ability to do things well. Each time we do something well, it feeds our belief that we are an effective person who can get things done. Even if we were lucky enough to have parents who taught us to believe in ourselves, this belief won't survive unless it is based on what we can actually do. The world quickly extinguishes beliefs that aren't grounded in reality. I have always been amazed by a story a friend told me that illustrates what happens if our belief in our self is not in line with what we can do. When my friend was a child, he almost drowned. He saw people swimming and thought, "Oh, I can swim." Fully embracing this belief, he jumped off the end of a dock and plummeted to the bottom of a lake. Luckily, he was rescued which is why he survived to tell the story.

Superstars actively build their beliefs in themselves by increasing their competencies and capacity to act effectively on the world. They engage in a process that first begins by learning how to do something well. They then use the positive feedback that they receive from their achievements to increase their belief in themselves. With each achievement, they gain the confidence to master something bigger and grander, thus creating an ever-expanding universe of areas in which they believe in themselves.

To engage in this process of building our belief in ourself, we must be willing to continually learn new competencies and skills. Superstars are always learning. As a child, Stan Shih was good at math and science but as he become older, he realized that his interpersonal skills were poor. He was painfully shy and introverted and avoided the spotlight. When he entered National Chiao-Tung University in Taiwan, he saw an opportunity to develop his interpersonal skills. At this time there were only 70 students and no clubs or teams at the university. He took the lead in establishing a series of university clubs and teams. He started a photography club, table tennis team, Go Game club, bridge club and volleyball team. By the time that he finished his studies, he had great confidence in his ability to lead, motivate and engage people in his projects. This belief in himself gave him the courage to start Acer and build it into an international power in the computer world.[51]

To achieve the level of mastery needed to believe in ourselves takes hard work and patience. When Roy Vagelos began working at the National Institutes of Health for Dr. Earl Stadtman, he was expected to attend Dr. Stadtman's journal club that met twice a week. At each session, a member of the group discussed and evaluated an important recent journal article in biochemistry. Roy had no confidence in his knowledge of biochemistry or ability to speak before a group.

> I was uncomfortable speaking to any group, even a small one, and I was miserable speaking to a group in which everyone knew more about the subject than I did. Naturally I hated making presentations.[52]

The task was made even more intimidating by the fact that Dr. Stadtman would become incensed by some of the findings reported in the papers that were presented. He would shout, "This *can't* be this way" or "These people are all wrong."[53]

For each of his presentations, Roy spent hours preparing. He not only read the assigned article but additional materi-

211

als in order to increase his knowledge of the subject matter addressed in the article. Gradually Roy acquired enough confidence to answer Dr. Stadtman's challenges and even defend the authors of the articles that he presented. As he slowly and steadily increased his knowledge of biochemistry and honed his presentation skills, his belief in himself grew. This belief in himself that he built played a key role in his later successes as head of the Department of Biological Chemistry at Washington University's School of Medicine and as CEO of Merck.[54]

In building our belief in ourselves, it is important to realize that we don't need to be perfect. Psychologists have found that striving for perfection can actually undermine our belief in ourself. Perfectionists set such high standards for themselves that they can't possibly meet them. As a result, they often never finish projects because they are overcome with the mental paralysis that befalls all of us when faced with an impossible task such as achieving perfection. With each failure, perfectionists become less confident and their belief in themselves steadily fades.

Superstars don't pursue perfection. They nourish and maintain their belief in themselves by setting reasonable standards for themselves based on what is possible for them under the circumstances. After Lance Armstrong had cancer, he didn't expect to immediately return to being a world-class racer. He knew that it would take time to achieve the level of fitness that he had before he became ill and rebuild his belief in himself as a top racer.[55]

Bill Gates would still be working on his original DOS operating system if he had insisted that it be perfect. Software for large computer systems is complex and there are so many ways in which bugs can arise that it is impossible to produce a perfect product. Bill Gates' approach is to develop good products and then work out the bugs that appear as people use the software.[56] Kozo Ohsone, general manager of Sony's Tape Recorder Business Division, took a similar approach when, in

1979, the heads of Sony came up with the idea for the highly successful Walkman. Given only four months to develop the Walkman, Ohsone met the deadline by deciding not to create the perfect Walkman but instead to only make sure that it was reliable. His philosophy was that reliability would be key to the Walkman's success, whereas styling and other features could easily be added later.[57]

Superstars also do not let unexpected circumstances threaten their belief in themselves. They know that they must adjust their standards to the circumstances that they face. When George Lucas makes a movie, he knows that it won't be perfect. During shooting, too many unexpected things go wrong.

> I like to tell students that I talk to that it's not a matter of how well you can make a movie. It's how well you can make it under the circumstances, because there's always circumstances and you cannot use that as an excuse. You can't put a title card at the head of the movie and say, "Well, we really had a bad problem. The actor got sick and it rained this day and we had a hurricane." You can't say the cameras broke down. You can't do that. You simply have to show them the movie and it has got to work.[58]

Learning how to believe in ourself is key to becoming a superstar. It involves accepting what we can do today and making a commitment to doing it better tomorrow. When we develop a strong solid belief in ourselves that is grounded in reality, it opens up new worlds for us. Like Dorothy, the Scarecrow, the Tin Man, and the Lion, it provides us with the courage to face the Wicked Witches in our lives and travel through the exciting and unknown lands that lie over the rainbow.

Take a Moment to Reflect

What are the areas in your life in which you are highly risk averse and avoid making changes?

On the page below, write down your thoughts about why you are risk averse in these areas.

Know How to Have Fun

One of the most powerful images in *The Wizard of Oz* is of Dorothy, the Scarecrow, the Tin Man, and the Lion linking arms and skipping down the Yellow Brick Road while they sing, "We're off to see the Wizard, the Wonderful Wizard of Oz." Despite the ups and downs that they face on their journey through Oz, they still have fun.

Knowing how to have fun is important to becoming a superstar. During our lives we will spend over 80,000 hours at work. This is a long time to do something that we don't like. In my research into the careers of the 60 superstars who appear in this book, I didn't find anyone who didn't enjoy what they did. Richard Branson only starts businesses that he thinks will be fun. The subtitle of his autobiography is *How I've Survived, Had Fun, and Made a Fortune Doing Business My Way.* In an interview discussing how he built Microsoft into a billion dollar company, Bill Gates commented, "I'd say that my job, throughout all this, has been, I think, the most fun job I can imagine having."[1] Warren Buffett similarly loves his work. He compares it to the exhilaration that Michelangelo must have experienced when he was painting the interior of the Sistine Chapel in Rome.[2] Bill Clinton has always loved campaigning. He is fascinated by people and the stories that they tell. After his first campaign trip for public office, he returned home "higher than a kite."[3]

It is when we are having fun that we often produce our best work. Richard Feynman, the Nobel Prize winning physicist, discovered the importance of having fun when he started teaching at Cornell after spending the years during World War II intensely working on the atomic bomb in Los Alamos, New Mexico. During his first year at Cornell, Feynman found that he no longer had any interest in pursuing his theoretical work in physics. As he contemplated his lack of motivation, he realized that the reason was that he no longer found physics fun.

> Physics disgusts me a little bit now, but I used to *enjoy* doing physics. Why did I enjoy it? I used to *play* with it. I used to do whatever I felt like doing-it didn't have to do with whether it was important for the development of nuclear physics, but whether it was interesting and amusing for me to play with. When I was in high school, I'd see water running out of a faucet growing narrower, and wonder if I could figure out what determines the curve. I found it was rather easy to do. I didn't have to do it; it wasn't important for the future of science; somebody else had already done it. That didn't make any difference: I'd invent things and play with things for my own entertainment.

> So I got this new attitude. Now that I *am* burned out and I'll never accomplish anything, I've got this nice position at the university teaching classes which I rather enjoy, and just like I read *Arabian Nights* for pleasure, I'm going to *play* with physics, whenever I want to, without worrying about any importance whatsoever.[4]

Once he decided to play at physics, Feynman again began to enjoy it. A week later he became fascinated with the wobble rate of spinning plates while watching a student in the cafeteria who was amusing people by throwing plates up in the air. Feynman started to spend his time working out equations to describe the motion of the plates. When he told Hans Bethe, a colleague, about his findings, Hans said, "That's pretty interesting but what's the importance of it?" Feynman replied, "There is no importance whatsoever. I'm just doing it for the fun of it." It was this work calculating the wobble rates of plates that ultimately led to his expanding the theory of quantum electrodynamics and winning the Nobel Prize in Physics in 1965.[5]

When we do work that we enjoy, we experience less stress. We are energized by our work rather than drained by it. Throughout his career Jack Welch worked long hours. As Vice President of General Electric he oversaw a number of plants. Many Monday mornings he and his team would fly out to visit these plants, returning home late Friday night. At each plant they would spend hours locked in a room reviewing issues and problems with the managers. Jack's wife, Caroline, commented that he was working himself to death, but from Jack's perspective it wasn't work because he loved what he was doing.[6]

Fred Smith has loved building Federal Express into a Fortune 500 company. When asked how he handles the stress of running Federal Express, he responded, "Business is a game. It's great fun. That's what it is all about. . . ."[7] When Katharine Graham stepped in to run *The Washington Post* after the trauma of her husband's unexpected suicide, she was filled with apprehension, but she soon fell in love with her job. In reflecting on her transition from wife to president, she writes:

> Yet, despite all my insecurities and misgivings, I was gradually beginning to enjoy myself. And unconsciously, somewhere along the line, I seem to have begun redefining my job and what it was I was doing. Indeed, within the first months of my new working life, the color started returning to my face, my jaw was beginning to unclench, and what I had once called "my initial girl-scout resolve" was turning into a passionate interest. In short, as I said at *Newsweek*, I "sort of fell in love." I loved my job, I loved the paper, I loved the whole company.[8]

Before he became a major star as Hawkeye on the television series M*A*S*H, Alan Alda took all sorts of jobs to support his family. He worked as a doorman, drove a taxi, sold mutual funds, served as a paid subject for a study of hypnosis, did cold calling, and even tried playing the horses. Every once in a while he would get an acting job. He recalls, "And that made me know that eventually we'd be all right. We'd make a living doing this thing that gave me so much pleasure. . . ."[9]

For superstars the journey itself is the source of enjoyment. Succeeding at something takes a long time and enormous amounts of energy. If we hate the process, we will never make it. Roger Federer plays tennis because he loves it-not because he wants to break records. Once Richard Branson has succeeded at one business, he starts another because figuring out ways to make businesses thrive is what he enjoys. When Coach Wooden, one of college basketball's most successful coaches, was asked about the joy he experienced winning national titles, he pointed out that the best part was pursuing the titles, not the happy ending.[10]

One of the most important things to remember is that becoming a superstar and having fun go hand in hand. They feed off each other. Fun provides the energy that we need to climb over the rainbow. Superstars, like Dorothy, the Scarecrow, the Tin Man, and the Lion, don't forget to have fun. They know that true success lies in expressing what is best in us in a way that we enjoy and that enhances the lives of others.

TAKE A MOMENT TO REFLECT

Do you find your work fun? Would you continue doing it if you won the lottery or suddenly became extremely wealthy? If not, what would you do?

On the page below, write down what you find fun about your work and what you would do if you didn't need to work.

The Wizard of Oz Story

The Wizard of Oz begins on a hot summer afternoon in Kansas when Dorothy and her dog, Toto, are swept away in their house by a cyclone. Twisting and twirling ever higher, the house lands with a crash on the Wicked Witch of the East in the magical land of Oz. The inhabitants of Oz are elated, but the Wicked Witch of the West soon arrives demanding to know who killed her sister. To protect Dorothy from the Wicked Witch, Glinda, the friendly Witch of the North, with a wave of her wand quickly transfers the Wicked Witch of the East's magical ruby red slippers onto Dorothy's feet. Enraged, the Wicked Witch of the West vows to take revenge on Dorothy and reclaim the slippers.

Dorothy is distraught at finding herself in Oz. She wants to return home to her Auntie Em and Uncle Henry in Kansas, but no one in Oz has ever heard of Kansas. At Glinda's suggestion, Dorothy and Toto set out down the Yellow Brick Road to the Emerald City to ask the Wizard of Oz for help. On her journey Dorothy meets the Scarecrow who dreams of having a brain, the Tin Man who yearns for a heart, and the Lion who longs for courage. Dorothy convinces each to come with her to ask the Wizard of Oz for help. In exchange, they proclaim that they will protect her from the Wicked Witch.

The group's journey is filled with danger and disappointment. At every turn of the road the group is threatened by the Wicked Witch. When they arrive at the Emerald City, the Wizard refuses to help them unless they bring him the Wicked Witch's broomstick. Courageously, the group travels to the Wicked Witch's castle through the dark and dangerous Enchanted Forest. As they approach the castle Winged Monkeys sent by the Wicked Witch sweep down from the sky, seize Dorothy and Toto, and fly them back to the Witch's castle. The Scarecrow, the Tin Man and the Lion run through the woods to the castle to rescue Dorothy. They find her imprisoned in a room at the top of the castle. After they free her, they rush to escape, but the Wicked Witch and her Winkie Guards soon trap them in a castle corridor. Gloating, the Wicked Witch lights her broomstick and sets the Scarecrow on fire. Intent on saving him, Dorothy picks up a bucket of water and throws it on the Scarecrow. Water splashes onto the Wicked Witch and she slowly melts, dissolving into a pool of dark liquid.

Triumphantly, the group returns to the Emerald City with the Wicked Witch's broomstick. In recognition of their achievement, the Wizard gives the Scarecrow a diploma, the Tin Man a heart shaped watch, and the Lion a medal for courage. He offers to take Dorothy and Toto back to Kansas in his hot air balloon, but the plan fails when Toto jumps out of the balloon to chase a cat and Dorothy sprints after him. The balloon comes free from its moorings and floats away without them. Dorothy with Toto in her arms stands steeped in total despair as she watches the balloon disappear. Glinda suddenly appears floating down from the sky in a bubble and lands next to her. She tells Dorothy that she has always had the power to return to Kansas. She only had to look inward. She then tells Dorothy to tap the heels of her ruby slippers together three times. Following her instructions, Dorothy and Toto are instantly transported back to Kansas and Auntie Em and Uncle Henry.

Recommended Additional Reading

Academy of Achievement, www.achievement.org.

Body and Soul: Profits with Principles: The Amazing Success Story of Anita Roddick & The Body Shop by Anita Roddick. Crown Trade Paperbacks, 1991.

"Exercising Influence" by Linda A. Hill. Harvard Business School Publishing, HBS No. 494-083.

Gifted Hands: The Ben Carson Story by Ben Carson, M.D. with Cecil Murphey. Zondervan, 1990.

Iacocca: An Autobiography by Lee Iacocca with William Novak. Bantam Books, 1986.

Jack: Straight from the Gut by Jack Welch with John A. Byrne. Warner Books, 2003.

It's Not About the Bike: My Journey Back to Life by Lance Armstrong with Sally Jenkins. Berkley Books, 2000.

Losing My Virginity: The Updated Story of the World's Greatest Entrepreneur by Richard Branson. Three Rivers Press, 1998.

Madame Secretary: A Memoir by Madeleine Albright with Bill Woodward. Miramax Books, 2003.

Managing Martians by Donna Shirley with Danelle Morton. Broadway Books, 1998.

"Managing Your Boss" by John Gabarro and John P. Kotter.

Harvard Business Review, May-June 1993.

"Managing Your Career" by Linda A. Hill. Harvard Business School Publishing, HBS No. 491-096.

Medicine, Science and Merck by Roy Vagelos and Louis Galambos. Cambridge University Press, 2004.

My Life by William Jefferson Clinton. Alfred A. Knopf, 2004.

Never Have Your Dog Stuffed: And Other Things I've Learned by Alan Alda. Random House, 2005.

No Bull: My Life In and Out of the Markets by Michael Steinhardt. John Wiley & Sons, 2001.

Of Permanent Value: The Story of Warren Buffett by Andrew Kilpatrick. AKPE, 2005.

Often Wrong, Never in Doubt: Unleash the Business Rebel Within by Donny Deutsch with Peter Knobler. Collins, 2005.

Personal History by Katharine Graham. Vintage Books, 1998.

Power and Influence: Beyond Formal Authority by John Kotter. The Free Press, 1985.

"Power Dynamics in Organizations" by Linda A. Hill. Harvard Business School Publishing, HBS No. 494-080.

Sam Walton: Made in America by Sam Walton with John Huey. Bantam Books, 1989.

Shutterbabe by Deborah Copaken Kogan. Random House Trade Paperbacks, 2000.

Soros on Soros: Staying Ahead of the Curve by George Soros with Byron Wien and Krisztina Koenen. John Wiley & Sons, 1995.

"Surely You're Joking Mr. Feynman!": Adventures of a Curious Character by Richard P. Feynman. W. W. Norton & Company, 1985.

This Just In: What I Couldn't Tell You on TV by Bob Schieffer. Berkley Books, 2003.

Notes and References

Introduction: The Power of Oz

1. Playboy Enterprises, Inc., "The Bill Gates Interview," About, http://beginnersinvest.about.com/od/billgates/l/billgatesint.htm.
2. Sam Walton with John Huey, *Sam Walton: Made In America* (New York: Bantam Books, 1992), p. 108.
3. Richard Branson, *Losing My Virginity: How I've Survived, Had Fun, and Made a Fortune Doing Business My Way* (New York: The Rivers Press, 1998), pp. 25–26.
4. Donna Shirley with Danelle Morton, *Managing Martians* (New York: Broadway Books, 1998), pp. 68, 75.
5. Bob Schieffer, *This Just In: What I Couldn't Tell You on TV* (New York: Berkley Books, 2003), p. 18.
6. Will Smale, "Profile: The Google founders," BBC News, April 30, 2004, http://news.bbc.co.uk/2/hi/business/3666241.stm.
7. Marjorie Coeyman, "Bragging rights," *Christian Science Monitor*, May 6, 2003, http://www.csmonitor.com/2003/0506/p13s02–lepr.html.
8. Karen D. Arnold, *Lives of Promise: What Becomes of High School Valedictorians* (San Francisco: Jossey-Bass Inc., Publishers, 1995), p. 17.

9. Jack Welch with John A. Byrne, *Jack: Straight from the Gut* (New York: Warner Books, 2003), pp. 15–18.

10. Melita H. Oden, "The Fulfillment of Promise: 40-Year Follow-Up of the Terman Gifted Group," *Genetic Psychology Monographs* 77, no.1 (1968): pp. 18–19, 53–90.

11. Academy of Achievement, "Oprah Winfrey Interview," www.achievement.org/autodoc/page/win0int-5.

12. Robert Waldron, *Oprah!* (New York: St. Martin's Press, 1987), p. 18.

13. Nancy Armour, "Kwan is Turin Bound; Cohen Wins 1st Title," *ABC News*, January 15, 2006, http://abcnews.go.com/GMA/wireStory?id=1507577.

Step One: Know Yourself

1. Bill George and Andrew N. McLean, "Oprah!," Case 9–405–087 (Boston: Harvard Business School, 2005), p. 6.

2. Paul Rudoff, "The Wizard Of Oz Movie Script," Un-official, http://www.un-official.com/The_Daily_Script/ms_wizoz.htm.

3. Sandra Blakeslee, "Car Calls May Leave Brain Short-Handed," *New York Times*, July 31, 2001.

4. Jack Welch with John A. Byrne, *Jack: Straight from the Gut* (New York: Warner Books, 2003), pp. 15–17, 27–28, 50.

5. Ibid., p. 53.

6. George and McLean, "Oprah!," p. 6; Oprah, "Oprah Winfrey's Biography," http://www2.oprah.com/about/press/about_press_bio.jhtml.

7. Robert Waldron, *Oprah!* (New York: St. Martin's Press, 1987), p. 116.

8. Ibid., p. 97.

9. Nancy F. Koehn and Erica A. Helms, "Oprah Winfrey," Case 9–803–190 (Boston: Harvard Business School, 2003), pp. 1–2.

10. Academy of Achievement, "Larry Ellison Interview," http://www.achievement.org/autodoc/page/ell0int-1.

11. Academy of Achievement, "Benjamin Carson Interview," www.achievement.org/autodoc/printmember/car1bio-1.

12. Ben Carson, M.D. with Cecil Murphy, *Gifted Hands: The Ben Carson Story* (Grand Rapids: Zondervan, 1990), p. 102.

13. Ibid., pp. 101–102.

14. Stephan Sharf, "Lee Iacocca as I knew him; he was certainly the right man at the right time. . . ," *Ward's Auto World*, May 1, 1996, http://waw.wardsauto.com/ar/auto_lee_iacocca_knew/.

15. Lee Iacocca with William Novak, *Iacocca: An Autobiography* (New York: Bantam Books, 1986), pp. 41–43, 65–82, 224–240.

16. Anita Roddick, *Body and Soul: Profits with Principles—The Amazing Success Story of Anita Roddick and The Body Shop* (New York: Crown Publishers, 1991), p. 51.

17. Ibid., pp. 68–69, 76.

18. Ibid., pp. 79–80.

19. Ibid., p. 64.

20. Ibid., pp. 80, 82.

21. Academy of Achievement, "Oprah Winfrey Interview," http://www.achievement.org/autodoc/page/win0int-8.

22. Academy of Achievement, "Jeff Bezos Interview," http://www.achievement.org/autodoc/page/bez0int-2.

23. Lance Armstrong with Sally Jenkins, *It's Not About the Bike: My Journey Back to Life* (New York: Berkley Books, 2000), p. 21.

24. Roy Vagelos and Louis Galambos, *Medicine, Science and Merck* (Cambridge: Cambridge University Press, 2004), p. 19.

25. Sam Walton with John Huey, *Sam Walton: Made In America* (New York: Bantam Books, 1992), p. 147.

26. Ibid., p. 111.

27. Richard Branson, *Losing My Virginity: How I've Survived, Had Fun, and Made a Fortune Doing Business My Way* (New York: The Rivers Press, 1998), p. 58.
28. Achievement, "Winfrey Interview," www.achievement. org/autodoc/page/win0int-2.
29. Rudoff, "Oz Movie Script," Un-official, http://www.un-official.com/The_Daily_Script/ms_wizoz.htm.
30. Michael Steinhardt, *No Bull: My Life In and Out of Markets* (New York: John Wiley & Sons, 2001), pp. 42, 44.
31. Deborah Copaken Kogan, *Shutterbabe* (New York: Random House Trade Paperbacks, 2000), p. 72.
32. Ibid., p. 11.
33. Walton with Huey, *Made In America*, pp. 72–73.
34. Ibid., p. 24.
35. Ibid., p. 29.
36. Ibid., p. 91.
37. Ibid., pp. 42–43.
38. Ibid., p. 31.
39. Rudoff, "Oz Movie Script," Un-official, http://www.un-official.com/The_Daily_Script/ms_wizoz.htm.
40. Achievement, "Bezos Interview," http://www.achievement.org/autodoc/page/bez0int-6.
41. Ibid.
42. Karen D. Arnold, *Lives of Promise: What Becomes of High School Valedictorians* (San Francisco: Jossey-Bass Inc., Publishers, 1995), pp. 40, 65.
43. Academy of Achievement, "Susan Butcher Interview," http://www.achievement.org/autodoc/page/but0int-4.
44. Academy of Achievement, "George Lucas Interview," http://www.achievement.org/autodoc/page/luc0int-1.
45. Roddick, *Body and Soul*, pp. 54, 60-69.
46. Ibid., pp. 69–70
47. Iacocca with Novak, *Iacocca: An Autobiography*, p. 33.
48. Achievement, "Lucas Interview," http://www.achievement. org/autodoc/page/luc0int-2.

49. Achievement, "Lucas Interview," http://www.achievement.
org/autodoc/page/luc0int-1.
50. Achievement, "Winfrey Interview," www.achievement.
org/autodoc/page/win0int-6.
51. Koehn and Helms, "Oprah Winfrey," p. 3.
52. CBS News, "Tiger Woods Up Close And Personal,"
March 26, 2006, http://www.cbsnews.com/stories/2006/
03/23/60minutes/main1433767.shtml.
53. Waldron, *Oprah!*, pp. 91–92.
54. George and McLean, "Oprah!," p. 5.
55. Academy of Achievement, "Johnny Cash Interview,"
http://www.achievement.org/autodoc/page/cas0int-2.
56. Welch with Byrne, *Straight from Gut*, p. xiv.
57. Ibid.
58. Ibid.
59. Academy of Achievement, "Michael Eisner Interview,"
http://www.achievement.org/autodoc/page/eis0int-1.

Step Two: Know Where You Are Going

1. Paul Rudoff, "The Wizard Of Oz Movie Script,"
Un-official, http://www.un-official.com/The_Daily_
Script/ms_wizoz.htm.
2. Jack Welch with John A. Byrne, *Jack: Straight from
the Gut* (New York: Warner Books, 2003), p. xii.
3. Academy of Achievement, "George Lucas Interview,"
http://www.achievement.org/autodoc/page/luc0int-1.
4. Donna Shirley with Danelle Morton, *Managing Martians*
(New York: Broadway Books, 1998), pp. 16–17.
5. Sam Walton with John Huey, *Sam Walton: Made In
America* (New York: Bantam Books, 1992), pp. 22–26.
6. Donny Deutsch with Peter Knobler, *Often Wrong,
Never in Doubt: Unleash the Business Rebel Within* (New
York: Harper Collins Publishers, 2005), pp. 19–24.
7. Ibid., p. 26.
8. Ibid., pp. 27–30.

9. Richard Branson, *Losing My Virginity: How I've Survived, Had Fun, and Made a Fortune Doing Business My Way* (New York: The Rivers Press, 1998), pp. 14–16.
10. Achievement, "Lucas Interview," http://www.achievement.org/autodoc/page/luc0int-1.
11. Academy of Achievement, "Jeff Bezos Interview," http://www.achievement.org/autodoc/page/bez0int-3.
12. Bill George and Andrew N. McLean, "Oprah!," Case 9–405–087 (Boston: Harvard Business School, 2005), p. 6.
13. Walton with Huey, *Made In America*, pp. 221–226.
14. Ibid., pp. 9–10.
15. Ibid., p. 10.
16. Branson, *Losing My Virginity*, p. 101.
17. Andrew Kilpatrick, *Of Permanent Value: The Story of Warren Buffett* (Birmingham: AKPE, 2005), pp. 7, 11.
18. Walton with Huey, *Made In America*, pp. 220-221.
19. Branson, *Losing My Virginity*, pp. 55, 269, 353.
20. Rudoff, "Oz Movie Script," Un-official, http://www.un-official.com/The_Daily_Script/ms_wizoz.htm.
21. Anita Roddick, *Body and Soul: Profits with Principles— The Amazing Success Story of Anita Roddick and The Body Shop* (New York: Crown Publishers, 1991), p. 80.
22. Academy of Achievement, "Frederick W. Smith Interview," http://www.achievement.org/autodoc/page/smi0int-2.
23. Kilpatrick, *Of Permanent Value*, p. 5.
24. David Margolik, "Strange Fruit," The Unofficial Billie Holiday Website, http://www.ladyday.net/stuf/vfsept98.html.
25. Ibid.
26. Academy of Achievement, "John Grisham Interview," http://www.achievement.org/autodoc/page/gri0bio-1.
27. Rudoff, "Oz Movie Script," Un-official, http://www.un-official.com/The_Daily_Script/ms_wizoz.htm.
28. Roy Vagelos and Louis Galambos, *Medicine, Science and Merck* (Cambridge: Cambridge University Press, 2004), p. 175.

29. Walton with Huey, *Made In America*, p. 28.
30. Ibid., pp. 34–35.
31. Ibid., p. 38.
32. Welch with Byrne, *Straight from Gut*, pp. 106–110.
33. Branson, *Losing My Virginity*, p. 12.
34. Vagelos and Galambos, *Medicine, Science and Merck*, p. 78.
35. Ibid., p. 101.
36. Ibid., p. 78.
37. Rudoff, "Oz Movie Script," Un-official, http://www.un-official.com/The_Daily_Script/ms_wizoz.htm.
38. J. Paul Getty, *As I See It* (Los Angeles: Getty Trade Paperbacks, 2003), p. 40.
39. Nancy F. Koehn & Erica A. Helms, "Oprah Winfrey," Case 9–803–190 (Boston: Harvard Business School, 2003), p. 3.
40. Ben Carson, M.D. with Cecil Murphy, *Gifted Hands: The Ben Carson Story* (Grand Rapids: Zondervan, 1990), pp. 127–135.
41. Academy of Achievement, "Larry King Interview," http://www.achievement.org/autodoc/page/kin0int-3.
42. John Campbell, *Margaret Thatcher: The Grocer's Daughter* (London: Jonathan Cape, 2000), p. 49.
43. Jennifer M. Suesse, "Margaret Thatcher," Case 9–497–018 (Boston: Harvard Business School, 1998), p. 10.
44. Campbell, *Margaret Thatcher*, p. 281.
45. Suesse, "Margaret Thatcher," pp. 13–17.
46. Achievement, "Smith Interview," http://www.achievement.org/autodoc/page/smi0int-3.
47. Academy of Achievement, "Jeong Kim Interview," http://www.achievement.org/autodoc/page/kim1int-4.
48. Katharine Graham, *Personal History* (New York: Vintage Books, 1998), pp. 461–462.
49. Achievement, "Smith Interview," http://www.achievement.org/autodoc/page/smi0int-4.
50. Achievement, "King Interview," http://www.achievement.org/autodoc/page/kin0int-1.

51. Ibid.
52. Achievement, "Smith Interview," http://www.achievement. org/autodoc/page/smi0int-1.
53. Bill Clinton, *My Life* (New York: Alfred A. Knopf, 2004), pp. 199, 210-212, 249.
54. Achievement, "Lucas Interview," http://www.achievement. org/autodoc/page/luc0int-3.
55. Clinton, *My Life*, pp. 210-211.
56. Shirley with Morton, Managing Martians, p. 95.

Step Three: Know How To Get There

1. Paul Rudoff, "The Wizard Of Oz Movie Script," Un-official, http://www.un-official.com/The_Daily_ Script/ms_wizoz.htm.
2. Acer Inc, "Acer Publications," Communications & Multimedia Laboratory, http://www.cmlab.csie.ntu.edu. tw/~chenhsiu/reading/metoo.pdf#search=%22%22is%20 not%20my%20style%22%20%22stan%20shih%22%22.
3. Academy of Achievement, "Benjamin Carson Interview," http://www.achievement.org/autodoc/page/ car1int-2.
4. Richard Branson, *Losing My Virginity: How I've Survived, Had Fun, and Made a Fortune Doing Business My Way* (New York: The Rivers Press, 1998), p. 56.
5. Ibid., pp. 58, 61–62.
6. Ibid., pp. 59–60.
7. Christopher A. Bartlett and Anthony St. George, "Acer, Inc: Taiwan's Rampaging Dragon," Case 9–399– 010 (Boston: Harvard Business School, 1999), p. 3.
8. John Campbell, *Margaret Thatcher: The Grocer's Daughter* (London: Jonathan Cape, 2000), p. 49.
9. Academy of Achievement, "Michael Eisner Interview," http://www.achievement.org/autodoc/page/eis0int-1.
10. Achievement, "Carson Interview," http://www.achievement. org/autodoc/page/car1int-8.
11. Rudoff, "Oz Movie Script," Un-official, http://www.un- official.com/The_Daily_Script/ms_wizoz.htm.

12. See Linda A. Hill, "Power Dynamics in Organizations," Note 9–494–083 (Boston: Harvard Business School Publishing, 1995).
13. Bill Clinton, *My Life* (New York: Alfred A. Knopf, 2004), pp. 212–228.
14. Madeleine Albright with Bill Woodward, *Madam Secretary: A Memoir* (New York: Miramax Books, 2003), p. 63.
15. Alan Alda, *Never Have Your Dog Stuffed: And Other Things I've Learned* (New York: Random House, 2005), p. 117.
16. David A. Whetten and Kim S. Cameron, *Developing Management Skills, 6th ed.* (Upper Saddle River, NJ: Pearson Prentice Hall, 2004), p. 262.
17. Personal observations based on my work with Charles Ogletree on legal cases and also my experiences as one of his students at Harvard Law School.
18. Sam Walton with John Huey, *Sam Walton: Made In America* (New York: Bantam Books, 1992), pp. 51–52, 148.
19. Branson, *Losing My Virginity*, pp. 133–134.
20. Anita Roddick, *Body and Soul: Profits with Principles—The Amazing Success Story of Anita Roddick and The Body Shop* (New York: Crown Publishers, 1991), pp. 69–71.
21. Rudoff, "Oz Movie Script," Un-official, http://www.un-official.com/The_Daily_Script/ms_wizoz.htm.
22. See Hill, "Power Dynamics in Organizations."
23. Albright with Woodward, *Madam Secretary*, p. 63.
24. Ibid., pp. 65–73.
25. Ibid., p. 65.
26. Whetten and Cameron, *Developing Management Skills*, p. 264.
27. Bob Schieffer, *This Just In: What I Couldn't Tell You on TV* (New York: Berkley Books, 2003), pp. 64–72.
28. Lee Iacocca with William Novak, *Iacocca: An Autobiography* (New York: Bantam Books, 1986), pp. 41–42, 65–82.

29. Donny Deutsch with Peter Knobler, *Often Wrong, Never in Doubt: Unleash the Business Rebel Within* (New York: Harper Collins Publishers, 2005), pp. 28–29.
30. See Hill, "Power Dynamics in Organizations."
31. Whetten and Cameron, *Developing Management Skills*, p. 262.
32. Roddick, *Body and Soul*, pp. 98–99.
33. Albright with Woodward, *Madam Secretary*, p. 83.
34. Clinton, *My Life*.
35. Katharine Graham, *Personal History* (New York: Vintage Books, 1998), p. 511.
36. Andrew Kilpatrick, *Of Permanent Value: The Story of Warren Buffett* (Birmingham: AKPE, 2005), pp. 51–52.
37. Lance Armstrong with Sally Jenkins, *It's Not About the Bike: My Journey Back to Life* (New York: Berkley Books, 2000), pp. 53–56.
38. Roland Lazenby, "Jackson takes his Jerry-mandering to L.A.," *Chicago Sun Times*, September 5, 2000, http://www.findarticles.com/p/articles/mi_qn4155/is_20000905/ai_n13873603.
39. Branson, *Losing My Virginity*, pp. 179, 184–185, 201.
40. Linda A. Hill and Katherine S. Weber, "Kevin Simpson at Haemonetics, Video," Case Video 9–494–516 (Boston: Harvard Business School Publishing, 1994).
41. Deutsch with Knobler, *Often Wrong, Never in Doubt*, p. 22.
42. Linda A. Hill and Katherine Seger, *Power and influence: Getting things done in organizations*, (Boston: Harvard Business School Publishing, 1995), pp. 39–49.
43. Linda A. Hill, "Exercising Influence," Note 9–494–080 (Boston: Harvard Business School Publishing, 1995).
44. Iacocca with Novak, *Iacocca: An Autobiography*, p. 61.
45. Frederick Herzberg, "One More Time: How Do You Motivate Employees?," *Harvard Business Review* Article R0301F (Boston: Harvard Business School, 2003), p. 4.
46. Jennifer M. George and Gareth R. Jones, *Understanding and Managing Organizational Behavior*, 4th ed. (Upper

Saddle River, New Jersey: Pearson Prentice Hall, 2005), pp. 181–183.

47. Deutsch with Knobler, *Often Wrong, Never in Doubt*, p. 84.
48. Ibid., p. 88.
49. Walton with Huey, *Made In America*, p. 179.
50. Deutsch with Knobler, *Often Wrong, Never in Doubt*, pp. 84–88.
51. Walton with Huey, *Made In America*, p. 181.
52. Roddick, *Body and Soul*, p. 99.
53. Walton with Huey, *Made In America*, pp. 199–201.
54. Roy Vagelos and Louis Galambos, *Medicine, Science and Merck* (Cambridge: Cambridge University Press, 2004), p. 126.
55. Bartlett and George, "Acer, Inc," pp. 2–3.
56. Kilpatrick, *Of Permanent Value*, p. 12.
57. Branson, *Losing My Virginity*, pp. 204–205.
58. Andrew Donoghue, "Google side-steps AI rumours," ZD Net UK, http://news.zdnet.co.uk/software/developer/0,39020387,39237225,00.htm.
59. Ibid.

Step Four: Know How to Create Your Personal Success Syndrome

1. Paul Rudoff, "The Wizard Of Oz Movie Script," Un-official, http://www.un-official.com/The_Daily_Script/ms_wizoz.htm.
2. John P. Kotter, *Power and Influence* (New York: The Free Press, 1985), p. 128.
3. Ibid., pp. 117–130.
4. Jack Welch with John A. Byrne, *Jack: Straight from the Gut* (New York: Warner Books, 2003), pp. 7, 15.
5. Ibid., pp. 17–18, 19.
6. Ibid., p. 19.
7. Ibid., pp. 23–24.
8. Ibid., p. 24.

9. Ibid., pp. 24–25.

10. Ibid., p. 36.

11. Ibid., p. 41.

12. Ibid., p. 77.

13. Ibid., p. 55.

14. Ibid., p. 80.

15. Ibid., p. 81.

16. Ibid., p. 77.

17. Academy of Achievement, "Benjamin Carson Interview," http://www.achievement.org/autodoc/page/car1bio-1.

18. Achievement, "Carson Interview," http://www.achievement.org/autodoc/page/car1int-1.

19. Achievement, "Carson Interview," http://www.achievement.org/ autodoc/page/car1int-3.

20. Ibid.

21. Ben Carson, M.D. with Cecil Murphy, *Gifted Hands: The Ben Carson Story* (Grand Rapids: Zondervan, 1990), p. 39.

22. Ibid., p. 106.

23. Ibid., p. 109.

24. Ibid., pp. 69–70.

25. Ibid., pp. 109–111.

26. Ibid., pp. 127–130.

27. Ibid., pp. 135.

28. Ibid., p. 133.

29. Ibid., p. 135.

30. Ibid., p. 154.

31. Ibid., p. 140.

32. Ibid., pp. 141–142, 148, 150-152.

33. Jennifer M. Suesse, "Margaret Thatcher," Case 9–497–018 (Boston: Harvard Business School, 1998), p. 1.

34. Gail Sheehy, "The Blooming of Margaret Thatcher," *Vanity Fair*, June 1989, pp. 110-111.

35. John Campbell, *Margaret Thatcher: The Grocer's Daughter* (London: Jonathan Cape, 2000), pp. 49–52.

36. Ibid., pp. 50, 56–57.

37. Margaret Thatcher, *The Path to Power* (London: HarperCollins, 1995), p. 49.
38. Ibid., pp. 43–45.
39. Campbell, *Margaret Thatcher*, pp. 52–54.
40. Ibid., pp. 71–73.
41. Ibid., pp. 75–79.
42. Thatcher, *The Path to Power*, p. 71.
43. Campbell, *Margaret Thatcher*, p. 76.
44. Ibid., p. 84.
45. Ibid., p. 92.
46. Suesse, "Margaret Thatcher," p. 5.
47. Campbell, *Margaret Thatcher*, p. 112.
48. Ibid., p. 113.
49. Suesse, "Margaret Thatcher," pp. 6–8.
50. Campbell, *Margaret Thatcher*, p. 141.
51. Ibid., p. 170.
52. Ibid., p. 188.
53. Suesse, "Margaret Thatcher," pp. 13–14.
54. Ibid., pp. 15–17.
55. Bill Gallagher (President of ADS Financial Services Solutions), Interview by Dr. White, February 24, 2005; April 22, 2005.
56. Other employees from the company also showed up to help even though none of them knew that the others were coming to help. Bill's partner, who lacked technical expertise to solve the problem, showed up with pizza.
57. Rudoff, "Oz Movie Script," Un-official, http://www.un-official.com/The_Daily_Script/ms_wizoz.htm.

Step Five: Know How To Get and Give Help

1. Academy of Achievement, "Oprah Winfrey Interview," www.achievement.org/autodoc/page/win0int-8.
2. Paul Rudoff, "The Wizard Of Oz Movie Script," Un-official, http://www.un-official.com/The_Daily_Script/ms_wizoz.htm.

3. Ben Carson, M.D. with Cecil Murphy, *Gifted Hands: The Ben Carson Story* (Grand Rapids: Zondervan, 1990), p. 112.

4. Academy of Achievement, "Larry King Interview," http://www.achievement.org/autodoc/page/kin0int-1.

5. Academy of Achievement, "Larry King Interview," http://www.achievement.org/autodoc/page/kin0int-2.

6. Ibid.

7. Ibid.

8. Based on over 150 interviews conducted with managers by students in the course Managing Workplace Performance, Harvard Extension School, 2003, 2004, 2005.

9. David A. Thomas and John J. Gabarro, *Breaking Through: The Making of Minority Executives in Corporate America* (USA: Thomas and Gabarro, 1999), p. 19.

10. Ibid., pp. 18–25.

11. Sam Walton with John Huey, *Sam Walton: Made In America* (New York: Bantam Books, 1992), p. 16.

12. Richard Branson, *Losing My Virginity: How I've Survived, Had Fun, and Made a Fortune Doing Business My Way* (New York: The Rivers Press, 1998), p. 102

13. Carson with Murphy, *Gifted Hands*, p. 354.

14. Cnettv.cnet.com. http://cnettv.cnet.com/60-minutes-steve-jobs/9742-1_53-50004696.html. Retrieved February 11, 2012.

15. Elaine Hatfield, John T. Cacioppo, and Richard L. Rapson, *Emotional Contagion* (Cambridge: Cambridge University Press, 1994).

16. Branson, *Losing My Virginity*, p. 58.

17. Ibid., pp. 133–134.

18. Carson with Murphy, *Gifted Hands*, p. 83.

19. Walton with Huey, *Made In America*, p. 163.

20. Ibid., pp. 163–164.

21. Rudoff, "Oz Movie Script," Un-official, http://www.un-official.com/The_Daily_Script/ms_wizoz.htm.

22. Branson, *Losing My Virginity*, 58.
23. Anita Roddick, *Body and Soul: Profits with Principles—The Amazing Success Story of Anita Roddick and The Body Shop* (New York: Crown Publishers, 1991), pp. 71–72.
24. Stephanie Strom, "Gates's Charity Races to Spend Buffett Billions," *New York Times*, August 13, 2006.
25. Rudoff, "Oz Movie Script," Un-official, http://www.un-official.com/The_Daily_Script/ms_wizoz.htm.
26. Jack Welch with John A. Byrne, *Jack: Straight from the Gut* (New York: Warner Books, 2003), p. 53.
27. Christopher Clarey, "Easy Putaway in Paris: Henin-Hardenne Wins Open Title," *New York Times*, June 5, 2005.
28. *Sports Illustrated*, "Bengals deal Dillon to Pats for second-rounder," April 20, 2004, http://sportsillustrated.cnn.com/2004/football/nfl/04/19/dillon.trade/.
29. Academy of Achievement, "Michael Eisner Interview," http://www.achievement.org/autodoc/page/eis0int-2.
30. Thomas and Gabarro, *Breaking Through*, p. 23.
31. Achievement, "Winfrey Interview," www.achievement.org/autodoc/page/win0int-8.
32. Branson, *Losing My Virginity*, p. 77.
33. Ibid., p. 77–78.
34. Roy Vagelos and Louis Galambos, *Medicine, Science and Merck* (Cambridge: Cambridge University Press, 2004), p. 122.
35. Academy of Achievement, "Jeff Bezos Interview," http://www.achievement.org/autodoc/page/bez0int-3.
36. Walton with Huey, *Made In America*, p. 104.
37. Ibid., p. 105.
38. Jack Welch with John A. Byrne, *Jack: Straight from the Gut* (New York: Warner Books, 2003), p. 96.
39. Linda A. Hill and Melinda B. Conrad, "Kevin Simpson," Case 9–492–041 (Boston: Harvard Business School, 1995), p. 6.

40. Branson, *Losing My Virginity*, p. 350.
41. Ibid., p. 351.
42. David A Whetten and Kim S. Cameron, *Developing Management Skills, 6th ed.* (Upper Saddle River, NJ: Pearson Prentice Hall, 2004), p. 228.
43. Jennifer George and Gareth Jones, *Understanding and Managing Organizational Behavior, 4th Ed.* (Upper Saddle River, NJ: Pearson Prentice Hall, 2005), pp. 107–109.
44. Acer Inc, "Acer Publications," Communications & Multimedia Laboratory, http://www.cmlab.csie.ntu.edu.tw/~chenhsiu/reading/metoo.pdf#search=%22%22is%20not%20my%20style%22%20%22stan%20shih%22%22.
45. Welch with Byrne, *Straight from Gut*, p. 19.
46. Sara Lawrence-Lightfoot, *I've Known Rivers: Lives of Loss and Liberation* (Reading, MA: Addison Wesley Publishing Company, 1994), pp. 116, 156–157.
47. Madeleine Albright with Bill Woodward, *Madam Secretary: A Memoir* (New York: Miramax Books, 2003), pp. 83–84.
48. J. Paul Getty, *As I See It* (Los Angeles: Getty Trade Paperbacks, 2003), p. 26.
49. Ibid., pp. 36–37.
50. Vagelos and Galambos, *Medicine, Science and Merck*, pp. 37, 42–43.
51. Ibid., p. 52.
52. Welch with Byrne, *Straight from Gut*, p. 129.
53. Thomas and Gabarro, *Breaking Through*, p. 22.
54. John J. Gabarro and John P. Kotter, "Managing Your Boss," *Harvard Business Review*, January 2005, p. 36.
55. Ibid., p. 37.
56. Ibid.
57. Ibid., p. 40.
58. Ibid., pp. 41–42.
59. Ibid., p. 40.

60. Walton with Huey, *Made In America*, p. 80.
61. Elizabeth Bumiller, "White House Letter; From Jenna's Ex to a Presidential Jeeves," *New York Times*, May 30, 2005.
62. Rudoff, "Oz Movie Script," Un-official, http://www.un-official.com/The_Daily_Script/ms_wizoz.htm.
63. Jennifer M. Suesse, "Margaret Thatcher," Case 9–497–018 (Boston: Harvard Business School, 1998), p. 5.
64. Peter Burrows with Peter Elstrom, "HP's Carly Fiorina: The Boss," *Business Week*, August 2, 1999, http://www.businessweek.com/1999/99_31/b3640001.htm.
65. Getty, *As I See It*, p. 41.
66. Academy of Achievement, "John Wooden Interview," http://www.achievement.org/autodoc/page/woo0int-3.

Step Six: Know How to Use the Power of Your Emotions

1. Paul Rudoff, "The Wizard Of Oz Movie Script," Un-official, http://www.un-official.com/The_Daily_Script/ms_wizoz.htm.
2. Rudoff, "Oz Movie Script," Un-official, http://www.un-official.com/The_Daily_Script/ms_wizoz.htm.
3. Daniel Goleman, Richard Boyatzis, and Annie McKee, *Primal Leadership: Learning to Lead with Emotional Intelligence* (Boston: Harvard Business School Publishing, 2002), p. 13.
4. Academy of Achievement, "Larry King Interview," http://www.achievement.org/autodoc/page/kin0int-2.
5. Ben Carson, M.D. with Cecil Murphy, *Gifted Hands: The Ben Carson Story* (Grand Rapids: Zondervan, 1990), p. 121.
6. Achievement, "King Interview," http://www.achievement.org/autodoc/page/kin0int-2.
7. Carson with Murphy, *Gifted Hands*, p. 121.
8. Richard Branson, *Losing My Virginity: How I've Survived, Had Fun, and Made a Fortune Doing Business My Way* (New York: The Rivers Press, 1998), p 16.

9. Rudoff, "Oz Movie Script," Un-official, http://www. un-official.com/The_Daily_Script/ms_wizoz.htm.
10. Academy of Achievement, "Jeff Bezos Interview," http:// www.achievement.org/autodoc/page/bez0int-5.
11. George Soros with Byron Wien and Krisztina Koenen, *Soros on Soros: Staying Ahead of the Curve* (New York: John Wiley & Sons, Inc., 1995), p. 57.
12. Jack Welch with John A. Byrne, *Jack: Straight from the Gut* (New York: Warner Books, 2003), p. 101.
13. Robert S. Weinberg and Daniel Gould, *Foundations of Sport and Exercise Psychology* (Champaign: Human Kinetics, 2003), p. 265.
14. Ibid., p. 266.
15. Academy of Achievement, "Larry Ellison Interview," http://www.achievement.org/autodoc/page/ell0int-5.
16. Weinberg and Gould, *Foundations of Sport*, pp. 85–94.
17. Soros with Wien and Koenen, *Soros on Soros*, p. 55.
18. Ibid., p. 57.
19. Madeleine Albright with Bill Woodward, *Madam Secretary: A Memoir* (New York: Miramax Books, 2003), p. 63.
20. Branson, *Losing My Virginity*, pp. 44–45.
21. Ibid., p. 45.
22. Sam Walton with John Huey, *Sam Walton: Made In America* (New York: Bantam Books, 1992), pp. 118–119.
23. Ibid., p. 156.
24. Ibid., p. 243.
25. Branson, *Losing My Virginity*, p. 346.
26. Achievement, "Ellison Interview," http://www.achievement. org/autodoc/page/ell0int-5.
27. Carson with Murphy, *Gifted Hands*, pp. 166–167.
28. Rudoff, "Oz Movie Script," Un-official, http://www. un-official.com/The_Daily_Script/ms_wizoz.htm.
29. Carson with Murphy, *Gifted Hands*, pp. 56–60.

30. Roy Vagelos and Louis Galambos, *Medicine, Science and Merck* (Cambridge: Cambridge University Press, 2004), p. 40.

31. Ibid., pp. 40-41.

32. Academy of Achievement, "John Wooden Interview," http://www.achievement.org/autodoc/page/woo0int-1.

33. Academy of Achievement, "Michael Eisner Interview," http://www.achievement.org/autodoc/page/eis0int-1.

34. Carson with Murphy, *Gifted Hands*, p. 118.

35. Vagelos and Galambos, *Medicine, Science and Merck*, p. 41.

36. Peter Burrows, *Backfire: Carly Fiorina's High-Stakes Battle for the Soul of Hewlett-Packard* (Hoboken: John Wiley & Sons, Inc., 2003), p. 90.

37. Ibid, pp. 90-92.

38. Rudoff, "Oz Movie Script," Un-official, http://www.un-official.com/The_Daily_Script/ms_wizoz.htm.

39. Elaine Hatfield, John T. Cacioppo, and Richard L. Rapson, *Emotional Contagion* (Cambridge: Cambridge University Press, 1994), p. 100.

40. Ibid., p. 102

41. Branson, *Losing My Virginity*, pp. 156–160.

42. Soros with Wien and Koenen, *Soros on Soros*, p. 48.

43. Ibid., p. 52.

44. *CNN*, "CNN Larry King Live: Interview with Wynonna Judd," September 29, 2005, http://transcripts.cnn.com/TRANSCRIPTS/0509/29/lkl.01.html.

45. Lee Iacocca with William Novak, *Iacocca: An Autobiography* (New York: Bantam Books, 1986), p. 65.

46. Burrows, *Backfire*, pp. 50-53, 61.

47. Walton with Huey, *Made In America*, pp. 152–153.

48. Branson, *Losing My Virginity*, p. 42.

49. Walton with Huey, *Made In America*, p. 201.

50. Ibid., p. 175.

51. Nora Ephron, "After the Love is Gone," *New York Times*, September 29, 2005.

52. Robert Browning, "The Pied Piper of Hamelin: Bibliographical Record," Indiana University, http://www.indiana.edu/~librcsd/etext/piper/text.html.

Step Seven: Know How To Manage Your Performance

1. Paul Rudoff, "The Wizard Of Oz Movie Script," Un-official, http://www.un-official.com/The_Daily_Script/ms_wizoz.htm.
2. Richard Branson, *Losing My Virginity: How I've Survived, Had Fun, and Made a Fortune Doing Business My Way* (New York: The Rivers Press, 1998), p. 93.
3. Ibid., p. 94.
4. Ibid., 96, 106–110.
5. Jennifer M. Suesse, "Margaret Thatcher," Case 9–497–018 (Boston: Harvard Business School, 1998).
6. Jack Welch with John A. Byrne, *Jack: Straight from the Gut* (New York: Warner Books, 2003), p. 51.
7. Jennifer M. George and Gareth R. Jones, *Understanding and Managing Organizational Behavior, 4th ed.* (Upper Saddle River, NJ: Pearson Prentice Hall, 2005), p. 118.
8. J. Paul Getty, *As I See It* (Los Angeles: Getty Trade Paperbacks, 2003), p. 25.
9. Roy Vagelos and Louis Galambos, *Medicine, Science and Merck* (Cambridge: Cambridge University Press, 2004), pp. 42, 52.
10. Ibid., p. 25.
11. Ibid.
12. Rudoff, "Oz Movie Script," Un-official, http://www.un-official.com/The_Daily_Script/ms_wizoz.htm.
13. Lee Iacocca with William Novak, *Iacocca: An Autobiography* (New York: Bantam Books, 1986), p. 20.
14. Walton with Huey, *Made In America* (New York: Bantam Books, 1992), p. 21.
15. Welch with Byrne, *Straight from Gut*, p. 18.
16. Lance Armstrong with Sally Jenkins, *It's Not About the Bike: My Journey Back to Life* (New York: Berkley Books, 2000), p. 244.

17. Branson, *Losing My Virginity*, p. 239.

18. Ibid., pp. 264–268.

19. Robert S. Weinberg and Daniel Gould, *Foundations of Sport and Exercise Psychology* (Champaign: Human Kinetics, 2003), p. 357.

20. Ibid., p. 352.

21. Ben Carson, M.D. with Cecil Murphy, *Gifted Hands: The Ben Carson Story* (Grand Rapids: Zondervan, 1990), p. 133.

22. Rudoff, "Oz Movie Script," Un-official, http://www.un-official.com/The_Daily_Script/ms_wizoz.htm.

23. Welch with Byrne, *Straight from Gut*, p. 76.

24. Academy of Achievement, "Larry Ellison Interview," http://www.achievement.org/autodoc/page/ell0int-6.

25. Bill Clinton, *My Life* (New York: Alfred A. Knopf, 2004), p. 258.

26. Madeleine Albright with Bill Woodward, *Madam Secretary: A Memoir* (New York: Miramax Books, 2003), p. 84.

27. Academy of Achievement, "Larry King Interview," http://www.achievement.org/autodoc/page/kin0int-2.

28. Peter Meyers, personal communication, October 14, 2005.

29. Academy of Achievement, "Oprah Winfrey Interview," www.achievement.org/autodoc/page/win0int-4

30. Iacocca with Novak, *Iacocca: An Autobiography*, p. 104.

31. Ibid., p. 121.

32. Ibid., p. 127.

33. Ibid., p. 134.

34. Achievement, "Ellison Interview," http://www.achievement.org/autodoc/page/ell0int-2.

35. Walton with Huey, *Made In America*, p. 148.

36. Welch with Byrne, *Straight from Gut*, p. 106.

37. Branson, *Losing My Virginity*, pp. 350-351.

38. Rudoff, "Oz Movie Script," Un-official, http://www.un-official.com/The_Daily_Script/ms_wizoz.htm.

39. Academy of Achievement, "John Wooden Interview," http://www.achievement.org/autodoc/page/woo0int-5.

40. Walton with Huey, *Made In America*, p. 18.
41. Academy of Achievement, "Susan Butcher Interview," http://www.achievement.org/autodoc/page/but0int-4.
42. Acer Inc, "Acer Publications," Communications & Multimedia Laboratory, http://www.cmlab.csie.ntu.edu. tw/~chenhsiu/reading/metoo.pdf#search=%22%22is%20 not%20my%20style%22%20%22stan%20shih%22 %22.
43. Donny Deutsch with Peter Knobler, *Often Wrong, Never in Doubt: Unleash the Business Rebel Within* (New York: Harper Collins Publishers, 2005), p. 4.
44. Ibid., p. 5.
45. Academy of Achievement, "Benjamin Carson Interview," http://www.achievement.org/autodoc/page/car1int-6.
46. Achievement, "Butcher Interview," http://www.achievement.org/autodoc/page/but0int-4.
47. Achievement, "Carson Interview," http://www.achievement.org/autodoc/page/car1int-1.
48. Achievement, "King Interview," http://www.achievement.org/autodoc/page/kin0int-1.
49. Armstrong with Jenkins, *It's Not About the Bike*, p. 60.
50. Carson with Murphy, *Gifted Hands*, p. 37.
51. Academy of Achievement, "Jeff Bezos Interview," http://www.achievement.org/autodoc/page/bez0int-4.
52. Peter Burrows, *Backfire: Carly Fiorina's High-Stakes Battle for the Soul of Hewlett-Packard* (Hoboken: John Wiley & Sons, Inc., 2003), pp. 49–50.
53. Armstrong with Jenkins, *It's Not About the Bike*, p. 29.
54. Achievement, "Butcher Interview," http://www.achievement.org/autodoc/page/but0int-2.
55. Iacocca with Novak, *Iacocca: An Autobiography*, p. 196.
56. Carson with Murphy, *Gifted Hands*, p. 106.
57. Peter Johnson, "White House Watchdog," *USA Today*, March 22, 1993.
58. Ibid.

59. Anita Roddick, *Body and Soul: Profits with Principles—The Amazing Success Story of Anita Roddick and The Body Shop* (New York: Crown Publishers, 1991), pp. 80-81.
60. Vagelos and Galambos, *Medicine, Science and Merck*, p. 149.
61. Ibid., pp. 155, 157.
62. Rudoff, "Oz Movie Script," Un-official, http://www.un-official.com/The_Daily_Script/ms_wizoz.htm.
63. J. Todd Arnedt et al., "Neurobehavioral Performance of Residents After Heavy Night Call vs After Alcohol Ingestion," *The Journal of the American Medical Association* 294, no.9 (September 2005): pp. 1025–1033.
64. Harris R. Lieberman et al., "The Fog of War: Decrements in Cognitive Performance and Mood Associated with Combat-like Stress," *Aviation Space and Environmental Medicine* 76, no. 7 (July 2005): pp. C7–C14.
65. Walton with Huey, *Made In America*, p. 186.
66. Branson, *Losing My Virginity*, p. 64.
67. Michael Steinhardt, *No Bull: My Life In and Out of Markets* (New York: John Wiley & Sons, 2001), pp. 153–155.
68. Academy of Achievement, "Martha Stewart Interview," http://www.achievement.org/autodoc/page/ste0int-1.

Step Eight: Know How to Manage Risk and Adversity

1. Paul Rudoff, "The Wizard Of Oz Movie Script," Un-official, http://www.un-official.com/The_Daily_Script/ms_wizoz.htm.
2. Academy of Achievement, "Michael Eisner Interview," http://www.achievement.org/autodoc/page/eis0int-2.
3. Academy of Achievement, "Donna Shirley Interview," http://www.achievement.org/autodoc/page/shi0int-2.
4. Academy of Achievement, "Jeff Bezos Interview," http://www.achievement.org/autodoc/page/bez0int-3.
5. Deborah Copaken Kogan, *Shutterbabe* (New York: Random House Trade Paperbacks, 2000), pp. 6–63.

6. Ibid., p. 51.

7. Ben Carson, M.D. with Cecil Murphy, *Gifted Hands: The Ben Carson Story* (Grand Rapids: Zondervan, 1990), pp. 81–83.

8. Ibid., p. 82.

9. Ibid., pp. 164, 170.

10. Garry Wills, "Lightning Rod," *The New York Review of Books* 50, no. 13 (August 2003), http://www.nybooks.com/articles/16510.

11. Academy of Achievement, "Frederick W. Smith Interview," http://www.achievement.org/autodoc/page/smi0int-2.

12. Katharine Graham, *Personal History* (New York: Vintage Books, 1998), pp. 448–450.

13. Rudoff, "Oz Movie Script," Un-official, http://www.un-official.com/The_Daily_Script/ms_wizoz.htm.

14. Academy of Achievement, "George Lucas Interview," http://www.achievement.org/autodoc/page/luc0int-5.

15. Lee Iacocca with William Novak, *Iacocca: An Autobiography* (New York: Bantam Books, 1986), p. 34.

16. George Soros with Byron Wien and Krisztina Koenen, *Soros on Soros: Staying Ahead of the Curve* (New York: John Wiley & Sons, Inc., 1995), p. 11.

17. Jack Welch with John A. Byrne, *Jack: Straight from the Gut* (New York: Warner Books, 2003), p. 53.

18. Achievement, "Eisner Interview," http://www.achievement.org/autodoc/page/eis0int-2.

19. The Board of Wisdom, "The Best Success Quotes," http://www.boardofwisdom.com/Default.asp?topic=1005&listname=Success.

20. *Stanford Report.* June 14, 2005. http://news-service.stanford.edu/news/2005/june15/jobs-061505.html. Retrieved February 12, 2012.

21. *ABC News*, "Fantasia's Memoirs Reveal Experiences With Illiteracy, Rape," September 30, 2005, http://abcnews.go.com/2020/OnlyinAmerica/story?id=1170655&page=1.

22. Sam Walton with John Huey, *Sam Walton: Made In America* (New York: Bantam Books, 1992), p. 50.
23. Anita Roddick, *Body and Soul: Profits with Principles— The Amazing Success Story of Anita Roddick and The Body Shop* (New York: Crown Publishers, 1991), p. 63.
24. Acer Inc, "Acer Publications," Communications & Multimedia Laboratory, http://www.cmlab.csie.ntu.edu. tw/~chenhsiu/reading/metoo.pdf#search=%22%22is%20 not%20my%20style%22%20%22stan%20shih%22%22.
25. J. Paul Getty, *As I See It* (Los Angeles: Getty Trade Paperbacks, 2003), pp. 34–35.
26. Roddick, *Body and Soul*, pp. 113–114.
27. Rudoff, "Oz Movie Script," Un-official, http://www. un-official.com/The_Daily_Script/ms_wizoz.htm.
28. Lance Armstrong with Sally Jenkins, *It's Not About the Bike: My Journey Back to Life* (New York: Berkley Books, 2000), p. 26.
29. In his speech Churchill didn't say "Never, never, never, never, never give up." The original words were, "Never, ever, ever, ever, ever, ever, ever, give in. Never give in. Never give in. Never give in." See Ron Kurtus, "Winston Churchill's "Never Give In" Speech of 1941," School for Champions, http://www.school-for-champions.com/ speeches/churchill_never_give_in.htm.
30. Academy of Achievement, "Johnny Cash Interview," http://www.achievement.org/autodoc/page/cas0int-1.
31. Achievement, "Lucas Interview," http://www.achievement. org/autodoc/page/luc0int-2.
32. Ibid.
33. Walton with Huey, *Made In America*, pp. 38–39.
34. Iacocca with Novak, *Iacocca: An Autobiography*, p. xiv.
35. Ibid., p. xvi.
36. Martin E.P. Seligman Ph.D., *Learned Optimism* (New York: Alfred A. Knopf, 1991), p. 99.

37. Associated Press, "Martha's Collegiate Euphemism for Prison," September 19, 2005, http://www.msnbc.msn.com/id/9403153/.
38. Achievement, "Lucas Interview," http://www.achievement.org/autodoc/page/luc0int-2.
39. Acer Inc, "Acer Publications," Communications & Multimedia Laboratory, http://www.cmlab.csie.ntu.edu.tw/~chenhsiu/reading/metoo.pdf#search=%22%22is%20not%20my%20style%22%20%22stan%20shih%22%22.
40. Armstrong with Jenkins, *It's Not About the Bike*, p. 197.
41. Ibid., p. 49.
42. Ibid., p. 65.
43. Achievement, "Lucas Interview," http://www.achievement.org/autodoc/page/luc0int-3.
44. Walton with Huey, *Made In America*, p. 39.
45. Academy of Achievement, "Jeong Kim Interview," http://www.achievement.org/autodoc/page/kim1int-4.
46. Richard Branson, *Losing My Virginity: How I've Survived, Had Fun, and Made a Fortune Doing Business My Way* (New York: The Rivers Press, 1998), p. 344.
47. Rudoff, "Oz Movie Script," Un-official, http://www.un-official.com/The_Daily_Script/ms_wizoz.htm.
48. Carson with Murphy, *Gifted Hands*, pp. 111–112.
49. Welch with Byrne, *Straight from Gut*, p. 5.
50. Ibid., p. 29.
51. Ibid., pp. 5–6.
52. Acer Inc, "Acer Publications," Communications & Multimedia Laboratory, http://www.cmlab.csie.ntu.edu.tw/~chenhsiu/reading/metoo.pdf#search=%22%22is%20not%20my%20style%22%20%22stan%20shih%22%22.
53. Roy Vagelos and Louis Galambos, *Medicine, Science and Merck* (Cambridge: Cambridge University Press, 2004), p. 42.
54. Ibid. p. 43.
55. Ibid., p. 42–43.

56. Armstrong with Jenkins, *It's Not About the Bike*, pp. 198–202.

57. Garry North, "When the Best Undermines the Good," Gary North's Specific Answers, www.garynorth.com/public/539print.cfm

58. Sony, "Walkman Episodes," http://www.sony.net/Products/walkman/brand/episode.html.

59. Achievement, "Lucas Interview," http://www.achievement.org/autodoc/page/luc0int-3.

Step Nine: Know How to Have Fun

1. David Allison, "Bill Gates Interview," National Museum of American History, http://americanhistory.si.edu/collections/comphist/gates.htm#tc30.

2. Andrew Kilpatrick, *Of Permanent Value: The Story of Warren Buffett* (Birmingham: AKPE, 2005), p. 5.

3. Bill Clinton, *My Life* (New York: Alfred A. Knopf, 2004), p. 214.

4. Richard P. Feynman, *Surely You're Joking, Mr. Feynman! (Adventures of a Curious Character)* (New York: W. W. Norton & Company, Inc., 1997), p. 173.

5. Ibid., p. 174.

6. Jack Welch with John A. Byrne, *Jack: Straight from the Gut* (New York: Warner Books, 2003), p. 53

7. Academy of Achievement, "Frederick W. Smith Interview," http://www.achievement.org/autodoc/page/smi0int-4.

8. Katharine Graham, *Personal History* (New York: Vintage Books, 1998), pp. 371–372.

9. Alan Alda, *Never Have Your Dog Stuffed: And Other Things I've Learned* (New York: Random House, 2005), p. 108.

10. Academy of Achievement, "John Wooden Interview," http://www.achievement.org/autodoc/page/woo0int-5.

Index

253

E

Effort, 44, 82, 104
Eisner, Michael, 36, 64, 72, 124, 155, 192, 199
Ellison, Larry, 14, 16, 17, 24, 148, 152, 174, 176, 188
Expertise, 44, 82, 104

F

Failure, 44, 82, 104
Fame, xv, 44
Federer, Roger, 218
Feedback, 44, 82, 104
Feynman, Richard, 216–217
Fiorina, Carly, 138, 157
Flexible, 44, 82, 104
Focus, 44, 82, 104
Fun, 44, 82, 104

G

Gallagher, Bill, 90, 91, 103, 111–112
Gates, Bill, 2, 4, 52, 123–124, 134, 212, 215
Getty, J. Paul, 52, 131, 138, 139, 168, 201–202
Giving Help Principle, 44, 82, 104
Graham, Katharine, 77, 196–197, 217

H

Heart, 24, 27, 44, 82, 104
Henin-Hardenne, Justine, 124
Hewlett, Bill, 161, 183
Holiday, Billie, 47

I

Iacocca, Lee, 14, 19–20, 31, 33, 74, 81, 160–161, 170, 175–176, 184, 198
IQ, 5

J

Jackson, Phil, 78
Jobs, Steve, xiii, 119, 199
Jordan, Michael, 199
Judd, Wynonna, 159

K

Kim, Jeong, 54, 208–209
King, Larry, 53, 55, 116–117, 143–145, 146, 175, 182
Kogan, Deborah Copaken, 25, 193–194

L

Listen, 44, 82, 104
Listener, 44, 82, 104
Listening, 44, 82, 104
Lucas, George, 29, 32, 33, 40–42, 56, 198, 204–206, 207, 213

M

Mentors, 44, 82, 104
Meyers, Peter, 175
Mini-strengths, 5, 44, 82, 104
Mission, 40, 44, 46, 82, 104
Mitchell, Andrea, 184, 185
Money, 44, 82, 104
Motivate, 44, 82, 104

O

Ogletree, Charles, 67, 130

P

Packard, Dave, 161, 183
Page, Larry, 4
Personal success syndrome, 44, 82, 104
Pivotal moments, 44, 82, 104

R

Relevance, 44, 82, 104

Follow Dr. White

Twitter: @DrMyraWhite
Facebook.com/SuperstarRoadmap
Go to www.SuperstarRoadmap.com for
The *Ask Dr. White* Blog, Motivational Exercises,
and Much More

CPSIA information can be obtained at www.ICGtesting.com
Printed in the USA
BVOW03s2203130415

396012BV00005B/15/P

9 780984 944903